HARM TO OTHERS

The MORAL LIMITS

VOLUME ONE

NEW YORK OXFORD

of the CRIMINAL LAW

Harm to Others

JOEL FEINBERG

OXFORD UNIVERSITY PRESS

Oxford University Press

Oxford   New York   Toronto
Delhi   Bombay   Calcutta   Madras   Karachi
Petaling Jaya   Singapore   Hong Kong   Tokyo
Nairobi   Dar es Salaam   Cape Town
Melbourne   Auckland

and associated companies in
Beirut   Berlin   Ibadan   Nicosia

Library of Congress Cataloging-in-Publication Data

Feinberg, Joel, 1926—
The moral limits of the criminal law.

Bibliography: p.
Includes index.
Contents: v. 1. Harm to others.
1. Criminal law—Philosophy.   2. Criminal law—
Moral and ethical aspects.   3. Crimes without victims.
I. Title.
K5018.F44   1986   345'.001   86-23924
ISBN 0-19-503409-0 (v.1)
ISBN 0-19-504664-1 (v.1; ppk.) 342.5001

Printing (last digit): 9 8 7 6 5 4 3 2 1

Printed in the United States of America
on acid-free paper

For Betty

Preface

Harm to Others is the first in a four–volume work, *The Moral Limits of the Criminal Law*. Volume 2, *Offense to Others*, will discuss offensive nuisances, profoundly offensive conduct (like mistreatment of dead bodies, desecration of sacred symbols, and the public brandishing of odious political emblems like swastikas and KKK garments), obscenity, and pornography. Volume 3, *Harm to Self*, will discuss the problems of legal paternalism, the nature of personal autonomy, and the concept of voluntariness. Volume 4, *Harmless Wrongdoing*, will discuss various positions often lumped indiscriminately under the heading "legal moralism," including the claims that criminal prohibitions can be justified by their role in preserving a way of life, enforcing true morality, preventing wrongful gain from exploitation even when it has no proper "victim," and elevating taste and perfecting character.

These volumes began as my contribution to a four–part collaboration on a study of the problem of "victimless crimes." My three collaborators at that time were all distinguished members of the faculty of the New York University Law School. Hyman Gross was to write an essay on the way the criminal law actually functions; Graham Hughes was to write about limits to criminalization implicit in the United States Constitution; Peter Zimroth was to write a kind of sociological essay on the collateral costs of criminalization. My task was to write a short chapter on the "philosophical part" of the problem. I promised the others that I could finish my assignment in a month or so.

Zimroth wrote his excellent essay quickly. Gross, plausibly enough, wanted to be able to read Hughes's contribution before starting his, and Hughes, equally plausibly, preferred to wait for my contribution before starting his. My "brief chapter" grew and grew. It seemed that I could not keep it short without falling back on empty liberal slogans and philosophical platitudes. I soon discovered, to my despair, that the "philosophical part" of the problem was itself a whole universe of problems that had never been systematically assaulted. I had fallen into a bog, and the collaboration, alas, collapsed.

The philosophical part of the problem of the limits of criminalization, I now realize, is its deepest and most difficult part. The philosopher not only formulates and applies principles; he analyzes or clarifies concepts. Each main part of this study focuses on a difficult critical concept: harm, offense, autonomy and voluntariness, and morality. Each main concept draws the analyst into a web of related notions: interests, wrongs, omissions, causes, consent, reasonableness, rationality, risk, exploitation, coercion, fraud, incapacity, neurosis, depression, choice, community, social change, character. At times it has seemed as if adequate treatment of any one of these topics presupposes adequate treatment of all the others. There may be some truth in that pessimistic thought, but if any progress toward enlightenment is possible, it requires that the topics be approached in some rational order, that the whole study be given a proper formal structure, first things first. That I have tried to do.

I am grateful to Gross, Hughes, and Zimroth, and to Elizabeth Sifton and the Viking Press, for their patience with me during the early years of this project, and to the John Simon Guggenheim Memorial Foundation, the National Endowment for the Humanities, and the Rockefeller Foundation for fellowship support at intervals during the subsequent period. The largest part of the labor was completed during a premature sabbatical year for which I am grateful to Dean Paul Rosenblatt of the University of Arizona.

Philosophical helpers have been too abundant to acknowledge individually in this limited space. I hope I have remembered them all in the notes. In any event, they know who they are, and I want them all to know that I am immensely grateful for their help. My former colleague Josiah S. Carberry will claim to be among their numbers. He may even go so far as to sue me for plagiarism. Let him sue; he won't have a chance.

J. F.
Tucson, Arizona
June, 1983

Acknowledgments

Various parts of this volume, from small passages to the major sections of whole chapters, have already been published in independent articles. I am grateful to their publishers for permission to republish these copyrighted materials here. Parts of Chapters 1 and 2 appeared as "Harm and Self-Interest" in *Law, Morality, and Society: Essays in Honour of H.L.A. Hart*, ed. P.M.S. Hacker and J. Raz (Oxford: Clarendon Press, 1977), pp. 289–308. A shortened version of Chapter 4, § 1–3, was presented to the 11th World Congress on Philosophy of Law and Social Philosophy, August 17, 1983 in Helsinki, Finland. It is reprinted here by special arrangement with the editors of the Congress proceedings. This essay was also published in *Criminal Justice Ethics*, Vol. 3, No. 3 (1984). Three paragraphs of Chapter 5, § 6, appeared in my article "Limits to the Free Expression of Opinion" in *Philosophy and Law*, 2d ed., ed. Joel Feinberg and Hyman Gross (Belmont, Cal.: Wadsworth Publishing Co., 1980), pp. 196–97. Section 7 of Chapter 5 was published as "The Interest in Liberty on the Scales" in *Values and Morals: Essays in Honor of William K. Frankena, Charles L. Stevenson, and Richard B. Brandt*, ed. Alvin I. Goldman and Jaegwon Kim (Dordrecht: Reidel, 1978), pp. 21–35, copyright © 1978 by D. Reidel Publishing Co., Dordrecht, Holland.

Contents

GENERAL
INTRODUCTION

1. The basic question of the book

This book is an attempt to find a general answer, albeit a complicated one, to the question: What sorts of conduct may the state rightly make criminal? Its subject, though broad, is still narrower than John Stuart Mill's famous concern in *On Liberty* with "the nature and limits of the power which can be legitimately exercised by society over the individual,"[1] since our concern is only with power exercised by the state by means of the criminal law. Unlike Mill, we shall be concerned here only with the exercise of political power, thus neglecting those interferences with individual liberty that come from private associations, public opinion, or the "despotism of custom." Moreover, we shall ignore the more subtle uses of state power, like taxation, indoctrination, licensure, and selective funding, so that we may focus more narrowly on statutory prohibitions enforced by penal sanctions. What our question has in common with Mill's broader one is its emphasis on determining the legitimacy of exercises of power.

My reason for restricting the inquiry to the criminal law is partly methodological. Even if one were concerned to give a complete account of social power, one would begin with the relatively blunt and visible forms of political coercion where interferences with liberty are "writ large." Later one could proceed, armed with the results of one's primary inquiry, to examine the more subtle forms of coercion. Mill himself might not have appreciated the point of this procedure since he was rightly impressed with the power of extrapolitical forms of social control, and extralegal forms of political control. As C. L. Ten points out, for Mill "extra-legal coercion was far more pervasive and insidious than the use of legal penalties because 'it leaves fewer means of escape, penetrating much more deeply into the details of life, and enslaving the soul itself.' "² But even though social pressures toward conformity will continue to have this impact on individual choices whatever the content of our criminal law, it is still not a matter of indifference for the cause of liberty what the criminal law decrees. Penal statutes can reenforce social pressures, and also create effective restrictions of their own. The threat of legal punishment enforces public opinion by putting the nonconformist in a terror of apprehension, rendering his privacy precarious, and his prospects in life uncertain. The punishments themselves brand him with society's most powerful stigma and undermine his life projects, in career or family, disastrously. These legal interferences have a prior claim on our attention then, not merely because of their greater visibility and theoretical accessibility, but also because of their immense destructive impact on human interests. Given the inherent costs of criminalization, when a particular legal prohibition oversteps the limit of moral legitimacy, it is itself a serious moral crime.

Our question can be understood as one posed for an ideal legislature in a democratic country. It is not my purpose to try to specify what such a body *would* choose to include in its ideally wise and useful penal code, but rather what it *may* include, if it chooses within the limits that morality places on its legislative decisions. This four-volume work, then, is an account of the moral constraints on legislative action. As such, it is an extended essay in applied moral philosophy. Even though it incidentally considers the rationale of various crimes, it does not provide detailed answers to legislative questions. Rather it attempts to provide a coherent and plausible set of moral principles to guide the legislator by locating the moral constraints that limit his options. The book will not consider the further questions of cost-benefit analysis that must guide the legislator in his choices among those alternatives that do fall within the recommended moral limits. Within the proper limits a legislator must consider the social utility of his various options, their likely effects on various private and public interests, constituent desires and pressures, even the demands of "politics" in a narrow sense (log-rolling, compromising, political debt-paying, etc.). Our primary question, however, is not one about social utility and practical wisdom. I do not offer suggestions here about what it would be "a good idea" to legislate within the scope of what *may* be legislated. This book is a quest not for useful policies but for valid principles.³

Neither is our basic question one of constitutionality within some actual system of law, American or other. Still, since our aim is to distinguish legitimate from illegitimate legislative purposes, our results could be useful for courts that must apply such standards in their review of otherwise valid statutes. And if some version of the natural law jurisprudence is applicable to (say) the American legal system, it will not be possible for a morally illegitimate statute to be legally valid within that system. In that case, this essay in applied moral philosophy would necessarily be an essay in constitutional law as well. But such an interpretation goes well beyond any claims I make for this work. The arguments are addressed to an ideal legislature, not to an ideal Supreme Court. I am quite prepared to assume at the start that (1) some constitutionally permitted statutes might not be morally legitimate, and yet are no less valid legally for that, and (2) some morally permissible or required statutes might not be constitutional. Whatever the overlap between legal validity and moral legitimacy in our system (and it is surely extensive), these are separate and independent concepts. If your jurisprudential theory leads you to hold that the United States Constitution embodies (without explicitly expressing) all relevant sound moral principles, *and* if you accept my thesis about what some of those principles are, then you will take this work to be a helpful interpretation of the Constitution. But if you hold that law is one thing and morality quite another, and that they need not perfectly coincide in a valid constitutional legal system, then you will take this work to be at most a moral guide to legislators. The present inquiry, in short, is meant to be neutral in respect to problems of philosophical jurisprudence. Its thesis is meant to be compatible with an extreme constitutional positivism, but if a natural law theorist should find it useful as a key to an "unwritten moral constitution" underlying our traditional written one and necessarily presupposed by it, he is welcome to it.

Even an extreme legal positivist, however, would approve of a court's applying its own moral standards, including standards of legislative legitimacy, wherever the Constitution seems to require that this be done. There is little doubt, I think, that the Constitution does provide the Supreme Court with a limited supply of moral blank checks. I have in mind those places where that document, or its accepted principles of interpretation, seem to invite the Court to apply its own standards of what is a *reasonable* or *unreasonable* search or seizure, what are *cruel* or *noncruel* punishments, what is *just* or *unjust* compensation, *excessive* or *unexcessive* fine or bail, what is *due* process or *equal* protection, and (especially) what are *legitimate* and *compelling* state interests. In any event, my assumption that some judicial discretion is moral discretion emboldens me here and there to criticize the judicial opinions of Supreme Court justices on such matters as obscenity and privacy.

These volumes might also be thought of (presumptuous as it sounds) as addressed to *ideal constitution-makers* in some hypothetical constitutional assembly. The draftsmen of the morally ideal constitution, in that case, would have to translate my criteria of moral legitimacy into constitutional rules of the form "Congress shall make no law . . . having such and such characteristics." Perhaps they would state that prohibitory laws with criminal sanctions must have a legitimate purpose, namely so and so, and must be at least arguably related to the achievement of that purpose, not overbroad and hence unnecessarily restrictive of liberty, and so on. That hypothetical constitution, if it embodied the correct principles of legislative legitimacy, would then be accepted as legally valid by the natural law theorist, and as soon as it was adopted its principles would be accepted (because of their enactment) by the positivist. The legal system that emerged from it then, in effect, would blend positivistic and natural law "rules of recognition" (criteria for the validity of statutes), being in effect a kind of enacted natural law document.

2. *The concept of moral legitimacy*

A basic distinction presupposed by this work, then, is that between criminal statutes that are *legitimized* by valid moral principles and those that are *justified* on balance as being both legitimate *and* useful, wise, economical, popular, etc. I have no intention of undertaking a deep philosophical analysis of the basic idea of moral legitimacy. That would be difficult, distracting, and because of that notion's intuitive familiarity, quite unnecessary. The idea of legitimacy is not an invention of arcane philosophy. It is part of the conceptual equipment of every man and woman "on the street." Consider an illustration of its everyday use.

If a red-headed stranger stops me as I am strolling north along Fifth Avenue and demands that I tell him where I am going, my first reaction will be to ask, in return, why he wishes to know. I will be genuinely curious, and also disposed to be polite and accommodating if he should have a good reason for his question. But if he brushes off my request and demands peremptorily that I answer his question or else "face the consequences," my mood will change abruptly. "Where I am going," I will say, "is *my business*, not yours. I am not answerable to you. You are not my owner, or my master, or a policeman. You have no authority over me of any kind, direct or delegated. Now stand out of my way."

If the stranger nevertheless persists in blocking my path and preventing me from proceeding in a northward direction, his interference with my liberty is *illegitimate*, *improper*, or *morally illicit*. These predicates, it should be noticed, are not legal or political terms. If the law gave all red-headed men the power to question and forcibly restrain all balding brunettes, that very legal authority would be morally illegitimate, and the statute confer-ring it would be morally unjustified, whatever its legal or constitutional status. The same would be true of a statute that simply outlawed walking in a northerly direction by specifying a criminal punishment and conferring enforcement power on policemen instead of civilians. It is *not the business of the state*, we might complain, to determine for no good reason the direction in which pedestrians may walk. Even if the constitution gave the legislature the right to make such a law, it would be *wrong* for the legislature to exercise its constitutional authority in such an arbitrary fashion. We can concede to the legal positivist, if only for the purposes of argument, that there can be legal *authority* to misrule in this fashion, even where there is no moral justification for its exercise. But authority is not what this book is about.

3. The idea of a liberty-limiting principle

We can also formulate the basic question of these volumes as one about the moral limits of individual liberty, understanding "liberty" simply as the absence of legal coercion. When the state creates a legal statute prohibiting its citizens from doing X on pain of punishment, then the citizens are no longer "at liberty" to do X. The credible threat of punishment working directly on the citizens' motives makes X seem substantially less eligible than before for their deliberate doing. We can think of every possible act as so related to a penal code that it must either be (1) required (a duty), (2) merely permitted (one we are "at liberty" to do or forbear doing), or (3) prohibited (a crime). Where coercive law stops, there liberty begins. The citizen's zone of liberty, therefore, corresponds to the second class, since (1) and (3) are alike in directing coercive threats at him. When we are required to do X (a duty), we are prohibited, under pain of penalty, from omitting to do X; when we are prohibited from doing Y we are required, under threat of penalty, to omit doing Y. The goal of this work then is to trace the contours of the zone in which the citizen has a moral claim to be at liberty, that is, free of legal coercion.

So conceived, the proper zone of liberty against the state might still have no moral barriers against penetration by other private individuals. To say of a person that he is at liberty to do X is to deny that he has a legal duty in respect to X. He has neither a duty to do X nor a duty not to do X. He may or may not do X as he pleases. But this says nothing about the duties of other individual citizens toward him in respect to his doing of X. Some may have duties not to interfere should he choose to do X, but no one has a duty of noninterference derived simply from another's being at liberty. Two or more people might both be at liberty to do the same thing if they can, even in competitive situations where at most only one of them *can* do what they both wish to do. Thus if *A* and *B* both see a $100 bill on the sidewalk, each is at liberty to take entire possession of it, but if they both wish to exercise that liberty, only the one who wins the race to the money will succeed.

On the other hand, my claim to the $100 bill now in my pocket is a much stronger thing, adding to my liberty to possess it or not as I choose a duty of noninterference incumbent on other people. I am at liberty to do what I wish with that money, and no one else is similarly at liberty with respect to it. That is to say that I have a *claim-right* to the money. In general a *claim-right* adds to my liberty a duty of others toward me (typically not to interfere).

The criminal law then not only regulates my liberty by imposing duties and extending liberties to me, it also confers rights on me against my fellow citizens and thereby protects me from *them* in the exercise of my liberties. A particular legal statute may impose a duty on everyone (say) not to assault John Doe, and in virtue of that general duty, Doe's liberty (to come and go as he wishes) is strengthened. Protecting him in the exercise of his liberty is the point of limiting everyone else's in this respect. But not all legal duties have liberty-protecting rationales. A criminal statute could simply impose a duty on everyone to do *X* (for example to say prayers every night), when the duty in question cannot be thought of as a duty of noninterference with another party's liberty.

It is important to distinguish between coercively imposed legal duties and other sources of *inability*. Not everything one is *unable* to do is something one is *not at liberty* to do. There are many other barriers to our actions than prohibitory rules backed by threats of punishment. I am not able to speak Russian, high-jump seven feet, write an original work in nuclear physics, or give birth to a baby. But it would be false and misleading to say that I am not free or not at liberty to do those things. Liberty is not the absence of just *any* kind of constraint or any kind of thing that can prevent me from doing something, but rather the absence of constraints of one particular kind, namely those imposed by enforced rules or commands. This point may at first seem a mere linguistic quibble, but it leads to an evaluative judgment of some importance. Liberty is an extremely valuable good, perhaps even necessary for a good life (see Chap. 5, §7, and Chap. 19, §3),* but it is by no means the only important good, and cannot therefore be sufficient. Both the rich and the poor in our free country are equally at

*These cross-references and others to follow refer to chapters and sections both in this volume and in Volumes 2, 3, and 4. The chapters are numbered sequentially from the first volume through the fourth, rather than starting afresh in each volume.

liberty to buy Cadillacs. The difference is that the rich enjoy two kinds of goods, liberty and money, while the poor have only their liberty. When it comes to car ownership, liberty without money is as useless as money without liberty.[4] And the same applies, in other compartments of life, to liberty without talent, knowledge, friendship, or health. Even good things in the purely juristic category are not exhausted by liberties and claim-rights. The legal *powers* to enter into contracts, to get married to any consenting party of one's choice, and to transfer one's property by will and testament are not the same thing as liberties (that is, they are not mere absences of duties to forbear); yet they are valuable legal instruments ("powers") that are so treasured that people have been willing to fight for them. (See Chap. 19, §6.)

While it is easy to overemphasize the value of liberty, there is no denying its necessity, and for that reason most writers on our subject have endorsed a kind of "presumption in favor of liberty" requiring that whenever a legislator is faced with a choice between imposing a legal duty on citizens or leaving them at liberty, other things being equal, he should leave individuals free to make their own choices. Liberty should be the norm; coercion always needs some special justification. That "presumption" together with its justifying reasons we can call the "presumptive case for liberty." We shall not pause long to try to make the case here (but see Chap. 5, §7, Chap. 18, and Chap. 19, §§3–5). Suffice it to say that the person deprived of a liberty will think of its absence as a genuine personal loss, and when we put ourselves in his shoes we naturally share his assessment. Moreover, loss of liberty both in individuals and societies entails loss of flexibility and greater vulnerability to unforeseen contingencies. Finally, free citizens are likelier to be highly capable and creative persons through the constant exercise of their capacities to choose, make decisions, and assume responsibilities. Perhaps these simple truisms, by no means the whole of the case for liberty, are nevertheless sufficient to establish some presumption in liberty's favor, and transfer the burden of argument to the shoulders of the advocate of coercion who must, in particular instances, show that the standing case for liberty can be overridden by even weightier reasons on the other side of the scales.

Thus, still another way of posing this work's basic question suggests itself: what kinds of reasons can have weight when balanced against the presumptive case for liberty? Answers to this question take the form of what I shall call "liberty-limiting principles" (or equivalently, "coercion-legitimizing principles"). A liberty-limiting principle is one which states that a given type of consideration is always a morally relevant reason in support of penal legislation even if other reasons may in the circumstances outweigh it. So conceived, the diverse liberty-limiting principles proposed by various philosophers, while distinct and separate, are nonetheless not rivals. More than one, and even all of them, could be true. As formulated here they do not contradict one another.

It is important to point out that these proposed coercion-legitimizing principles do not even purport to state necessary and sufficient conditions for justified state coercion. A liberty-limiting principle does not state a *sufficient condition* because in a given case its purportedly relevant reason might not weigh heavily enough on the scales to outbalance the standing presumption in favor of liberty. That presumption is not only supported by moral and utilitarian considerations of a general kind;[5] it is also likely to be buttressed in particular cases by appeal to the practical costs, direct and collateral, of criminalization. A new crime on the books might put a strain on court facilities, divert police resources from more serious respon- sibilities, crowd prisons, and provide markets for the monopolistic and criminogenic enterprises of organized crime.[6] So merely to show that there is a morally relevant reason for a particular penal statute is not yet to show that it is a sufficient or conclusive reason in the case at hand. In particular legislative contexts there are always equally relevant reasons on the other side that must be overridden. Moreover, no liberty-limiting principle claims to put forth a *necessary condition* for the justification of criminal statutes either. No one of them makes any claim about the truth or falsity of the other principles that have been proposed, and indeed there is nothing in a principle's formulation to preclude any or all of the others from being valid too. If more than one coercion-legitimizing princi- ple is correct in stating an always relevant reason for criminalization, then no one of them can state a necessary condition for all justified criminaliza- tion. In short, each liberty-limiting principle puts forth a kind of reason it claims always to be relevant—always to have some weight—in support of proposed legal coercion, even though in a given instance it might not weigh enough to be decisive, and even though it may not be the only kind of consideration that can be relevant.

4. Commonly proposed liberty-limiting principles

About the propriety of one class of crimes there can be no controversy. Willful homicide, forcible rape, aggravated assault, and battery are crimes (under one name or another) everywhere in the civilized world, and no reasonable person could advocate their "decriminalization." Almost as non- controversial as these serious "crimes against the person" are various serious "crimes against property": burglary, grand larceny, and various offenses involving fraud and misrepresentation. The common element in crimes of these two categories is the direct production of serious harm to individual persons and groups. Other kinds of properly prohibited behavior, like reckless driving and the reckless discharging of lethal weapons, are banned not because they necessarily cause harm in every case, but rather because they create unreasonable risks of harm to other persons.

Still other crimes that have an unquestioned place in our penal codes are kinds of conduct that rarely cause clear and substantial harm to any specific person or group, but are said to cause harm to "the public," "society," "the state," public institutions or practices, the general ambience of neighborhoods, the economy, the climate, or the environment. Typical of crimes in this general category are counterfeiting, smuggling, income tax evasion, contempt of court, and violation of zoning and antipollution ordinances. The harms produced by such crimes can be labeled "public" as opposed to "private" harms provided it is kept in mind that the public is composed of private individuals standing in complex social and legal relations to one another. In some cases of public harm—for example the poisoning of a city's water supply or the undermining of a government's currency—the harm to many or all private citizens is direct and serious. In other cases—for example, a single instance of tax evasion—the harm to any given individual is highly dilute and unnoticeable. Crimes of the latter sort do have a tendency, of course, to weaken public institutions in whose health we all have a stake, and if they were allowed to become general, the institutions in question would be undermined to our great collective loss.

Generalizing then from the clearest cases of legitimate or proper criminalization, we can assert tentatively that it is legitimate for the state to prohibit conduct that causes serious private harm, or the unreasonable risk of such harm, or harm to important public institutions and practices. In short, state interference with a citizen's behavior tends to be morally justified when it is reasonably necessary (that is, when there are reasonable grounds for taking it to be necessary as well as effective) to prevent harm or the unreasonable risk of harm to parties other than the person interfered with. More concisely, the need to prevent harm (private or public) to parties other than the actor is always an appropriate *reason* for legal coercion. This principle, which we have tentatively extracted from the clearest cases of legitimate interference, can be called "the harm to others principle" or "the harm principle" for short, and recommended to legislatures as part of a moral guide to the limits of their proper activity. John Stuart Mill argued in effect that the harm principle is the *only* valid principle for determining legitimate invasions of liberty, so that no conduct that fails to satisfy its terms can properly be made criminal. We would be better advised, however, to begin in a cautious way with the claim that the harm principle is *a* valid legislative principle (though not necessarily the *only* one), and then, applying it hypothetically to the difficult and controversial areas case by case, try to determine to what extent, if any, it must be modified or supplemented to achieve moral adequacy.

The harm principle then is a useful starting place for our inquiry, but it could hardly be advanced, at this stage in the argument, as our final conclusion without begging some of the most controversial questions of public policy. Moreover, in its present form, the principle is too vague to be of any potential use at all. Clearly not every kind of act that causes harm to others can rightly be prohibited, but only those that cause avoidable and substantial harm. Since the effect of legal coercion may itself be harmful to the interests of the actor it restrains, one would think that only the prevention of still more serious harms to others could justify its infliction. (But see Chap. 5, §2.) So the harm principle must be made sufficiently precise to permit the formulation of a criterion of "seriousness," and also, if possible, some way of grading types of harms in terms of their seriousness. Without these further specifications, the harm principle may be taken to invite state interference without limit, for virtually every kind of human conduct can affect the interests of others for better and worse to *some* degree, and thus would properly be the state's business.

So far, despite such misgivings, we have endorsed the view that considerations of harm prevention are always relevant reasons in support of coercion. The more radical view of Mill's that such considerations are the only relevant reasons cannot be evaluated until the classes of reasons put forth by other candidate principles have been examined. Most writers would accept at least some additional kinds of reasons as equally legitimate. Three others, in particular, have won widespread support. It has been held (but not always by the same person) that it is always a good and relevant reason in support of penal legislation that: (1) it is reasonably necessary to prevent hurt (see Chap. 1, §4) or offense (as opposed to injury or harm) to others (the *offense principle*); (2) it is reasonably necessary to prevent harm to the very person it prohibits from acting, as opposed to "others" (*legal paternalism*); (3) it is reasonably necessary to prevent inherently immoral conduct whether or not such conduct is harmful or offensive to anyone (*legal moralism*). An especially interesting position, and one which deserves separate discussion, is that formed by the intersection of moralism and paternalism which holds that a good reason for restricting a person's liberty is that it is reasonably necessary to prevent moral (as opposed to physical or economic) harm to that person himself. This view, which provides one of the leading rationales for the prohibition of pornography, can be labeled *moralistic paternalism*. (See Chap. 2, §1, and Chap. 12, §2.)

The liberty-limiting principles listed above, since they do not purport to specify necessary conditions for legitimate state coercion, are not mutually exclusive. It is logically open to us to hold only one of them, rejecting all the others (as Mill did), or to hold two or more of them at once, even all of them together, and it is possible to deny all of them (as an anarchist might). Our strategy here will be to begin by accepting the harm principle and then examine controversial classes of crimes not legitimized by that principle, to determine whether the harm principle requires supplementation by one or more of the others.

The alternative principles suggest an orderly classification of the various categories of criminal statutes that are the objects of current controversy. The *offense principle*, for example, could provide reason for creating such "morals offenses" as open lewdness, solicitation, and indecent exposure, and for criminalizing the distribution or sale of pornography, activities and materials offensive to religious or patriotic sensibilities, and racial and ethnic slurs. *Legal paternalism* would provide support for criminal prohibitions of self-mutilation, suicide, euthanasia, drunkenness, possession and use of psychoactive drugs, and various forms of gambling, as well as requirements, enforced by criminal sanctions, that hunters wear red caps and motorcyclists wear crash helmets, that motorists use seat belts, that doctors' prescriptions be required for the purchase of various medicines, and so on. *Legal moralism* provides grounding for statutes prohibiting deviant sexual activities—homosexual or extramarital sexual intercourse and "perversions" especially shocking to the legislators, even when performed in private by consenting adults—adultery, bigamy, prostitution even when discreetly arranged, and live sex shows or bloody gladiatorial contests presented by voluntary performers before consenting audiences.

Most of the controversial criminal statutes that receive apparent blessing from the principles alternative to the harm principle, however, have often been said to have support also from the harm principle itself. Often the consequences of lewdness, homosexuality, drug-taking, or gambling are said to be harmful to others in some very subtle way, or produced by some partially concealed or indirect causal process. So much confusion has resulted from these allegations that it has become far from evident just which crimes now on the books satisfy the harm principle and which do not. That confusion can only be dispelled by a careful analysis of the concept of harm, and the formulation of relatively precise maxims to mediate the application of the harm principle to hard cases. My purpose in this volume will be to provide that necessary clarification. (A fuller list of liberty-limiting principles and their more exact definitions follows this Introduction on p. 26.)

5. Liberalism

"A liberal, I suppose one could say, is a person who believes in liberty, as a nudist is a person who believes in nudity."[7] So much is true, but the degree of the liberal's commitment can vary from mere lip service to fanatic extremes. Liberalism applied to the problem of the limits of the criminal law would require commitment to the presumption in favor of liberty, but that presumption could be thought of, at one extreme, as powerful enough to be always decisive, and at the other, as weak enough to be overridden by any of a large variety of liberty-limiting principles, even when minimally applicable. If the word "liberal" is to have any utility in this context, it should refer to one who has so powerful a commitment to liberty that he is motivated to limit the number of acknowledged liberty-limiting principles as narrowly as possible, and to require in particular cases that in order to override the presumptive case for liberty, a valid liberty-limiting principle must exert a substantial part of its weight on the scales, considerably more than a mere token presence.

As we have seen, no responsible theorist denies the validity of the harm principle, but the liberal would prefer if possible to draw the line there, and deny validity to any other proposed ground for state interference. Most liberals, however, have been forced to give a little more ground, and acknowledge the offense principle (duly refined and qualified) as well. Even John Stuart Mill, after his bold initial claim that "the *only* purpose for which power can be rightfully exercised over any member of a civilized community, against his will, is to prevent harm to others,"[8] comes to appreciate the offense principle, in a later chapter, as a kind of afterthought: ". . . there are many acts which, being directly injurious only to the agents themselves, ought not to be legally interdicted, but which if done publicly, are a violation of good manners and, coming thus within the category of offenses against others, may rightly be prohibited. Of this kind are offenses against decency, on which it is unnecessary to dwell. . . ."[9] When offensive behavior is irritating enough, and those offended cannot conveniently make their escapes from it, even the liberals among them are apt to lose patience, and demand "protection" from the state, as the widespread acceptance of criminal nuisance statutes attests. That being so (the point is argued in detail in Chapter 7), we can define liberalism in respect to the subject matter of this work as the view that the harm and offense principles, duly clarified and qualified, between them exhaust the class of morally relevant reasons for criminal prohibitions. Paternalistic and moralistic considerations, when introduced as support for penal legislation, have no weight at all.

Having so defined "liberalism," I must now express in all candor my own liberal predilections. I frankly intend in these volumes to make the best possible case for liberalism so defined, and if the attempt fails to persuade the skeptical reader that liberalism is true doctrine, it will nonetheless be a success if it convinces him that its formulation here makes it as plausible as it can be while still properly called "liberalism." I will attempt to define, interpret, qualify, and buttress liberalism in such ways that in the end we can say that the refined final product is what liberalism must look like to have its strongest claim to plausibility. Even the opponent of liberalism then will be pleased to know that the theory he rebuts is not a mere "straw man" or "dead horse." This work, by the same token, will be an effort to vindicate the traditional liberalism derived from Mill's *On Liberty*, not by slavishly adhering to its every contention and argument, but by salvaging a central part of it, qualified and reformulated in the light of the many accumulated difficulties and criticisms. The highly qualified view presented here will be at the very least faithful to Mill's liberal motivating spirit.

In the beginning I will try to placate the unreconstructed "extreme liberals" who are unwilling to acknowledge *any* ground for legitimate interference with liberty beyond the harm principle. My procedure, having "assumed" the correctness of the harm principle, will be to adopt a properly liberal skeptical stance toward all other liberty-limiting principles, and to try to go as far as possible with the harm principle alone, acknowledging additional valid principles only if driven to do so by argument. Every effort will be made to keep the list of valid coercion-legitimizing principles as short as possible. I will begin in a cautious way with the claim that the harm principle (which was extracted from the clearest cases of intuitively legitimate criminalization) is *a* valid legislative principle (though not necessarily the only one), and then, applying it to the difficult and controversial areas case by case, try to determine to what extent, if any, it must be modified or supplemented to achieve moral adequacy.

Some mention here should be made of the currently popular ideology that bears the name of "libertarianism." Libertarians are very likely to accept the liberal position on the moral limits of the criminal law, and their support is surely welcome. But the liberal arguments deployed in this book give little support to the other central doctrines of libertarianism. As I understand it, libertarianism embraces three positions: *laissez-faire* in economic policy, isolationism in foreign policy, and liberalism on the question of criminal prohibitions. This triad of views is described pithily (though informally) by Edward H. Crane III of the libertarian Cato Institute: "I see what many people have interpreted as a conservative trend in our country as really more of a libertarian trend; a growing sophistication among people who reject the authority of the alleged leaders of society who presume to tell us how much of our money we can keep, where we've got to fight, and what kind of sexual life we can have."[10] The liberal agrees emphatically that the state may not try to determine what kind of sexual life we may have. The question of military conscription is a more difficult one, but the liberal is surely not opposed to it in an absolute way in any and all circumstances. Sometimes, after all, failure to serve is to inflict a social *harm* that the state is entitled to prevent, and in those circumstances, therefore, conscription receives support from the harm principle. Other questions of foreign affairs and economic management are questions of policy rather than principle, unaddressed by liberalism in the sense of this work. As for taxation (decreed by those who "presume to tell us how much of our money we can keep"), the libertarian's adamant opposition can only be a source of amazement to the liberal, who appreciates the great social harms (and not mere loss of benefits) that would be incurred were tax revenues to disappear, and also the extent to which individual income and wealth is a product of social conditions rather than the fruit of individual effort, in the first place.[11]

6. Methodology

The reader who is unfamiliar with academic philosophy may be impressed by the extent to which this work "deals with abstractions." It does not probe deeply into the facts or discuss, for example, the varieties of drug addiction, or the effects of pornography on children, or the degree of physical protection provided by seat belts in the various types of automobile accidents. It does not provide specific and detailed recommendations for legislation. But its aim is to be *practical* anyway. Philosophical inquiries into principles and concepts *can* have practical usefulness if only because in the present stage of public discussion of legislative issues, the abstract level is where the most serious confusions are located. All practical reasoning involves the application of principles to the facts. The principles, in turn, must be clarified and tested tentatively against hypothetical possibilities. They must be rendered compatible with our more confident "intuitions," that is with our deeply entrenched informed convictions in particular cases, and rendered harmonious with one another. But the principles at hand, at least as simply stated, are rarely clear. They must be fleshed out; otherwise they are mere rhetorical slogans, empty of meaning.

Often the unclarity of principles derives from the vagueness of the central

concepts in whose terms they are too simply formulated. Conceptual clarification is the most distinctively philosophical of enterprises. We cannot
discuss the moral limits of the criminal law without heavy reliance on the
concepts of harm, benefit, interests, wants, injuries, wrongs, action, omission, causation, offense, nuisance, obscenity, invective, harassment, liberty,
autonomy, voluntariness, consent, risk, reasonableness, rationality, coercion, threats and offers, a community, a community's morality, manipulation, exploitation, welfare, and character—to name only some. All of these
concepts, and more, are subjected to analysis in context, in the pages that
follow.

Conceptual clarity is neither more nor less important for public policy
than factual discovery. Each is vitally necessary, and the two are mutually
dependent. Facts are important for the social philosopher not only for the
proper application of his principles but also for their convincing derivation,
since if the facts are such that tentative hypothetical testings of principles
yield consistently unsatisfactory results in particular cases, then the principles themselves are defective as formulated, and must be revised. But conceptual clarification is what the philosopher by training and experience does
best, and empirical studies he must leave, in a spirit of interested cooperation, to his social scientific colleagues.

To take one example of the different character of related conceptual and
empirical inquiries, consider the questions raised in this volume about one
of the central concepts, *harm*. I do not make any empirical determination of
the extent to which pornography, for example, causes harm. That question,
of vital importance to the legislator, is left to those who can design ques-
tionnaires, statistical studies, and experiments. But I do ask questions about
harm that social scientists rarely raise—whether corruption of character
without effect on interests is a harm, whether harm can be vicarious,
whether a person can be harmed by his own death or by events after his
death, or by his conception or birth, whether one can harm by omission, or
by mere suggestion, whether one can consent to being harmed, or be exploited without being harmed. Until these questions are answered one cannot have a firm grasp of the concept of harm; one cannot know how to
interpret results of empirical studies of harm; one cannot confidently apply
a "harm principle" to legislative problems.

Technical philosophers too may find the approach in these volumes
skewed, although in a different direction. They will find no semblance of a
complete moral system, no reduction of moral derivatives to moral primi-
tives, no grounding of ultimate principles in self-evident truths, or in "the
nature of man," the commandments of God, or the dialectic of history. It
would be folly to speculate whether the moral theory implicit in this work

is utilitarian, Kantian, Rawlsian, or whatever. I appeal at various places, quite unselfconsciously, to all the kinds of reasons normally produced in practical discourse, from efficiency and utility to fairness, coherence, and human rights. But I make no effort to derive some of these reasons from the others, or to rank them in terms of their degree of basicness. My omission is not due to any principled objections to "deep structure" theories (although I must confess to some skeptical inclinations).[12] I do not believe that such an approach is precluded, but only that it is unnecessary. Progress on the penultimate questions need not wait for solutions to the ultimate ones.

Even though this work abjures the more systematic treatment that would make proofs and demonstrations possible, it contains an abundance of argumentation of the sort that led Santayana, with forgivable hyperbole, to write that "there can be no other kind of argument in ethics" than the *argumentum ad hominem*.[13] The appeal in such arguments is made directly "to the person" of one's interlocutor, to the convictions he or she is plausibly assumed to possess already. If the argument is successful, it shows to the person addressed that the judgment it supports coheres more smoothly than its rivals with the network of convictions he already possesses, so that if he rejects it, then he will have to abandon other judgments that he would be loath to relinquish. The argument may attempt to demonstrate to the addressee that the denial of the judgment to be provided would logically entail other propositions which he could not himself embrace without great embarrassment. A *reductio ad absurdum* argument in geometry proves a proposition by showing that its denial logically entails a false proposition. Its *ad hominem* counterpart in ethics purports to show only that the entailed proposition is already *believed to be false* by the person addressed. This "coherence method"[14] obviously presupposes a great deal of common ground between arguer and addressee (reader) to begin with. If two persons possessed no important moral beliefs in common, they could not expect to reach agreement by appealing to the beliefs they "already have." My assumption, however, is that almost all my readers share with me a large number of values and ideals, and that they all would be willing to modify or relinquish some of their beliefs if they could be shown that by so doing, they would strengthen the support for others that are more fundamental, and increase internal coherence generally. As for the logically possible but not very likely person whose moral beliefs are all logically contradictory to my own, there is nothing relevant that I can say to him. Whether reason has further resources to "refute" the consistent fascist, or convince the hypothetical skeptic, are questions for moral epistemology whose genuineness and importance I do not deny. But they are not the questions addressed in this book.

The *ad hominem* method may employ any of a great variety of techniques, some subtle, all familiar and eminently rational. I cite here only three examples from the text. In Chapter 7, I try to convince the "extreme liberal" of the state's legitimate interest in preventing offensiveness as such. I tell a fanciful story there of a hypothetical bus ride in which the reader is asked to imagine himself as a very reluctant passenger. All of the conditions for a legitimate application of the offense principle are present, and I assume that the honest reader will respond by making the desired concession, so that his spontaneous response to the hypothetical story will be more smoothly integrated into his own conviction network. The "argument" may fail, but it should at least show the adamant reader that holding on to one of his prior convictions carries a certain cost, and that may be a point he had not previously noticed. In Chapters 18 and 19, I try to persuade the reader to share my conception of personal autonomy by presenting a full portrayal of it in the hope that he will "recognize" it as a conception in fact presupposed by, or implicit in, his own everyday attitudes. In Chapter 29, I try to convince the reader that essential changes in a "way of life" are not tragic losses by urging him to reject the misleading model of "cultural genocide" for the more pertinent models of biological evolution and linguistic change. He does not grieve for the loss of *Eohippus* or the Etruscan language; why then, in all consistency, I ask, should he grieve for the gradual passing of "ways of life"? Again, the appeal is direct and personal, and makes no claim to have "proved" anything. But then why should it?

There are, of course, dangers and limitations in the *ad hominem* method. There is little gain in convincing only the already convinced. But I hope to do more than that: I hope to convince many who share my basic ideals and attitudinal outlook also to share less obvious specific judgments about the particular subject matter of the book. And even the "already convinced" may find here a useful framework of reasons to render more clear and secure their prior convictions, and that is some gain. A greater danger is the one Santayana himself pointed out in his criticism of Bertrand Russell's way of arguing "whenever he approaches some concrete ethical question," namely that the vivid image employed in the *ad hominem* may merely reenforce the addressee in his prejudices and leave him ignorant of possibilities for belief that have not had a fair hearing in his narrow experience. The apparent cogency of the argument in that case may simply be the consequences of want of imagination.[15] The reader is forewarned.

7. Primary and derivative crimes

Some penal statutes have a very simple formal structure. They describe a certain kind of conduct, place it under an interdiction, and threaten punishments for engaging in it. The laws against homicide, battery, rape, theft, kidnapping, arson, forgery, public drunkenness, open lewdness, and cruelty to animals, among many others, are *direct prohibitions* of this kind. Punishment for violations of these statutes is of course "punishment for disobedience," but only in the trivial sense in which all punishment is for noncompliance with law. There is also something else, something primary, that the punishment is *for*, namely killing, beating, raping, stealing, and so on. The whole purpose of the criminal prohibition is to discourage the particular antisocial behavior that is forbidden, and that behavior can be characterized quite independently of the legal statute that forbids it. Criminal punishment plays a different, and less direct, role in other sorts of crime. Sometimes it is a mere "back-up sanction" held in reserve to enforce the provisions of rules that define other techniques[16] of social service or control. For example, the law of torts is not meant simply to prohibit antisocial conduct by threat of sanctions. Its aim is to repair damage done by one party to another through forced payments of compensation. But if the court orders the defendant to pay the plaintiff's damages, and the defendant flatly refuses, then the court order will be backed up by legal force. The disobedient litigant will pay up whether he chooses to or not, and he may be punished to boot for contempt of court. In that case his punishment is not for his prior negligence (say) to the plaintiff; it is for disobedience to authority, plain and simple. That conduct could not even be clearly characterized independently of that system of rules which provides, as a public service, a system for settling private disputes, and defining incidentally the authority of judges. The backup sanctions then are in a sense derivative, rather than primary. It is not the central purpose, the *raison d'être*, of the law of torts to punish contempt of court, any more than it is the purpose of legal marriage to prevent adultery; but it is the whole point of the law of criminal homicide to prevent and punish wrongful killings. Statutes whose sanctions are primary in this way are also "natural crimes" in a familiar eighteenth-century sense, whereas sanctions attached to rules that have purposes other than simple prohibition are relatively "artificial." One can wrongfully kill whether or not there is a criminal law of homicide, but one cannot commit contempt of court unless there is already in existence a complex legal structure (the court system) whose rules confer powers and immunities, and define authority.

In addition to contempt of court, other crimes in the "derivative-artificial" category are tax evasion, draft evasion, practicing medicine without a license, issuing prescription drugs without a physician's prescription, driving without a license, possessing an unregistered firearm, and perhaps perjury, bribery, bail-jumping, and escape from prison. Other criminal sanctions are clearly primary but attached to crimes that are to some degree "artificial."

For example, the aim of the statute against counterfeiting is to prevent the private manufacture of fake currency, "plain and simple." That statute is clearly a part of the criminal law proper, and not merely an incidental enforcement of authority defined by rules in some other branch of the law, like torts or administrative regulation. But the scale from "natural" to "artificial" is more a matter of degree. Counterfeiting is more of an artificial crime than murder, because one can wrongfully kill a person in a state of nature prior to any civil government or criminal code at all, whereas one cannot commit counterfeiting unless there is already in existence a monetary system with an official currency. But counterfeiting is more "natural" a crime than (say) contempt of court because it can be defined independently of the penal statute that forbids it, whereas contempt of court is a mere backup to power-conferring rules defining an institutional practice, and inconceivable without those rules.

I restrict my attention in this book almost entirely to the rationales for crimes in the "primary" category, where "punishment is used in the first instance" and not merely "as a last resort,"[17] where punishment is clearly *for* something other than (or in addition to) mere disobedience to authority as such, and it can be specified what punishment is for independently of the rules of legal institutions set up for some purpose (e.g. reparation, regulation by licensure, revenue-raising, recruiting military personnel, etc.) other than criminalization *per se*. Without such a restriction there could be no limit to our subject, and discussion would wander over the entire range of economic and political policy. Where criminal punishments are mere backup sanctions in noncriminal legislation, liability to the sanctions is simply a corollary of authority, the other side of its coin. If we are going to confer authority on designated officials in order to make some governmental program or institution work, we are committed thereby to granting them enforcement powers, since unenforcible authority is, in effect, no authority at all. If we want to decide whether a rule creating this kind of "derivative" criminal liability is morally legitimate, we must first decide whether there is adequate justification for the program or institution requiring this kind of power in the first place. But it would take us much too far afield if we tried to review here the pros and cons of taxation schemes, of military conscription, of regulation of the drug industry and the pharmacy profession, of licensing programs for medical practice, automobile driving, firearm possession, and so on. One of the places where we come closest to considering such derivative crimes is in the final chapter when we consider whether individuals may be coerced so that others benefit, but our concern there will not be with the justification of public policies, but rather with the conceptual distinction between harms and nonbenefits.

8. Alternatives to the criminal law

For every criminal prohibition designed to prevent some social evil, there is a range of alternative techniques for achieving, at somewhat less drastic cost, the same purpose. Instead of outright banning of the conduct in question, for example, we could enpower judges, upon receiving complaints, to issue warning injunctions or "cease and desist" orders, themselves backed by punitive sanctions. We could require, alternatively, that complaints be made formally to the police and that complaining parties themselves initiate prosecution by pressing charges in criminal court. The former alternative gives discretionary powers to judges to evaluate complaints in individual cases, before putting the offending parties on warning that their intended actions, or continuance in actions already begun, will lead to prosecution. The latter gives the offending party no chance to reconsider, but it does limit discretion to prosecute to instances where a private citizen lodges a complaint.

Instead of passing an ordinary criminal statute against the antisocial behavior, a legislature might rely on nonpenal sanctions, creating any of a range of civil disabilities, through such measures as withholding licenses, withdrawing professional certification, refusing to enforce certain kinds of contracts, job dismissals by public agencies, suspending governmental subsidies or financial support, child custody discontinuances, and so on. Technically, most of these are examples of the withholding of legal powers rather than the invasion of liberty, and the apparatus of the criminal law is not involved in their infliction except as the usual backup threat in support of the authority of official orders. (And even that is not involved in some of the examples, like withholding of funds.) Yet, in some way, the sanctions are strongly punitive, and meant to control behavior by threat. Other measures do invade "liberty" (in the broader sense of the absence of barriers of one kind or another imposed by government against possible choices) even though they threaten no criminal punishment. Legislation requiring manufacturers to install safety devices is sometimes enforced by fines, but often by orders to withdraw defective products from the marketplace at great loss, or by new liabilities to civil suits.[18] Another way in which political liberty in this broad sense can be limited is by "prior restraint" as an alternative to various crimes of expression like criminal libel, sedition, and the like. Under such a system, writers would be "free" to say in print anything they pleased without fear of incurring criminal liability as a direct consequence of their writing. The catch is that the writing would have to be passed by a government censorship board before it could be published, and the restraining judgments of that board would be backed up by criminal sanctions. If punishment were to enter the picture it would be punishment for disobedience to valid legal orders, not (except indirectly) for one's expressed opinions *per se*. (Small consolation!) The system of prior restraint is a good example of a liberty-limiting technique alternative to direct criminalization that can be *more* oppressive even than the usual method of defining crimes in advance and then prosecuting their commission. A criminal trial for sedition guarantees the accused his due process and a public airing, necessitates the use of fixed and public rules, and imposes a heavy burden of proof on the prosecution. Prior censorship is a much more efficient (and oppressive) means of suppressing unpopular opinions, and is therefore, in a sense, an even greater threat to liberty.

Nevertheless, the technique of direct prohibition through penal legislation, *on the whole*, is a more drastic and serious thing than its main alternatives, if only because criminal punishment (usually imprisonment) is a more frightening evil than lost inducements, increased taxes, and various civil disabilities, and in a sense to be explained (Chap. 23), more coercive. The existence of alternative techniques of social control, however, sometimes creates difficulties for my arguments about the limits of primary criminalization. Occasionally I argue (on certain factual assumptions) against direct criminalization of a certain kind of conduct, but suggest that control of that kind of conduct by other measures which only incidentally employ criminal sanctions as a last resort would be permissible. That kind of distinction always poses a problem of consistency when there is a valid liberty-limiting principle that appears to apply equally to both techniques. I follow Michael Bayles,[19] for example, in preferring the method of injunctive discretion to that of direct legislative prohibition in the control of obscene billboards (Chap. 8, §1), although the liberty to display what one wishes on a billboard is equally diminished by both kinds of control. The former method, however, would require a citizen complaint; it would allow the deciding official discretion to permit continuance of the display if he chooses; and it would threaten punishment only for defiance of the eventual order to remove the display, not for obscenity as such. The would-be displayer may be equally constrained but he runs lesser risk of disastrous punishment. On balance, then, the discretionary injunctive technique is less intrusive, more efficient, and less subject to abuse.

The problem is more severe in other instances when I oppose criminalization of a kind of conduct (for example, smoking) while not opposing other governmental means of discouraging it (for example, taxation). I object to criminalization of smoking because it is supported only by a paternalistic liberty-limiting principle that I find invalid, but I do not oppose taxing

cigarette use, even though it too is *coercive* in a proper sense, and its rationale would be equally paternalistic. After all, if "Your money or your life"
is a coercive threat when uttered by the gunman, then "Your money or no
cigarettes" is coercive in the same sense, though of course to a much lesser
degree. How then can the differing judgments about criminalization and
taxation be reconciled?

There are at least two possible approaches to reconciliation. In the first
place the legal coercion exerted by penal statutes is not only typically
greater than the coercion of bills of taxation; there is also a difference in the
mode of coercion so significant that it amounts to a difference in kind as
well as degree. The typical criminal sanction is imprisonment, which is not
only a severe deprivation of liberty in all its important dimensions, but also
a brand of censure and condemnation that leaves one, in effect, in permanent disgrace.[20] Punitive fines are less stigmatic, and therefore fall on a scale
of coerciveness somewhere between punishment proper and taxation. Taxation, however, is a much more impersonal transaction than exacting fines.
There is nothing pointed and condemnatory about it, no symbolic judgment of censure, no stigma of disgrace. These differences make plausible
the view that criminal sanctions are special enough to require their own
liberty-limiting principles, and among all the common techniques of official
coercion, are opposed initially by the strongest presumptive case. One can
imagine other techniques that could be employed by the state to discourage
smoking whose coercive threats would be so great that even without the
punitive stigmata, they would be as morally improper as criminalization.
Imagine, for example, laws permitting cigarette smoking but only on condition that the smoker, for each carton consumed, must serve a year in the
army, or become a subject in a medical experiment. Those examples also
differ in degree of coercion from mere taxation to such an extent that they
amount to a difference in kind.

The second approach is to examine the multiple rationales that can always be found for a given bill of taxation. When the tax is levied against a
particular activity like smoking which is thought to be dangerous to those
who engage in it, then it appears, plausibly enough, to be intended to
discourage that activity, and to do so for the sake of the very persons who
would otherwise engage in it. But if the harms caused by that activity,
taken all together, approach the threshold of harm to the public, then the
discouragement may be just sufficient to keep the total harm within the
bounds that society can afford, and can be justified, whatever its original
motivation, on liberal principles.

There is also a point about distributive justice. Whatever else taxation
does, it also raises revenues for governmental expenditures. Given that we

must have such funds, the legislature must decide how to raise them. When it puts a disproportionately great tax burden on the consumption of products that are dangerous to physical health, it in effect permits that consumption while requiring the dangerous activity to pay its fair share of the considerable social costs (lost productivity, hospitalization, medical care, etc.). In that case there is a rationale available other than the paternalistic one that "coercive pressure is being applied for the smoker's own good." Now the state tells him, "Smoke if you must, but pay your fair share of the indirect costs to all the rest of us." Even if the tax revenues extracted from smokers go into a general fund, the effects would be almost the same as if they were earmarked for costs directly connected with smoking, for more funds would be available from the general fund for those special purposes. Nonsmokers, moreover, would have proportionately smaller taxes to pay, so the tax on smokers would be a kind of benefit to them, a positive inducement not to take up smoking. This could be classified as an inducement rather than a threat in virtue of the prior duty all citizens have to support legitimate government programs with their tax contributions. It would be quite implausible, on the other hand, to think of criminal punishments of smoking as "positive inducements" to nonsmokers. There is no prior duty of all citizens to undergo periodic incarceration.

9. Skepticism

Writers who have given serious attention to the problem of this work have emphasized its complexity. Mill claimed to have answered our question adequately by defending "one simple principle," but as many of his critics have since pointed out, neither Mill's principle nor the principles he rejects are simple and unitary. Ernest Nagel, in an important article,[21] is so impressed with the complexities often masked by simple-sounding formulae that he despairs of any "wholesale answer" to the question at all. "There is no general answer to the question whether certain categories of action should be legally controlled and whether certain standards of conduct should be legally enforced. The question can be resolved only case by case. . . ."[22] Nagel writes with great sensitivity about this issue, and there is little for me to disagree with in his analysis except the way he formulates his conclusion. His argument shows not that there is no *general* answer, but only that there is no *simple* one.

Nagel reminds us that we count as "harmful" inflictions of physical injury by one person upon another in duels and feuds but not in boxing matches or self-defense, and that other societies classify these effects in different ways. It is obvious then that if Mill's "simple principle" (the harm principle) is not to include far too much in the category of prohibitable harmfulness, it must first argue for some systematic conception of what is to count as "harm or evil to others." That project, in turn, "cannot escape references to some more or less explicit and comprehensive system of moral and social assumptions—more fully articulated than Mill's."[23] Nagel is certainly right about this, and I have taken his point seriously by attempting a thorough analysis of the critical concept of "harm," by articulating maxims to mediate application of the harm principle in living contexts, by taking moral stands about the relation of consent to harm, by recommending priority rankings of conflicting interests in situations where harm seems unavoidable, and more. In the end, the reader may have difficulty distinguishing between my complicated conclusions and Nagel's denial that "general conclusions" are possible, and if my system of qualified theses should be radically unsatisfactory, then these volumes themselves may be an unintended confirmation of Nagel's skepticism.

Definitions of Liberty-Limiting Principles

1. *The Harm Principle:* It is always a good reason in support of penal legislation that it would probably be effective in preventing (eliminating, reducing) harm to persons other than the actor (the one prohibited from acting) *and* there is probably no other means that is equally effective at no greater cost to other values.*

2. *The Offense Principle:* It is always a good reason in support of a proposed criminal prohibition that it is probably necessary to prevent serious offense to persons other than the actor and would probably be an effective means to that end if enacted.†

3. *The Liberal Position* (on the moral limits of the criminal law): The harm and offense principles, duly clarified and qualified, between them exhaust the class of good reasons for criminal prohibitions. (The "extreme liberal position" is that only the harm principle states a good reason . . .)

4. *Legal Paternalism* (a view excluded by the liberal position): It is always a good reason in support of a prohibition that it is probably necessary

---

*The clause following "and" is abbreviated in the subsequent definitions as "it is probably necessary for . . . ," or "the need to . . ." Note also that *part* of a conjunctive reason ("effective *and* necessary") is itself a "reason," that is, itself has some relevance in support of the legislation.

†The clause following "and" goes without saying in the subsequent definitions, but it is understood. All of the definitions have a common form: X is probably necessary to achieve Y (as spelled out in definition 1) and is probably an effective means for producing Y (as stated explicitly in definitions 1 and 2).

to prevent harm (physical, psychological, or economic) to the actor himself.

5. *Legal Moralism* (in the usual narrow sense): It can be morally legitimate to prohibit conduct on the ground that it is inherently immoral, even though it causes neither harm nor offense to the actor or to others.

6. *Moralistic Legal Paternalism* (where paternalism and moralism overlap *via* the dubious notion of a "moral harm"): It is always a good reason in support of a proposed prohibition that it is probably necessary to prevent *moral harm* (as opposed to physical, psychological, or economic harm) to the actor himself. (Moral harm is "harm to one's character," "becoming a worse person," as opposed to harm to one's body, psyche, or purse.)

7. *Legal Moralism* (in the broad sense): It can be morally legitimate for the state to prohibit certain types of action that cause neither harm nor offense to anyone, on the grounds that such actions constitute or cause evils of other ("free-floating") kinds.

8. *The Benefit-to-Others Principle:* It is always a morally relevant reason in support of a proposed prohibition that it is probably necessary for the production of some *benefit* for persons other than the person who is prohibited.

9. *Benefit-Conferring Legal Paternalism:* It is always a morally relevant reason in support of a criminal prohibition that it is probably necessary to *benefit* the very person who is prohibited.

10. *Perfectionism* (Moral Benefit Theories): It is always a good reason in support of a proposed prohibition that it is probably necessary for the improvement (elevation, perfection) of the character—
    a. of citizens generally, or certain citizens other than the person whose liberty is limited (the *Moralistic Benefit-to-Others Principle*), *or*
    b. of the very person whose liberty is limited (*Moralistic Benefit-Conferring Legal Paternalism*).

Principles 8, 9, and 10b are the strong analogues of the harm principle, legal paternalism, and moralistic legal paternalism, respectively, that result when "production of benefit" is substituted for "prevention of harm."

HARM TO OTHERS

I

Harms as Setbacks to Interest

1. Meanings of "harm"

The criminal law is not the state's primary tool for the reduction of harms generally. At the most, it shares this useful function with public health agencies, safety inspectors, equipment maintenance and repair departments, regulatory commissions, and like agencies. But the criminal law system is the primary instrumentality for preventing people from intentionally or recklessly harming one another. Acts of *harming* then are the direct objects of the criminal law, not simply states of harm as such. From the legislative point of view, however, states of harm are fundamental, for they determine in part which acts are to count as acts of harming, and to become thereby proper targets of prohibitory legislation. An act of harming is one which causes *harm* to people. To vary the idiom slightly, a harmful act (or type of act) is one which has a tendency to cause harmed states or conditions in people. A *harmed* condition of a person may or may not also be a *harmful* condition, depending on whether it has itself the tendency to generate further harm. A blistered finger may be to some small degree a harmed condition, but unless the finger is on the hand of a concert pianist or a baseball pitcher, it may not be at all harmful. In any event, the idea of a harmed condition seems more fundamental conceptually than an act of harming, since one must mention harm in the explanation of what it is for one person to harm another, whereas one can hope to analyze the idea of harm (harmed condition) without mentioning causally contributory actions.

The word "harm" is both vague and ambiguous, so if we are to use the harm principle to good effect, we must specify more clearly how harm (harmed condition) is to be understood. In its bare formulation, without further explanation, the harm principle is a mere convenient abbreviation for a complicated statement that includes, among other things, moral judgments and value weightings of a variety of kinds. The simple English word "harm" is well chosen for the role of stand-in for this more complicated statement. It does as well as any other single word in expressing its motivating spirit. But insofar as it is ambiguous, we must select among its normal senses the one or ones relevant for our normative purposes, and insofar as it is vague in those senses, it should be made more precise—a task that requires some degree of stipulation, not simply a more accurate reporting of current usage. Conditions we may not wish to count as harm for our present purposes (for example, unrequited love) may be clear examples of harm as the term is used in ordinary language, and conditions that we should probably count as harm for our purposes (perhaps death is an example) may seem near yet beyond the boundaries of that term as ordinarily used. Indeed, because of the vagueness of the ordinary senses, there may be some examples whose classification as harmful or not may be simply indeterminate, an untidy state of affairs which the theory-maker understandably would like to correct by stipulation of more exact senses. Since it is no part of our purpose to provide an accurate dictionary definition of a word that is simply a useful peg, we can revise the boundary lines here and there with a clear conscience, while remaining generally faithful to the spirit of the word's customary use.

We can begin by distinguishing three senses of "harm" that are in general circulation. The first of these is a derivative or extended sense, and I mention it only to dismiss it, but its dismissal is important. I refer to the sense in which we can say that any kind of thing at all can be "harmed." By smashing windows, vandals are said to harm people's property; neglect can harm one's garden; frost does harm to crops. Quite clearly this is harm in a transferred sense; we don't feel aggrieved on behalf of the windows or the tomatoes, nor are they the objects of our sympathies. Rather our reference to their "harm" is elliptical for the harm done to those who have interests in the buildings or the crops, those who have in a manner of speaking "invested" some of their own well-being in the maintenance or development of some condition of those objects. By breaking windows, the vandals have done direct harm to the interests of the building's owner; they have harmed *windows* only in a derivative and extended sense.

It might be thought that there is a nonderivative sense in which mere things can be harmed even when they are objects of no one's interests. Better words than "harm" for this sense are "damaged" and "broken."

Roget also lists terms like "mangled," "cut," "spoiled," "decayed," "rotted," "split," "rent," "torn," "slashed," "mutilated," "shattered," "smashed," "ruptured," "sprung," "burst," "cracked," "chipped," and "burned." These things *can* be done to a mere thing even if no person has an interest in it. But I doubt that we would say, in that case, that the thing was *harmed* in any sense. It is interesting to note, further, that although far more things are capable of being damaged or broken than of being harmed (in a proper sense), not everything we can name is capable even of being damaged or broken. It is impossible, for example, to break or damage the number seven or the law of gravity. Even so mundane an object as a rock is not the sort of thing that can be broken or damaged in normal circumstances, though it can be split, shattered, chipped, and the like. For a rock to be coherently described as broken or damaged, it must either have some special value to a human being (say, as an art object) or have some function in a larger complex that has now been impaired. Machines and organisms are proto-typical examples of the sorts of objects that can cease "working" or "work-ing properly" because of part-functional impairment. Machines and organisms behave in certain ways because their component parts or subsystems behave in certain ways (and vice versa). So if the characteristics of at least one component part are crucially altered, then the complex whole can no longer behave in the way it normally does, and we say that, because of its impaired function, it is broken. (A simple rock, as such, has no such func-tion, though we can imagine rocks put to use, for example as supports for structures, and they can in those cases be *broken* when they are cracked or split.) But if no one has an interest in a machine's unimpaired functioning then it is *only* broken, not harmed even in the derivative sense mentioned above.

The second genuine sense of "harm" is that from which the transferred sense derives, namely harm conceived as the thwarting, setting back, or defeating of an interest. The term "interest" when used in this way is obviously not meant to refer to "money due on loans" or "the excitement of attention or curiosity," perhaps its most common senses. There is, how-ever, a familiar commercial-legal sense of the word that can serve as a helpful model for understanding the word in the sense in which it is linked to harm. I refer to the sense in which a person has an interest in a company when he owns some of its stock. If I have an interest, in this sense, in the Apex Chemical Company, I have a kind of *stake* in its well-being. All interests are in this way types of risks: the word "stake" has its primary or literal use to refer to "the amount risked by a party to a wager, or match, or gamble, a thing whose existence, or safety, or ownership depends on some issue." In general, a person has a stake in X (whether X be a company, a career, or some kind of "issue" of events) when he stands to gain or lose depending on the nature or condition of X.[1] To say that I have a stake in Apex Chemical is to say that the better off it is financially, the better off I am financially. I may have a small or large interest, a big or little stake in it, depending on how much I have invested in it. If I have only a few shares, then I am not made much worse off if it collapses. I have a very large stake indeed, however (and not merely in a financial sense), in the furtherance of my professional career, the protection of my total assets, the peace and prosperity of my country, and the well-being of my family and loved ones. It is greatly *in my interest* that these causes flourish.

One's interests, then, taken as a miscellaneous collection, consist of all those things in which one has a stake, whereas one's interest in the singular, one's personal interest or self-interest, consists in the harmonious advancement of all one's interests in the plural. These interests, or perhaps more accurately, the things these interests are *in*, are distinguishable components of a person's well-being: he flourishes or languishes as they flourish or languish. What promotes them is to his advantage or *in his interest;* what thwarts them is to his detriment or *against his interest*. They can be blocked or defeated by events in impersonal nature or by plain bad luck. But they can only be "invaded" by human beings, either by myself, acting negligently or perversely, or by others, singly, or in groups and organizations. It is only when an interest is thwarted through an invasion by self or others, that its possessor is harmed in the legal sense (though obviously an earthquake or a plague can cause enormous harm in the ordinary sense). One person harms another in the present sense then by invading, and thereby thwarting or setting back, his interest. The test, in turn (as we shall see), of whether such an invasion has in fact set back an interest is whether that interest is in a worse condition than it would otherwise have been in had the invasion not occurred at all.

The third sense of harm, while closely related to the second, is in fact a distinct notion that can often be at variance with it. This is a kind of normative sense which the term must bear in any plausible formulation of the harm principle. To say that A has harmed B in this sense is to say much the same thing as that A has wronged B, or treated him unjustly. One person *wrongs* another when his indefensible (unjustifiable and inexcusable) conduct violates the other's right, and in all but certain very special cases such conduct will also invade the other's interest and thus be harmful in the sense already explained. Even in those exceptional cases in which a wrong is not a harm on balance to interests, it is likely to be a harm to some extent even if outbalanced by various benefits. For example, so-called harmless trespass on another's land violates the landowner's property rights and thereby "wrongs" him even though it does not harm the land, and even might incidentally improve it. But the law does recognize a proprietary interest in the exclusive possession and enjoyment of one's land, and for whatever it is worth, the trespass did invade *that* interest. It is "harmless" only in the sense that it doesn't harm any *other* interests, and certainly no interest of a "tangible and material kind." Another hard example is the wrongly broken promise that redounds, by a fluke, to the promisee's advantage. This wrong violates a kind of interest of the "victim's" in liberty, that is, an interest in himself tying down the future in a certain respect and determining through his own choice what is to happen. Insofar as *that* interest was invaded, he was *harmed* (as well as wronged), but in the example, no other interest of his is harmed and some are actually promoted, so that on balance, he actually benefits. Most such apparent examples of wrongs that are not harms to interests can be interpreted in this way. There *can* be wrongs that are not harms *on balance*, but there are few wrongs that are not *to some extent* harms. Even in the most persuasive counterexamples, the wrong will usually be an invasion of the interest in liberty.

Though almost all harms in the special narrow sense (wrongs) are also harms in the sense of invasions of interest, not all invasions of interest are wrongs, since some actions invade another's interests excusably or justifiably, or invade interests that the other has no right to have respected. The interests of different persons are constantly and unavoidably in conflict, so that any legal system determined to "minimize harm" must incorporate judgments of the comparative importance of interests of different kinds so that it can pronounce "unjustified" the invasion of one person's interest of high priority done to protect another person's interest of low priority. Legal wrongs then will be invasions of interests which violate established priority rankings. Invasions that are justified by the priority rules are not legal wrongs though they might well inflict harm in the nonnormative sense of simple setback of interest.

One class of harms (in the sense of set-back interests) must certainly be excluded from those that are properly called wrongs, namely those to which the victim has consented. These include harms voluntarily inflicted by the actor upon himself, or the risk of which the actor freely assumed, and harms inflicted upon him by the actions of others to which he has freely consented. I have not wronged you if I persuade you, without coercion, exploitation, or fraud to engage in a fair wager with me, and you lose, though of course the transaction will set back your pecuniary interest and thus harm you in that sense. The harm principle will not justify the prohibition of consensual activities even when they are likely to harm the interests of the consenting parties; its aim is to prevent only those harms that are wrongs. That is why the harm principle needs to be supplemented by an elaborate set of mediating maxims, interest-rankings, principles of justice, and the like, before it can be applied to real legislative problems.

Legal commentators sometimes recommend that the courts, in some noncriminal contexts, provide remedies for admittedly nonharmful wrongs. Charles Fried,[2] for example, argues for the enforcement of some gratuitous unilateral promises, even when a breach has only disappointed the promisee without affecting in any visible way his interests. Suppose Mary, pointing at a window display, tells John that she would love to have that $10,000 diamond necklace. Promptly John replies: "It's as good as yours. I'll buy it for you as soon as I receive some money I'm expecting." "Oh John," says Mary, "you won't change your mind?" "No way. I promise you I'll have it for you on Monday." Then suppose that John does change his mind. Has Mary been *harmed?* She has not given John anything in exchange for his promise that she will now lose; nor has she acted in reliance on John's promised performance. In respect to necklace ownership, she is no worse off than she was before. She has only been disappointed. But Fried eloquently protests that she has been *wronged.* John has, in the exercise of *his* autonomous freedom, created a genuine right in her which he then proceeded to violate, and that violation (wrong), Fried argues, calls for a legal (but of course not a criminal) remedy.

What then is the sense of "harm" employed by the harm principle, as we will here understand it? Since we have distinguished harms (setbacks to interest) from wrongs ("harm" in the third sense), and allowed for the existence both of rare nonharmful wrongs and common nonwrongful harms, which of these combinations captures the sense of "harm" in the liberty-limiting principle? Whatever the correct policy may be for the law of contracts, the harm principle as a guide to the moral limits of the criminal law does not license liability for acts that tend to cause only nonharmful wrongs. It is more obvious still that no plausibly interpreted harm principle could support the prohibition of actions that cause harms without violating rights, for example setbacks to interest incurred in legitimate competitions, or harms to the risk of which the "victim" freely consented. The sense of "harm" as that term is used in the harm principle must represent the overlap of senses two and three: only setbacks of interests that are wrongs, and wrongs that are setbacks to interest, are to count as harms in the appropriate sense. The remainder of this and the following chapter will be concerned with one of these two components of legal harm: setbacks to interest.

2. Welfare interests and ulterior interests

The importance of an interest to the well-being of its possessor can be determined by two different standards. According to one of these, a person's more ultimate goals and aspirations are his more important ones: such aims as producing good novels or works of art, solving a crucial scientific problem, achieving high political office, successfully raising a family, achieving leisure for handicraft or sport, building a dream house, advancing a social cause, ameliorating human suffering, achieving spiritual grace. By a quite different and equally plausible standard, however, a person's most important interests are by no means as grand and impressive as these. They are rather his interests, presumably of a kind shared by nearly all his fellows, in the necessary means to his more ultimate goals, whatever the latter may be, or later come to be. In this category are the interests in the continuance for a foreseeable interval of one's life, and the interests in one's own physical health and vigor, the integrity and normal functioning of one's body, the absence of absorbing pain and suffering or grotesque disfigurement, minimal intellectual acuity, emotional stability, the absence of groundless anxieties and resentments, the capacity to engage normally in social intercourse and to enjoy and maintain friendships, at least minimal income and financial security, a tolerable social and physical environment, and a certain amount of freedom from interference and coercion. These are interests in conditions that are generalized means to a great variety of possible goals and whose joint realization, in the absence of very special circumstances, is necessary for the achievement of more ultimate aims. In one way, then, they are the very most important interests a person has, and cry out for protection, for without their fulfillment, a person is lost. But in another way, they are relatively trivial goods, necessary but grossly insufficient for a good life. They are the "basic requisites of a man's well-being,"[3] but by no means the whole of that well-being itself.

These minimal but nonultimate goods can be called a person's "welfare interests." When they are blocked or damaged, a person is very seriously harmed indeed, for in that case his more ultimate aspirations are defeated too; whereas setbacks to a higher goal do not to the same degree inflict damage on the whole network of his interests. Moreover, as Nicholas Rescher has argued, welfare interests, taken together, make a chain that is no stronger than its weakest link. "Deficiencies in one place are generally not to be compensated for by superiority in another; there are few, if any, trade-offs operative here—just as cardiovascular superiority does not make up for a deficient liver so added strengths in one sector of welfare cannot cancel out weaknesses in another."[4] In general then, an invasion of a welfare

interest is the most serious, but not the only kind of harm a person can
sustain.

3. Interests and wants

There is perhaps little that is controversial in our account of harm thus far,
but there are several further questions about the nature of interests that
have divided philosophers. One controversy is over whether or not we can
say everything we have to say about interests in the terminology of wants
or desires. (See Chap. 2, §1.) Certainly, there must be a very close connection between a person's interests and his wants. If a person has an interest
in some outcome when he "has a stake" in it, and he has a stake in it when
he stands to gain or lose depending on its issue, then it would be very odd
indeed for a person with an interest in Y to deny that he wants Y to happen.
Such a denial, after all, would imply that the person does not prefer gaining
to losing, which on its face would seem highly irrational. To be sure, there
are situations in which a person does not know his own interests. In such
cases, there is nothing paradoxical in the person having an interest in Y but
not wanting Y. What would be genuinely paradoxical, however, would be
to *believe* that one has an interest (a stake) in Y but not want Y. Even this
situation is approached, however, in the case of the person who is torn
between duty or principle and what he takes to be his self-interest. If he
freely chooses to sacrifice his interest in order to do what is right, it may
seem that he is doing what he "really wants" in sacrificing interest for duty,
so that he did not "really want" to do what he believed was in his interest.
It would be more natural, however, to describe this case as a conflict of
wants, in which the wants connected with interests are overridden by the
desire to do one's duty, and there is nothing paradoxical about that. It
seems safe to conclude, therefore, that "Jones believes that he has an interest (stake) in Y" implies that "Jones to some degree wants Y," at least insofar
as Jones is minimally rational. The qualification "to some degree" is necessary to explain the case in which Jones wants some Z, which he believes
incompatible with Y, even more than he wants Y.

Most of the controversy about the relation between interests and wants,
however, concerns the analysis of another common idiom, namely, "X is in
Jones's interest." Here we should distinguish initially between two interpretations: (1) "X promotes some one particular interest of Jones," e.g. his
interest in pecuniary accumulation or in artistic achievement, and (2) "X
promotes Jones's self-interest," i.e. all of his interests as a group. Much the
same sorts of things can be said about (1) as were said earlier about the
idiom "Jones has an interest in Y." X may indeed be in one of Jones's

interests without Jones wanting X, as for example when X is bitter-tasting medicine which will promote Jones's interest in health, and yet Jones so hates its taste that he refuses to take it. Jones may not want some X that in fact promotes his interest in Y, either because he does not believe that X promotes Y, or because he does not believe that he has an interest in Y (i.e. that Y is one of his interests). He may, on the other hand, want X to some degree because he believes that X will promote his interest in Y, yet not choose X because he also believes that X will impede his interest in Z, which he believes to be a stronger interest, or because X is ruled out by one of his moral principles. In either case, he will have a conflict of wants which is resolved against his desire for X. He may not choose X, finally, because he finds it too repugnant, distasteful, or frightening (as in the bad-tasting medicine example). In this case there is not conflict of *interests*, but rather a conflict between a desire to promote an interest, on the one hand, and sheer fear or repugnance, on the other. (This is a typical example of a conflict between reason and "blind emotion.") In none of these cases then is there a belief that X promotes an interest in Y in the absence of a want or desire (however weak) that X occur, even though it is clear that a person may not want X because he is ignorant of its connection to Y or of Y's status as one of his interests, or may not choose X even though wanting it, because of stronger conflicting wants, principles, or passions.

The analysis of (2) "X is in Jones's self-interest" is more complicated, and its relation to wants more obscure. As a start, we can say that this idiom means that X somehow promotes Jones's interests (the things he has a stake in) as a group. We have already suggested that this in turn means that X contributes to the harmonious advancement of Jones's interests. (The term "advancement" is preferable to the term "fulfillment" which suggests that well-being consists in the permanent and final achievement of all goals with no unfulfilled aspirations left over.) At this point in the analysis difficulties begin. What sorts of conditions count as "harmonious advancement"? Three kinds of cases should be distinguished. In the first (which since it is the most interesting and difficult, will be discussed last) X advances Jones's interests "harmoniously" by promoting *all of them*, either equally or un-equally. In the second, X promotes a particular interest Y of Jones's, or a set of such interests, without impairing any of his other interests. In the third case, X promotes some of Jones's interests and impairs others, but the ones promoted are superior in some relevant way to those that are impaired, so that the result is a net gain for Jones on the whole.

The third case distinguished above is possible only when the interests compared are truly commensurable so that trade-offs are possible between them. There are many homely examples where this condition is satisfied, but many equally familiar ones in which it is not. The easiest cases involve conflicting interests in the same category, for example pecuniary accumulation. Suppose X will cause Jones to gain $2,000 from one source and to lose $1,000 from another source. Clearly X would cause—in the most literal sense—a net gain for Jones. Similarly, X may help a fat man to lose weight at some cost to another of his "health interests"; perhaps it will cause him to lose sleep for a period of weeks. Yet on balance the cost may be worth the gain. Even interests in different categories may be susceptible to trade-offs, as when going alone to Europe to do research for a few months may present unique opportunities for professional achievement to a professor while also creating family strains. Damage to his "family interests" might be reparable later, while an equal professional opportunity may never come again, in which case, he may calculate that the trip would be a net gain for his personal interest. On the other hand, if Jones has a genuine and equal interest in the well-being of two other individuals, say his wife and his daughter, he can find no gain in an X that will leave the one (either one) dead and the other rich. In general, X will not be in a person's interest all told if it advances his interest in Y at unacceptable cost to his interest in Z.

Where X promotes some of Jones's interests without affecting the remainder one way or the other (our second case above), there is of course no problem. X represents pure gain at no cost, and "harmony" is not disrupted. But in what ways could an X promote *all* of Jones's interests (the first case above)? There are at least three ways in which this could happen. In the first, X promotes harmony directly either by *modifying* various interests so that they are not to the same degree as before in conflict, or else by modifying one's *circumstances* so that there are more opportunities for joint advancement of interests that would otherwise be competing. Two interests are "conflicting" in the strongest sense when one is an interest in Y and the other in *not-Y*, so that it is logically impossible for both of them to be advanced at once. The unfortunate person who suffers this condition must be in a state of partial personal disintegration. His salvation can be achieved only by some psychological equivalent of the "withdrawal of investment" from one or both of the conflicting causes, thus eliminating their corresponding interests. The more familiar, and less pathological, form of conflict between two of a person's interests consists in their "competition" for the scarce resources that can advance them both. An interest in Y competes in this sense with an interest in Z when the circumstances are such that Y cannot be advanced without impairing Z, and vice versa; that is, there is a shortage, or in the extreme case a complete absence, of Xs that can promote the one interest without impairing the other. Where the shortage is complete and uncorrectable in the very nature of the case, a person can avoid harm to self-interest as a whole only by modifying or "eliminating" at least one of the competing interests. But where the shortage of instruments for joint advancement can be corrected, then the indicated remedy for the troubled person who suffers the conflict is to attempt to modify the circumstances that create it.

The second way in which a person's act or policy can promote all of his interests is through the deliberate creation of new interests that "compete," in a certain sense, with some of the interests he has already. I have in mind here a kind of psychological analogue to the practice of prudent investors who "diversify their investments" or "balance their portfolios" so as to protect their (financial) interest as a whole by guarding against the most likely threatening contingencies. When all one's eggs are in the same basket, one calamitous event can destroy them all; hence prudence dictates a variety of baskets. Moreover, protective diversification is often achieved by arranging one's interests so that what harms some of them necessarily helps others, and what helps some necessarily harms others. In this way one is "guaranteed" that the interests so arranged will not sink below a certain level, even at the cost of an equally strong expectation that they will not substantially rise above that level either. Prudence (so conceived) is hardly the only self-regarding practical virtue. Its aim is to *protect* personal interest by preventing some component interests from falling below a minimal level of fulfillment. The happy, well-balanced person whose personal interest maximally flourishes, however, will be equally concerned to *advance* (and not merely protect) some of his interests, and there may be no wiser way of doing that than by assuming large risks of harm and failure.

The third way in which all of a person's interests might be advanced is by the mediation of some act or policy which produces or improves a generalized means to the advancement of his various ulterior interests. For almost all normal persons in our society, anything that promotes their "welfare interests" in health, economic sufficiency, emotional stability, political liberty, and so on, by that very fact improves the prospects for their various ulterior interests, whatever they should happen to be. Indeed the most important generalized means will be effective ones not only to the achievement of present actual ends, but to a variety of future goals that have not even suggested themselves yet to the person who will one day have a stake in them.

Corresponding to these three ways in which a person's interest can be advanced are three ways in which it can be impaired, and the person himself harmed. The "invader" of personal interest can (1) modify an interest directly so that it comes into conflict or competition with another interest, or else modify the circumstances to make scarcer the means of joint satisfaction of two or more already competing interests; (2) diminish the extent to which prudential interests are protectively diversified; or (3) directly impair a welfare interest (for example, the interest in health, or financial adequacy), thereby diminishing the person's means to advance his various ulterior interests.

So far, this analysis of the phrase "X is in Jones's interest" has been able to do without reference to wants. We have seen that people tend to want, at least to some degree, what they believe they have a stake in, at least insofar as they are minimally rational. But in respect at least to welfare interests, we are inclined to say that what promotes them is good for a person *in any case*, whatever his beliefs or wants may be. A person's interest in health, for example, would in fact *be* one of his interests, even if he mistakenly believed the contrary, and even if he desired ill health and decay instead of good health and vitality. In respect to this particular interest, at least, there may be a correspondence between interest and want, but the existence of the former is not dependent upon, nor derivative from, the existence of the latter.

Welfare interests, however, normally achieve their status as interests in virtue of their being generalized means, often indispensable ones, to the advancement of more ulterior interests. Our question about the role of wants in the analysis of interests is merely postponed, therefore, until we consider the nature of our more ulterior interests themselves. In respect to these interests, wants seem to have an essential role to play, for it is difficult at best to explain how a person could have a direct stake in certain developments without recourse to his wants and goals. How could I have an interest in my professional achievement, or in gaining political power, or in building a dream house—how could I have such a stake in these things that I stand to gain or lose depending on their issue—without having invested some desire in them for their own sakes? My health may be good for me whether I want it or not, but in respect to some of my more ulterior interests, at least, I seem to have a stake in them because I desire their fulfillment, rather than the other way round. In these instances, if my wants changed, my interests would too.

On the other hand, it does not seem likely that wants, even strong wants, are *sufficient* to create interests. John Doe, a baseball fan, may have a very powerful desire that the Dodgers win the pennant, but that alone would hardly constitute grounds for saying that he has an interest in a Dodger victory. If he bets his whole fortune on the outcome, however, he will have a strong interest indeed. Richard Roe, a Dodger player, on the other hand, may have a powerful personal stake in a Dodger victory, and the pride in shared achievement, the financial bonus, tributes, invitations, etc., that will follow in its wake. There is, I suppose, a sense in which anyone who has a strong desire for anything at all stands to "gain" or "lose" depending on whether it is satisfied. The pleasant state of mind we call satisfaction is itself a kind of reward or form of "gain" (although it does not come automatically when we get what we desire), and intense disappointment is itself a kind of "loss." But one cannot do without the quotation marks. There is a distinction, crucial for our present purposes, between being disappointed *because* one has suffered a personal loss, and the "loss" that consists entirely in disappointment; and between the "gain" that consists entirely in satisfaction at some outcome and the satisfaction that occurs *because* there has been some personal gain. The "losses" and "gains" in quotation marks have no necessary or direct connection with interests or with harms. We are commonly enough disappointed, dissatisfied, even frustrated, without suffering harm.

Very few baseball fans have invested so much of a psychic stake in the outcome of a season's play that they are personally harmed if their team loses (though it is easy enough to conceive of a hypothetical extreme case approaching this description). And very few of us have interests in contented states of mind or in avoiding disappointment as such. Rather, our interests and desires both are typically aimed at external things, not internal states. Both when we have a stake in Y's happening and when we want Y to happen, the object of our interest or want is Y, not the satisfaction or avoidance of disappointment that may come in Y's wake. These mental states could be objects of other interests and wants derivative from the interest in and want for Y, but they rarely are. If our stake in and desire for Y are genuine and powerful, they will overshadow any separate, self-regarding concern for our own states of mind, and paradoxically, the occurrence of the desirable mental state is likely to depend on our indifference to its coming about, through our preoccupation with the pursuit of Y itself. In general then, an interest in, and desire for, some development Y does not imply an interest in or desire for a satisfied state of mind, or for the avoidance of a disappointed state of mind in respect to Y. What we have a stake in is Y itself, not the avoidance of disappointment.

Some of our most intense desires then are not of the appropriate kind to ground ulterior interests since (like a sudden craving for an ice cream cone) they are unlinked to our longer-range purposes, or they are insufficiently stable and durable to represent any investment of a stake. When such desires are frustrated, our complex web of interests might shake, but every strand holds. Our psyches are sturdy; we can take a certain amount of disappointment without our interests being affected, that is, without suffering harm.

What then must a desire be like in order to create a stake in some outcome for its own sake? One can only answer this question in cautious psychological generalizations. People differ, and some eccentric ones are capable of psychological investments that seem impossible to the rest of us. So we must avoid all suggestion of necessity in listing the features generally characteristic of interest-creating desires. Generally speaking, however, various interest-making characteristics can be listed. To begin with, wants of the appropriate sort are generally associated with realistic hopes and expectations. Mere ideal wishes or fantasies will not do. A person is not harmed by his inability to travel to Mars or to live forever. Secondly, the wants must obviously be for objects that are desired, at least in part, for their own sakes, and not merely as a means to the advancement of other, preexistent interests. If an object is desired entirely for the purpose of making money, then it is in the desiring person's interest, but not *because* he desires it, but *only* because it promotes interests of other kinds that he already has.

It is widely though not necessarily true, thirdly, that the want in question, if it is to be the ground of an interest of the most ulterior kind, that is an *ultimate* interest, should be capable of promotion by human efforts, particularly by the efforts of the person whose want it is. Though there are exceptions, the most typical wants underlying ultimate interests are not only desires but also conscious goals or objectives. (The Dodger fan might well have made an interest-investment in his team if only there was something he could have *done*, apart from ineffectual rooting, to help them win.) I may have an interest either in the advancement of my own career or in the advancement of another's career. But in order for another's achievement to be an ultimate interest of *mine*, there usually must be something I can do to help. If I have an ultimate interest in *his* mastering the clarinet, there must be some ways in which I can assist him, if only indirectly. I cannot master the clarinet for him, and not being a clarinetist myself, I may not be able to teach him how to do so. In that case, it may be an overstatement to say that his achievement is *my goal*. But there may be indirect ways I can help, say by cheering him up or paying his bills, so that my "goal" can properly be said to be to do whatever I can to help him achieve *his* goal. Without that special relation to personal effort that converts a mere want into an objective, it is not likely that the appropriate sort of "investment" can be made that is needed to create a "stake" in the outcome. The importance of that relation is asserted here as a psychological generalization about the capacities of people to create stakes for themselves rather than as a matter of conceptual analysis. For all I know, some Dodger fans may have the extraordinary psychological capacities to create ultimate interests for themselves in desired outcomes that are wholly beyond their powers to influence.

The kind of want that creates a relatively ulterior interest is not just a desire of the moment, like the desire to "go to the cinema to enjoy myself,"[5] which can create a "stake" only in its own satisfaction or avoidance of disappointment, but a relatively deep-rooted and stable want whose fulfillment, as we have seen, can be both reasonably hoped for and (usually) influenced by one's own efforts. It can usually be called with propriety a general aim, goal, or objective. An ulterior interest of this kind is at once an end which gives value to all reasonable instrumentalities (these are said to be *in* its interest) and also a kind of means to the enhancement of a great variety of other ends to which it is linked. In most persons, there is no one supreme "end of all ends" whose achievement is the "be all and end all" of human existence. Rather our ultimate interests characteristically resemble what C. L. Stevenson has called "focal aims," ends (not *the* end) which are also means to many other divergent ends. Our more important (in the sense of "ultimate") ends satisfy Stevenson's formal definition of a focal aim: "an end which is also such an exceptionally important means to so many divergent ends that if anything else is not, in its turn, a means to this, it will be without predominating value."[6] Thus, building a dream house is a means to the entertainment of house guests, to the private pursuit of studies and pleasures, to hours of aesthetic contemplation, and so on; the achievement of political power is a means to the advancement of favorite causes and policies; and the solution of a scientific problem is a means to the further advance of knowledge and technology, to say nothing of personal glory.

4. Harms, hurts, and offenses

Not everything that we dislike or resent, and wish to avoid, is harmful to us. Eating a poorly cooked dish may be unpleasant, but if the food is unspoiled, the experience is not likely to be harmful. So it is with a large variety of other experiences, from watching a badly performed play to receiving a rude comment. These experiences can distress, offend, or irritate us, without harming any of our interests. They come to us, are suffered for a time, and then go, leaving us as whole and undamaged as we were before. The unhappy mental states they produce are motley and diverse. They include unpleasant sensations (evil smells, grating noises), transitory disappointments and disillusionments, wounded pride, hurt feelings, aroused anger, shocked sensibility, alarm, disgust, frustration, impatient restlessness, acute boredom, irritation, embarrassment, feelings of guilt and shame, physical pain (at a readily tolerable level), bodily discomfort, and many more. In all but exceptional cases (to be noted below), people do not have as ulterior focal aims, interests simply in the avoidance of these states as such.[7] And like various pleasures of the moment, these passing unpleasantnesses are neither in nor against one's interests. For that reason, they are not to be classified as harms.

If these unpleasant experiences are intense or prolonged enough, however, or if they recur continuously or occur at strategically untimely moments, they can get in the way of our interests. A grating noise or evil smell is just an unpleasant sensation to be put up with grudgingly, irritating to be sure, but not harmful or injurious; but if it keeps one awake all night, then it interferes with one's interest, in the way ill health might, by making it impossible to work efficiently the next day. Similarly, an affront or an insult normally causes a momentary sting; we wince, suffer a pang or two, then get on with our work, unharmed and whole. But if the experience is severe, prolonged, or constantly repeated, the mental suffering it causes may become obsessive and incapacitating, and therefore harmful.

Unhappy but not necessarily harmful experiences can be divided into two categories: those that *hurt* and those that *offend*. The most prominent hurts, of course, are physical pains, and they can serve as a model of comparison for identifying "mental pains" which are also "hurts" if only by courtesy of metaphor. Offended mental states can also be compared in a certain respect with familiar physical analogues, namely, the motley assortment of nonpainful physical discomforts. Physical pains include pangs, twinges, aches, stabs, stitches, cricks, and throbs, as caused by cuts, bruises, sores, infections, muscle spasms, over-dilated or contracted arteries, gas pressures, and the like. Roughly analogous to these are various forms of mental suffering (they "hurt" too): "wounded" feelings, bitterness, keen disappointment, remorse, depression, grief, "heartache," despair. Nonpainful forms of physical unpleasantness include nausea (which can be even more miserable a condition than pain, but does not, strictly speaking, *hurt*), itches, dizziness, tension, hyperactivity, fatigue, sleeplessness, chills, weakness, stiffness, extremes of heat and cold, and other discomforts. For our present purposes, these can be lumped together with physical pains as forms of physical discomfort. Analogous to them, however, are various nonpainful mental states, which are of sufficient interest to be placed in a separate category, and labeled "forms of offendedness." Like their physical analogues, these form a great miscellany of conditions that have little in common except that they don't hurt but are nevertheless universally disliked. Some of the more prominent mental states in this category have already been mentioned: unpleasant sensations, disgust, shocked sensibilities, irritation, frustration, anxiety, embarrassment, shame, guilt, boredom, and certain kinds of responsive anger and fear.

The distinction between hurtful and offended states is to some degree arbitrary, based as it is on somewhat obscure analogies, and lumping to-

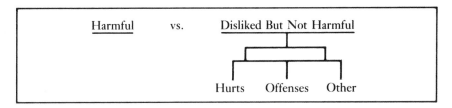

Diagram 1

gether, as it does, quite disparate conditions under common labels, in some instances with considerable linguistic strain. Anxiety, for example, is not strictly speaking an *offended* state, but it is a not-necessarily-harmful state that doesn't fit neatly under any of our headings. And at least one type of boredom—the solitary, footloose kind—is not in any usual sense a way of being *offended*, but it is not in itself harmful or painful either, though it can be a very unpleasant state indeed.

Most of the linguistic strain can be removed if we distinguish between states of mind that are "offended" in the strict and narrow sense and those disliked but not hurtful states of mind that form a miscellany, and are "forms of offendedness" only in a misleadingly extended sense. Then our classification scheme could be charted as in Diagram 1, or perhaps as in Diagram 2. The "Other" category could then include anxiety, embarrassment, shame, disappointment, frustration, and (some) boredom, among other unpleasant states of mind that can be produced by the actions of others.

What is important for our present purposes, however, is not the distinctions among hurts, offenses, and "other" disliked states, but rather the generic contrast between harmful conditions and *all* the various unhappy and unwanted physical and mental states that are not states of harm in themselves. That contrast can be made out in quite parallel ways for hurts, offenses, and the miscellaneous category.

There is no interest in not being hurt as such, though certainly we all want to escape being hurt, and the absence of pain is something on which we all place a considerable value. Not everything valuable is such that its absence is harmful; nor is everything that is undesirable such that its presence is harmful. An undesirable thing is harmful only when its presence is sufficient to impede an interest. When a given condition becomes extremely painful, of course, it does interfere with the pursuit of various goals and objectives, and that incapacitating effect renders it harmful as well as hurtful. Even a moderate hurt, if it be constant and unrelenting, can distract a person from his business, and harm his various interests, but in that case, it

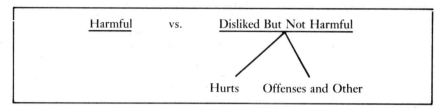

Diagram 2

is the capacity of the condition to distract, rather than its inherent character as a hurt, that renders it a harm.

The distinction between hurt and harm raises one especially interesting question for public policy, and suggests how it is to be answered. We must include in the category of "hurts" not only physical pains but also, as we have seen, forms of mental distress. Our question is whether, in applying the harm principle, we should permit coercion designed to prevent mental stress merely, when the distress is not likely to be followed by hurt or harm of any other kind. Some forms of mental distress (e.g. "hurt feelings") can be ruled out simply on the grounds that they are too minor or trivial a matter to warrant interference. Others, of course, are so severe that they can lead to mental breakdowns. In that case, however, it is the consequential harm to mental health and not the mere fact of distress that clearly warrants interference. Thus a convenient criterion for determining whether a hurt is sufficiently serious to qualify as a harm suggests itself: the hurt is serious enough if and only if it is either a symptom of a prior or concurrent harm of another order (as a pain in an arm may be the result and sign of a broken bone) or else it is in itself the cause of a consequential harm (e.g. mental breakdown) of another order.

It should be emphasized that even though a given hurt may not qualify under these criteria as a harm, and will not therefore warrant preventive coercion *under the harm principle*, it is nevertheless an *evil* of its own kind, and perhaps in some circumstances a sufficiently serious evil to warrant protective intervention under an alternative liberty-limiting principle. We can interpret the offense principle as authorizing legal coercion to prevent "offenses" in the widest possible interpretation of that term, in which it includes offenses proper (e.g. revulsion and disgust), hurts (e.g. "harmless" throbs and pangs), and "others" (e.g. shame and embarrassment). Surely if "offenses proper," for example those caused by obscene posters or racial slurs, can rightly be punished by the criminal law, then any intense pains that somehow fail to qualify as harms might also be preventable by similar means.

It is plausible, of course, to think of prolonged states of intolerably intense pain as "harmed conditions" in themselves, quite apart from their relations to other interests, on the grounds that we all have a basic interest of a not wholly instrumental kind in avoiding such things. (It would be stretching things though to think of such an interest as a predominant life-purpose or focal aim.) In other words, to suffer an intensely painful experience is to be in a *harmed condition* quite apart from whether it is a *harmful condition* or not. We can imagine (just barely) intense pain produced in such a way as to cause no (further) harm to mind or body, and to leave the victim with full capacity for normal action in the aftermath. Suppose A imposes on B, by force, intermittent electric shocks of sufficient intensity and frequency to cause great pain, but keeps them just below the threshold at which B's (other) interests would be impaired. That is, B's nervous system and mental health, though strained, are not damaged. After several days of this torture, A gives B a pill which destroys all memory of the painful experiences. One might ask, out of purely conceptual puzzlement, whether B has been harmed or "merely hurt." But however we answer the conceptual question, there is nothing "mere" about that kind of hurt! Intense pain, even if it does not set back an interest, can be as great an evil as severe harm, and its wanton infliction on another would clearly be punishable under the broadly interpreted offense principle (and under legal moralism too), even if it is not classified as a harm. In any event, it is plausible to attribute to all normal people an ulterior interest in not undergoing torture even when the experience is not harmful as measured by its effects on *other* interests. Having the torture experience described in the fanciful hypothetical example then would count as being in a condition of harm, though not in a harmful condition.

The problem of classifying "offended and other unpleasant" states can be treated in a fashion parallel to our treatment of hurts, with one big difference. It is much less plausible to attribute to most people an independent, noninstrumental *interest* in being unoffended. It is unlikely then that being in an intensely offended state could *ipso facto* amount to being in a harmed state. More like the common tolerable kinds of hurts, offended states of mind, even intense ones, are not in themselves harms; but also like the common hurts, they are sometimes symptoms or consequences of prior or concurrent harms, and more often, the causes of subsequent harms, as for example, when provoked ill will leads to violence or riot. A sufficiently intense offended state of mind can become harmful to its possessor by incapacitating or obsessively preoccupying him at a cost to his other interests. But unless common hurts and offenses are of a sufficient magnitude to violate other interests, for example the interests in health and peace, they are not harms, and the use of the criminal law to prevent them cannot be justified by the harm principle as it is here interpreted.

There is one kind of offended state that can probably never satisfy this requirement, namely the shock or disappointment occasioned by the bare knowledge that other persons are doing, or may be doing, immoral things in private with legal impunity. (See Chap. 8, §1.) It is conceivable, I suppose, that there could be a person whose moral sensibilities are so tender that such knowledge would lead to a mental breakdown; but in such a case, it would be more plausible to attribute the breakdown to abnormal susceptibilities than to the precipitating cause. If a sneeze causes a glass window to break, we should blame the weakness or brittleness of the glass and not the sneeze. In general, the application of the harm principle requires some conception of normalcy. (See Chap. 5, §1.) It is the person of normal vulnerability whose interests are to be protected by coercive power; the person who, figuratively speaking, can be blown over by a sneeze cannot demand that other people's vigorous but normally harmless activities be suspended by government power. He can demand protection only against conduct that would harm the normal person in his position. The further protection he needs he must provide himself by noncoercive methods.

Before leaving this subject, I must concede that there could be persons, and indeed that there have in fact been persons, who have as a predominant focal aim the avoidance of hurt, disappointment, and offense as such. The ancient Epicurean moral philosophers even put forth this negative condition as life's highest and most realistic ideal. Live not for pleasure, they taught, but rather for the reduction, even the total elimination, of pain and emotional turbulence. These philosophers, if they practiced what they preached, did indeed have as genuine ulterior *interests*, the absence of hurt and offense as such. The appeal of their teachings has always been greatest to those persons who have known such great suffering, whether from illness, depression, or violent emotion, that they have been vividly impressed with the truth that life cannot be worth living except in the absence of such extremities. The person in the grip of severe pain may be willing to settle for *anything*, if only the pain would go away. If he can get rid of suffering, any alternative condition would seem a blessing. That is understandable, but it is a strange notion indeed that anything alternative to what is intolerable is a supreme good, that avoiding the worst that can happen is itself the best that can happen. What is a supremely important *necessary condition* of well-being (the absence of incapacitating suffering), by a confusion comes to be thought of as a *sufficient condition*, all by itself, for the good life. The confusion is then compounded by the unwarranted judgment that even tolerable alternatives to the intolerable are intolerable in a good life, that is, that even transitory and moderate hurts and offenses are in themselves to be totally avoided as part of one's highest purpose, and avoided for their inherent character as hurtful or offensive rather than for their power to incapacitate.[8]

The absence of incapacitating suffering is a welfare interest in everybody's interest system, but it is as empty and ignoble a guiding ideal as the desire for oxygen to breathe or any other welfare interest. Still the law, following the harm principle, will protect the Epicurean like everyone else from indefensible inflictions of severe suffering, which usually violate the standard person's welfare (instrumental) interests, and failing that, the standard person's ulterior interest in being free of extreme pain as such. It can hardly protect the Epicurean, however, from inflictions of minor hurts and offenses that are not incapacitating, even though such conditions are harmful to him, being direct invasions of his peculiar ulterior interest in being unhurt, unriled, and unoffended ever. It is improper to use coercion to protect him from these invasions, not because his negative goals are not real interests, not because minor hurts, annoyances, and offenses are not real harms to him, but rather because by falling short of harm to the interests the law ascribes to the standard person, they are deemed to be less serious harms than those that would come from restricting the liberty of others. The Epicurean's peculiar self-created interests, like any other interests, demand respect, and carry some weight on the legislative balancing scales inevitably employed to compare the "seriousness" of harms (see Chap. 5, §6.) But criminal statutes, to be effective, must employ general terms without the endless qualifications and refinements that would be needed to accommodate the whole range of idiosyncratic vulnerabilities. Besides, the Epicurean, if he is true to his creed, has acquired his own disciplined immunities. He will not let himself be hurt by his ill treatment at the hands of others, especially by the noncriminal conduct of others under a code derived from the harm principle as applied to standard interests.

5. The manner in which acts and other events affect interests when they harm them

The reader may already have noticed the profusion of terms employed to characterize the effect of harmful acts on interests. The acts (and sometimes but not always the events) that harm people have been said (alternatively) to be those that (1) violate, (2) invade, (3) impair, (4) set back, (5) defeat, (6) thwart, (7) impede, and (8) doom their interests. These terms for the effect on interests are not all exact synonyms, so it is worth sorting them out in the expectation that some may be more apposite than others.

The term "violate" fits acts of harming in the "relatively narrow sense" that we will assign to "harm" as that word is understood in the harm principle. (*Supra*, Chap. 1, §1.) Harm in that sense has two components, one a violation of the victim's rights (a wrong to him) and the other a certain deleterious effect on his interests, which we are here trying to make clearer. The word "violate" suggests the element of wrongfulness, but does not add anything to our understanding of the nature of the effect on interests. It is by no means an inappropriate term to use when characterizing wrongful harms, but it has no analytic power to explain what it is to have a damaging impact (wrongful *or* innocent) on interests. Natural events like fires and earthquakes cause harm in the purely interest-affecting sense, but only persons acting improperly "violate" interests. Strictly speaking, it is the victim's *rights* that are violated when his interests are wrongfully damaged, and as we have seen (Chap. 1, §1), rights can be violated even without harm to interests.

The term "invasion of interests" is frequently used, and to good effect, in legal contexts. In fact, legal harm is commonly defined in jurisprudential works as "the invasion of a legally protected interest," apparently another way of saying "violation of a legal right," except that there is the further assertion that underlying the right is an interest to be protected. There is no good objection to this legal terminology, but the term "invasion," if used in an explanation of the nature of specifically harmful effects on interest, is subject to the same objection already made to the term "violation." The term "invade" and the closely related terms "transgress" and "interfere," as John Kleinig points out, "are clearly intended to indicate human agency."[9] An invasion is a (usually hostile) crossing of another person's boundaries, an encroachment on the other's territory. To enter wrongfully the sphere of another person's proper self-government is to violate his autonomy, that is to infringe his right of self-determination. (See Chap. 18, §5, and Chap. 19.) But the invading conduct *can* in some circumstances wrong the other party without causing any harm to his interests, unlikely and infrequent as that might be, in which case the characteristics that make that conduct "invasive" are not the same ones that make it harmful or damaging. Kleinig provides an ingenious example:

> Suppose that a young child, *X*, is abducted, but is rescued not long after. At the time it may be said: "*X* was found unharmed," the implication being that *X* suffered no *bodily* harm. Later on it may also be said, "*X* was not harmed by the experience," by which it is at least implied that *X* suffered no *psychological* harm. Being a young child, we may also suppose that *X*'s abduction did not lead to the thwarting of any significant projects. Now, if we think of harm simply as *interference* with welfare interests, then *X* was most certainly harmed

in being abducted. But harm normally involves more than mere interference; it implies *impairment*.[10]

To impair something, Kleinig goes on to say, is "to make it worse or cause it to deteriorate." But strictly speaking, this cannot be what harmful events do to interests. It is not the *interests* that "become worse." Rather, it is the person's whole situation that worsens or deteriorates when his interests are affected in the manner we are still trying to clarify. A more common application of the term "impairment" is to abilities and capacities which are impaired when they are weakened and lose their effectiveness. A broken arm is an impaired arm, one which has (temporarily) lost its capacity to serve a person's needs effectively, and in virtue of that impairment, its possessor's welfare interest is harmed. Impairment of function is not the only way in which interests are harmed but it is the most common form of setback to welfare interests, and perhaps the mode characteristic of the most serious harms to persons.

There are only minor differences among terms (4) through (7), so they can be treated as a group. These are the terms, I think, that best explain what it is that an event does to an interest in virtue of which its possessor is harmed. All of them involve a kind of directional metaphor. To *set back* an interest is to reverse its course, turn it away, put it back toward the point from which it started. In terms of its associated goals, it is to reverse its progress, to put it in a worse condition than it was formerly in. To *defeat* an interest is to put it to utter rout, to conclusively and irrevocably set it back by destroying the conditions that are necessary for its advancement or fulfillment, as death for example can set back some interests once and for all. (See Chap. 2, §3.) To *thwart* (or block, or frustrate) an interest is to stop its progress without necessarily putting it in reverse; to successfully oppose it, and prevent it, at least for the time being, from making an advancement or improvement. To *impede* an interest is to slow its advancement without necessarily stopping or reversing it, to hinder or delay. Common to all these notions is the idea of a starting point or "baseline" from which the direction of advance or retreat is charted and measured. The ordinary idea of an interest is vaguer than that of a business ledger or bank account, but in theory it too could be charted on graph paper in a curve that moves along the X and Y axes in a positive (upward) or negative (downward) way, with upward progress representing gain or improved condition, and downward plunges representing loss, or becoming "worse off."[11]

The interests that are affected for better or worse by events are already ongoing concerns with their own direction and momentum before the harming or benefiting events occur. If the current point of the curve is already near the top of the graph paper, so to speak, then an event which has the effect of merely keeping it there has a protective or preservative influence and can be thought of as beneficial. If it has the effect of only weakening upward momentum without actually stalling or reversing it, then I suppose its effect is harmful, though not seriously so. If the curve, already high in the positive region, is made to decline a bit, then the cause may be said to have harmed the interest without having put it into a "harmed state," that is without having brought it below the center line. The sense of "harm" we have been working with is clearly a relativistic notion: whether one is harmed by an event is determined by reference to where he was before, and whether his position has improved or regressed. But another, nonrelativistic, concept waits in the wings, always ready to replace the main performer. In that conception, one is harmed only when one's interest is brought below the centerline, and thus put into a "harmed condition."[12] Similarly, when one's interest, say in adequate food supplies, languishes near the bottom of the chart, any crumb thrown one's way may advance the curve in an upward direction, but if it does not bring it to the point where nutritional deficiency is cured (the centerline) it may not seem much of a benefit, and if it does not bring it even to the point where imminent starvation can be avoided, it may be no benefit at all. Measurement of harms and benefits is thus influenced in very complicated ways by the prior locations of interest states on the chart, their directions of movement, and their momentum. At the extreme ends (top and bottom) of the chart especially, interest-affecting events have eccentric effects. One might think of the diminishing marginal utility of money as a model. A penny given to a pauper is much more of a benefit to him (given his starting place) than the same amount given to a millionaire, and a penny taken from him could be a disaster, whereas the same deprivation would be beneath the millionaire's notice. These puzzles are complicated enough in the economic realm. When it comes to human well-being in general, they are without answers. Our everyday conception of self-interest is only roughly and vaguely based on the economic analogy. It would be fruitlessly digressive to attempt to make it more precise until some philosophic issue is seen to require it. We will return to the interest-graph in Chapter 4, when we will be confronted with the challenging and unavoidable distinction between harms and mere nonbenefits.

A final way of harming a person is to *doom* one of his interests, to foreordain its defeat. Once a person invests enough in a given goal to make it one of his ulterior interests, while unknown to him, another party has destroyed (or will destroy) the conditions necessary for its fulfillment, then from that moment on, his hopes and labors will be in vain. To pursue or hope for a result that is so important to one that one's good depends on it, when those hopes and efforts are not to come to fruition, is to play a losing game from the start. An observer who knows that the other's interest is doomed may think of him as already in a harmed condition though that appraisal cannot be confirmed until the interest is in fact defeated, perhaps years later. To be pouring one's energies vainly into a doomed enterprise is in itself to be in a condition that can only inspire pity from the better-informed observer, not only for what is to come, but also for what is already happening. A person who invests his savings regularly in a doomed bank is harming himself even before the bank finally fails. Another person who is driving to the airport where he shall board a plane that will crash shortly after take-off is in a harmed condition, we might say, from the moment his life interests are doomed. If *we* knew what he is doing we would think of him as a poor fellow rushing off to his own destruction, not a happy state to be in, even though he is unaware of its harmfulness at the time. This notion of doomed interest will be used further in a discussion of the harmfulness of death in Chapter 2, §6.[13]

6. The concept of an interest network

There are countless ways in which human interests might be classified: in terms of ulteriority, minimality, degree of comprehensiveness, the type of associated fulfilling activity, the characteristic mode of invasion, whether self or other-regarding, and many more. Several of these bases for classification are subject to differences in degree, and thus could provide helpful scales for ordering the seriousness or "importance" of corresponding types of harm.

Consider, for example, the related characteristics of ulteriority and minimality. As we have seen, some degree of ulteriority, stability, and permanence is necessary to the very existence of an interest. A mere "passing desire," however genuine or intense, does not establish an interest. A sudden craving for an ice cream cone on a hot summer day, when plenty of cold water is available, does not itself make it true that ice cream is "in one's interest" at that time. To say that something would be "in my interest" is to say that it would increase my ability or opportunity to satisfy those of my ulterior wants that are themselves the bases of interests, those goals in whose advancement I have a stake. In Brian Barry's example, I may desire to go to the cinema, and I may then go and enjoy myself very much, "but was it 'in my interests' to go to the cinema? We can imagine a situation in which this could truly be said, but it would be a situation where some ulterior purpose would be served by going, for example, impressing my employer with my highbrow tastes and thus disposing him to give me a [raise]."[14] In the ordinary case, however, where *all* there is to gain by seeing the film is enjoyment, "going to the cinema . . . is neither *in* one's interests nor *contrary* to one's interests."[15] Satisfaction of an immediate want is in one's interest, then, only when it is a means to the promotion of more ulterior ends in which one *has* an interest.

At the other extreme, the most ulterior and comprehensive goals, for quite different reasons, must be excluded from the realm of interest. There is a sense in which all rational persons desire their own ultimate good (however that be conceived) or the harmonious fulfillment of their *other* desires as a group, or their own well-being, or happiness. But these tacit objectives are rarely conscious goals deliberately aimed at, and even when we do make them our deliberate aims, as in moments of calculating prudence, it would be somehow redundant to say that we had an *interest* in these things. The happiness that persons rarely seek directly is a "dominant end"; whereas the happiness that all rational persons can be understood to be pursuing indirectly when they consciously aim at other things is an "inclusive end." Anthony Kenny explains the distinction in this way: "If happiness is thought of as a dominant end, then it is the object of a single prime desire: like that say, for money, or for philosophy. If it is thought of as an inclusive end, then the desire for happiness is the desire of the orderly and harmonious gratification of a number of independent desires."[16] To say that we have an interest in our own happiness conceived as an *inclusive* end would be to say something virtually tantamount to the statement that we have an interest in our interest, or that what promotes our interest is in our interest, which is certainly unenlightening and trivial. It is conceivable, on the other hand, that some rare persons do have an interest in their own happiness conceived as a *dominant end*, that is, as a kind of chief interest among equals. Happiness so conceived might be understood in hedonistic terms. Just as some avaricious or miserly persons have as ulterior focal aims the acquisition of as much wealth as possible, so some calculating hedonists might aim primarily at the enjoyment of pleasant feeling tones, and find no value in anything that is not a means to contentment and serenity. Considering how desirable pleasant states of mind are to all of us, it is surprising how few persons, if any at all, make the cultivation of such mental states a conscious predominating aim.

Having eliminated passing wants of the moment and inclusive ends as objects of interests, we are left with wants and goals of an intermediate range of ulteriority. In an ascending order of ulteriority these are of three sorts. First, there are immediate wants whose fulfillments, unlike the desire for an ice cream cone or to go to the cinema under normal conditions, *are* linked up, either as means or as necessary conditions, to the advancement of more ulterior goals. It may be in a person's interest at a given time to take some exercise or to decline a rich dessert, since these activities and omissions will promote the interest which he most assuredly has in his own health. Similarly, it may be in one's interest to go to bed early, or contrariwise to work late for overtime pay, depending on the circumstances. There is usually no particular *interest in* working late, taking exercise, and the like, as such; but these things may nevertheless be *in our interests* because they are means to the advancement of more general, stable, and permanent goals like health and financial sufficiency in which we certainly do have an interest. We can call desires of this class *instrumental wants.*

In the second class are those *welfare interests* which have already been discussed. Essential to all of the wants on which these interests are based is their character as bare minima. Our interest in welfare, speaking quite generally, is an interest in achieving and maintaining that minimum level of physical and mental health, material resources, economic assets, and political liberty that is necessary if we are to have any chance at all of achieving our higher good or well-being, as determined by our more ulterior goals. Personal welfare, as the term is used here, is an indispensably necessary condition for the achievement of ultimate well-being, but by no means a sufficient condition. One cannot get anything else if one does not have it, but one does not usually have much when one has only it. On the other hand, while one cannot live on bread alone, without bread one cannot live at all.

Corresponding to many of the basic welfare interests are possible ulterior interests, which some of us do and some of us do not have, in achieving a much higher level of a particular element of welfare than is actually required. Thus the interest in becoming prosperous or affluent resembles the welfare interest in having enough money for a decent life in that both of them are economic interests, and would be so categorized in a different scheme of classification. But an interest in affluence, while differing only in degree from the welfare interest in financial sufficiency, is by no means itself a welfare interest. Similarly, the interest in putting oneself in vibrant blooming health and the very best athletic condition is a kind of physical interest like the welfare interest in not being sick, but is not itself a welfare interest.

Welfare interests, to summarize, have the characteristics of bare minimality, stability, and durability. They are also, as we have seen, so linked together that they are no stronger than their weakest link. All the money in the world won't help you if you have a fatal disease, and great physical strength will not compensate for destitution or imprisonment. Finally, the value of the welfare interests seems at first sight to be entirely instrumental, not in the sense that welfare is a guaranteed efficacious means to the achievement of other goals, but rather in the sense that it is an indispensable necessary condition.

At this point, however, we must hesitate. There do seem to be some beings, for example animals and human infants, who have no interests more ulterior than their welfare ones. Some animals, for example, can plausibly be supposed to have no "higher good" above and beyond satisfaction of the mundane requirements of simple survival. Yet they most assuredly have welfare interests. It is in their interest that their food supply not be diminished or destroyed, that parasites not weaken their vigor, that microbes not cause infections, that predators be kept at bay, and so on. Some of these welfare interests are interconnected so that fulfillment of one is a means to the fulfillment of another. The male lions keep scavenging beasts away from the kill, for example, so that the pride's food supply can be preserved and consumed. But it is less clear that any single leonine welfare interest or even the whole collection of their welfare interests are pursued in order to promote ulterior interests valued in part as ends in themselves. However, if welfare interests are "entirely instrumental," and lions' apparent interests are means to nothing at all beyond themselves, it seems to follow that the apparent welfare interests of animals are not true interests at all, that animals have no good or welfare of their own, and can neither be benefited nor harmed. Two centuries ago, that conclusion might have been congenial to most people. Today it seems to be a reduction of otherwise plausible premises to absurdity.

In fact, we now tend to think of animals (at least the "higher" ones that can be thought to have their own conscious wants and purposes) as having their own distinct kind of good, corresponding to what I have called mere "welfare" in humans rather than to the distinctively human sort of well-being that is based on ulterior interests and focal aims. But if that is the case, it would follow that the welfare interests they seem to have cannot be entirely instrumental. Even some human beings—at certain times and places, *most* human beings—have as their highest good something resembling mere welfare. For these hardy souls, *just making it*, surviving from day to day, is triumph enough. Finding the minimal means for bare survival under trying conditions can be a challenge to toughness and ingenuity, and small successes a source of typically human pride. For these unfortunates ("unfortunate" at least in *our* eyes), mere welfare is one and the same as well-being, and it has a value that is not *entirely* instrumental after all, in virtue of the investment of the same sorts of wants that in others are the ground of more ulterior interests.

There are other possible ways out of our quandary, but we cannot pursue them here. Some of the higher animals, primates for example, might be thought to have some genuinely ulterior interests, even if primitive by human standards, after all. These might include advancement in a social hierarchy, collection of a harem, protection of the newborn, and in some species (wolves and geese, for example), raising a "family." Even in less advanced species, where this account is implausible, there might be a kind of natural interest in the fulfillment of inherited biological propensities,[17] an interest that is pursued through (but not "by means of") the promotion of the welfare interests. For these species, developed enough to have conscious wants and aims, but too primitive to have ulterior interests, their ultimate well-being may consist in simply doing well "what comes naturally" throughout a normal life-span, even though *all* that comes naturally is the direct pursuit of welfare interests. They do not achieve fulfillment by pursuing welfare interests as a conscious *means* to it. Rather, *in* pursuing their welfare they are *ipso facto* achieving their fulfillment.

In summary, welfare interests are typically instrumental, though in exceptional circumstances and in some animals they are evidently more than that. Welfare interests (defined ostensively as the interest in staying alive, not sick, with minimally adequate resources, etc.) can be goals as ultimate as any that one has. It follows that in these cases we can describe an interest as a welfare interest while denying that it is valued as a means to any more ulterior interest, acknowledging at most its instrumental value to other welfare interests. Even in the normal case where the intrinsic value of a welfare interest is not so evident, it might nevertheless have some such value to its possessor. To determine whether that is true in one's own case, one should conduct a thought experiment in which one asks oneself how one would value one's welfare interests (defined ostensively) *if* one had no more ulterior interests. The answer to that speculative hypothetical question might well carry implications about the nature of the value those interests actually have to their possessor *now*.

The third group of wants that create interests are those associated with the more ulterior goals that we have called focal aims. These vary in number and type, though with much overlap, from person to person. No doubt they can be classified in a large number of criss-crossing and overlapping ways. Some are extensions of welfare interests to trans-minimal levels; some are different in kind from welfare interests. Some are "economic," or "political," or "physical," or "educational." Some aim at possession or accumulation; others at personal achievement; others at power or glory. Most are self-regarding; some are other-regarding or publicly oriented. Some of the self-regarding interests are self-confined; others aim at self-centered relations with other persons. Common to all of them, however, is their character, at least in part, as ends in themselves. These aims are as "ulterior" as our dominant ends can be, and their value cannot be entirely instrumental. Still, for the most part, their value is not entirely intrinsic either, since their advancement or fulfillment invariably produces benefits of a great many kinds throughout the whole network of personal wants and interests. Thus, when we have an ulterior *interest in Y, Y* will also be *in* our interests, in that its achievement will promote other ulterior interests as well (and also foster satisfaction, and enjoyment of an immediate kind that may be unrelated to interest).

Diagram 3 lists the types of wants and interests discussed above, and the examples used to illustrate each.

Passing Wants	Instrumental Wants	Welfare Interests	Focal Aims
To eat an ice cream cone.	To forego dessert.	In physical health and vigor.	Building a dream house.
To go to a movie.	To get exercise.	In the absence of obsessive pain.	Writing a book.
	To start a savings account.	In the absence of grotesque disfigurement.	Winning fame or glory.
	To go to bed early.	In intellectual competence.	Acquiring political power.
	To work overtime.	In emotional stability.	Acquiring religious holiness.
		In economic sufficiency.	Advancing a cause.
		In a tolerable environment.	Solving a scientific problem.
		In minimal political liberty.	Raising a family.
			Achieving leisure.

Diagram 3

Our classification of interests (and some noninterests too) in terms of relative ulteriority can then be depicted as in Diagram 4.

The chart shows the structure of a typically human *interest network*, and traces some of the relations between interests and wants. It does not include those ulterior interests, which some people have, that are not *objectives* which they can further by their own efforts, and hence not focal aims, though they are not exactly welfare interests either. A person's focal aims are, of course, *his* interests, but, as the chart indicates, their advancement also promotes his other interests, including his other focal aims (as well as other wants), and hence is *in* his interest too. If we now add to the picture some symbolic indication of its ongoing character, with key interests being

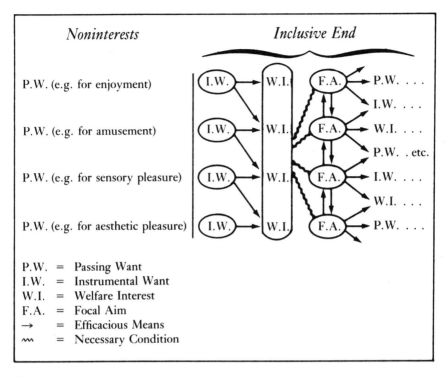

Diagram 4

self-regenerative, and new interests regularly emerging from old ones to be advanced harmoniously with their progenitors, we have a reasonably accurate depiction of that human happiness which is for most rational persons in nondesperate times their most inclusive end.

7. Legally protectable interests

Jurisprudential writers have classified in various ways the interests that are safeguarded by the law. One of the more common lists includes "Interests of Personality" (absence of harmful bodily contacts and the apprehension thereof, freedom from confinement, absence of emotional distress), "Interests of Property" (the exclusive enjoyment and possession of land and chattels and their good physical condition), "Interests in Reputation," "Interests in Domestic Relations" (family solidarity, marital fidelity), "Interests in Privacy" (absence of physical intrusions upon solitude, absence of unpermitted disclosure of intimacies), among others. Not all of the interests in this list are protected by the criminal law; some of them are protected instead by the willingness of the state, under law, to compel compensation for harm to them. For the most part, they are welfare interests of the most vital kind. Inflictions of harm to one's bodily or mental health; diminutions of one's security by the creation of new threats and dangers; reductions of one's liberty of movement through abduction or false imprisonment; depletions of one's material resources through larceny, or robbery, or fraud: all attack one's entire personal well-being, by attacking the welfare interests necessary to it.

Our more ulterior interests, which since they include our highest aspirations are in a sense the most important elements of our well-being, are for the most part not *directly* protectable by the law. If I have an interest in making an important scientific discovery, creating valuable works of art, or other personal achievements, the law will protect that interest by guarding my welfare interests that are essential to it. But given that I have my life, health, economic adequacy, liberty, and security, there is nothing more that the law (or anyone else, for that matter) can do for me; the rest is entirely up to me. If my highest interest is in pecuniary accumulation as such, or in such uses of wealth as the purchase of a yacht or a dream house, the law can protect that interest indirectly by protecting me from burglary and fraud, but it cannot protect me from bad investment advice, personal imprudence, the unpredictable dependencies of others, the lack of personal diligence or ingenuity, and so on. If my boss reduces my salary as a consequence of his low assessment of my work, that act may set back one of my ulterior interests; but the law cannot protect me in this instance from my boss without invading *his* liberty (a vital welfare interest) intolerably. Similarly, I may have invested so much hope and desire in the developing moral character of my children that their eventual personal excellence is one of *my* interests. (See Chap. 2, §2.) This other-regarding ulterior interest can be protected from kidnappers, Fagins, brainwashers, and white slavers, but the rest of the job—including the deliberate choice of schools, neighborhoods, and moral exemplars—is up to me (or up to chance). The law cannot protect me by interfering with the liberty of those whose character and life-style falls below my standards, without oppressive invasion of *their* liberty. In general, those who invade my ulterior interests in any way other than by invasion of my welfare interests, either do so simply in the exercise of their own proper liberty without moral blame, or, if they do incur blame, do so in subtle ways not preventable as a practical matter by the law.

The one clear kind of exception to the reluctance of the law to protect ulterior interests directly is constituted by those ulterior goals that simply extend elements of welfare beyond minimal levels. Material wealth is the best example. The law of burglary protects not only the pauper who would be ruined by the theft of his welfare check, but also the millionaire for whom a thousand-dollar bill has less utility than a penny has for a child. There would be enormous practical difficulties in attempting to apportion degrees of protection according to the actual seriousness of harm. Moreover, protection of the wealthy person from minor thefts does not interfere with the normal everyday exercise of individual liberty, as in the other examples. Furthermore, it is not only the miserly and megalomaniacal ulterior interests of millionaires that are protected, but also their interests in liberty (the interest in being the person who decides how the accumulated funds are to be spent) and security (even his welfare interests might be *threatened* by the act that invades his financial interest, especially if the invasive act employs force or coercion, or seems likely to be frequently repeated). Moreover, the invasion of any person's financial interests threatens the general security of property, and the orderliness and predictability of financial affairs in which everyone has an interest, however small.

The latter remark suggests still another way of classifying interests and correlative harms. Until now we have been discussing only the interests, self- and other-regarding, of individual persons. There are other interests, however, of a widely shared character, belonging to large groups, institutions, and corporate entities, that have always received protection from the criminal law. These are sometimes called "public interests," though that term is too ambiguous to be of immediate use. (But see Chap. 6, §2.) Two groups of interests come to mind. The first are so important to the individuals who have them that they amount to elements of their individual welfare, and yet they are so widely shared that they can be said to be possessed by the community itself. Public peace, health, security from foreign enemies, and a sound economy are the clearest examples. The second group of interests are those normally ascribed to the government rather than the community. Governmental interests are "those generated in the very activities of governing,"[18] such as collecting taxes, registering aliens, conscripting an army, customs-inspecting, conducting trials and court hearings, operating prisons, etc. These are the interests violated in such "impersonal crimes" as tax fraud, failure to register, perjury, bribing a government official, and escaping from prison. Like community interests, governmental interests in the last analysis belong to individual citizens. But the maintenance or advancement of a specific government interest may be highly dilute in any given citizen's personal hierarchy. *I* am not seriously harmed by a single act of contempt of court or of tax evasion, though *if* such acts became general, various government operations that are as essential to my welfare as public health and economic prosperity would no longer be possible. An act of poisoning the water supply invades a community interest and directly harms me; the bribing of a public official harms me only indirectly or remotely, but it *threatens* direct harm insofar as it endangers the operation of government systems in whose efficient normal functioning we all have a stake.

2

Puzzling Cases

1. Moral harm

A harms *B* in the strict and narrow sense employed by the harm principle when (1) *A* sets back *B*'s interests, and (2) *A* does this in such a manner as to violate *B*'s rights (i.e. wrong him). The analysis proposed in Chapter 1 of what it is for *B*'s interests to be set back (the first component of *harming* in the full sense) should fit the clear cases of harm quite unproblematically. There are various types of hard cases for the application of the concept of harm, however, where the fit is by no means certain. Some of these are borderline cases, problematic alike for our analysis and for the ordinary usage of the term "harm," which has a large area of vagueness. For these cases, we are forced to refine our analysis by stipulation since the vagueness cannot be tolerated in a concept that is to be put to such important normative uses. The process of stipulation cannot be entirely arbitrary either, even though unguided by a clear light from ordinary language; otherwise we shall find ourselves defending the legitimacy of state interferences with liberty that, preanalytically, we would find dubious or wrong. In other kinds of hard cases, our analysis classifies the example clearly enough either as harm or nonharm, but in ordinary discourse the case is not so much indeterminate as essentially controversial. Whether "we would ordinarily say" that the condition in question is harm depends upon the way in which we initially classify the data from which we extract our criterion, and some persons, already influenced by the theory they will eventually arrive at, classify the data one way, while others, perhaps equally influenced by *their* tacitly presupposed theory, classify in the opposite way.

A good example of this second kind of puzzle is the ancient controversy over whether there can be such a thing as purely moral harm. No doctrine was more central to the teachings of Socrates, Plato, and the Stoics than the thesis that a morally degraded character is itself a harm quite independently of its effect on its possessor's interests. On this issue, the implications of our own analysis of harm in terms of set-back interest are clear. If a wicked person has no ulterior interest in having a good character, and if such a character is not *in* his (other) interests, then his depraved character is no harm to him (*pace* Plato, *et al.*), and even if he becomes worse, he does not necessarily become worse off.

Plato, of course, has an elaborate theory in support of his own view of the matter. What he does in *The Republic* is to interpret human psychology in political terms. The mind is so constituted by its nature that one "part of the soul" is meant to rule over the others. It is the natural function of reason (or what we might call "conscience") to bear this rightful authority, just as it is the natural function of the heart to pump the blood. When one bodily organ usurps the function of another, or when one lower-ranked part of the soul usurps the authority of the ruling part, then the whole bodily econ- omy, in the one case, or spiritual harmony, in the other, is thrown out of kilter, and the human person is unable to function properly. This impaired condition is precisely what we mean by sickness, whether physical or men- tal, and there is no doubt that illness is a harm.[1]

That moral corruption is essentially sickness, and therefore necessarily harmful in itself to the "morally sick" person, is one of the Great Ideas of intellectual history, though it has probably caused as much mischief (through its confusion of categories) as inspiration. The important point for our purposes here, however, is that this theory was designed by Plato to account for what he already assumed to be the case as one of the mere data of his problem in *The Republic*. Socrates never doubts that wickedness is essentially unprofitable to the wicked person. The question posed at the end of Book I, in effect, is *how can this be possible?* But it is not one of the presuppositions of the present inquiry that the wicked must necessarily be in a harmed condition, that "they can't be getting away with it *really*." So Plato's ingenious theory, even though it does explain the data *he* assumes, has little probative force against us.[2]

A platonist, of course, could reply that my theory of harm has no more cogency against him, since at best it accounts for the data assumed by me, but not by him. To this I can only counter that the key datum assumed here seems more plausible initially, and less question-begging, than the opposite one assumed by Plato. When a remorselessly wicked person *appears* to be flourishing, and there *appear* to be no reasons to suppose he is not, then I "assume" that he is indeed profiting from his wickedness, and try to fashion my theory of harm and benefit to save the appearances. Plato begins with an equally powerful commitment, only his is to the ultimate moral propriety of things. His reason for assuming that the wicked person suffers is that he (Plato) finds it intolerable that he should not. Plato fashions his theory not to "save" but to explain away the appearances.

These divergences find expression in a more modern controversy: whether the notion of interest employed in the analysis of harm is to be construed (as I have) as a wholly "want-regarding" concept or whether that analysis leaves out something important. The label "want-regarding" comes from Brian Barry,[3] who contrasted it with what he called "ideal-regarding" concepts and principles. A concept is want-regarding if it can be analyzed entirely in terms of the "wants which people happen to have," whereas it is ideal-regarding if reference must also be made to what would be ideal, or best for people, their wants notwithstanding, or to the wants they ought to have whether they have them in fact or not. Barry's own analysis of interest is uncompromisingly want-regarding. To say that X is in Jones's interest, according to him, is to say that X increases Jones's opportunities, or "puts him in a better position" to satisfy his various ulterior wants, whatever they should happen to be, into the indefinite future.[4] As for those familiar cases, made so much of by moralists, where what a person wants is *not* in his interest, or where he doesn't want what is in his interest, Barry concludes as his definition requires: "The contrast is . . . not between want-satisfaction and something other than want-satisfaction, but rather between want-satisfaction now and want-satisfaction later."[5]

The ideal-regarding theory holds that it is in a person's interest ultimately not only to have his wants and goals fulfilled, but also (and often this is held to be more important) to have his tastes elevated, his sensibilities refined, his judgment sharpened, his integrity strengthened: in short to become a better person. On this view, a person can be harmed not only in his health, his purse, his worldly ambition, and the like, but also in his character. One's ultimate good is not only to *have* the things one wants, but (perhaps more importantly) to *be* an excellent person, whatever one may want. We not only degrade and corrupt a person by making him a worse person than he would otherwise be; on this view, we inflict serious harm on him, even though all his interests flourish. Socrates and the Stoics even went so far as to hold that this "moral harm" is the *only* genuine harm. Epictetus was so impressed with the harm that consists simply in having a poor character that he thought it redundant to punish a morally depraved person for his crimes. Such a person is punished enough, he thought, just by being the sort of person he is.

To a certain extent, the conflict between the two accounts of interest is entirely academic. That is because most forms of excellence, most of the time, tend to promote want-based interests. If there is an antecedent desire for excellence, as there often is, then the achievement of excellence is want-satisfying, and even in the absence of such a desire, personal excellence is likely to contribute to the joint satisfaction of other wants. But contrary to Plato and many other ancient sages, there is no necessity that excellence and happiness always coincide, no impossibility that morally inferior persons can be happy, and excellent persons miserable. There is still room for controversy then over what is truly good for persons in the latter two cases. In particular, philosophers have disagreed over whether it is *in the interest* of the contented moral defective to become a better person. This disagreement can persist even when it is agreed on all sides that it is desirable that the defective's character improve. Desirable, yes; a good thing, to be sure; but in *his* interest? That is another thing.

The source of the appeal of the ideal-regarding theory, I think, is evident. Few of us would wish to exchange places with people we regard as morally flawed, no matter how content they seem to be. It is easy to understand and sympathize with Epictetus's attitude toward the morally depraved criminal. We would not want to be *him* even if he escaped punishment, indeed even if he profited richly from his crime and suffered no remorse for it. Neither would we wish to be contented and vulgar, contented and dull, contented and stupid. We would in fact be prepared to sacrifice a good deal of our (other) want-fulfillments to avoid becoming flawed in these ways. But that is surely because we already have *desires* for excellences of character construed in accordance with our own standards. It is because we have such wants that we think it in our interest to be excellent, or at least not defective. Without those antecedent wants, it would not be in our interest to be excellent at all, except of course indirectly through the happy effects (not always to be relied upon) of excellent character on popularity and material success. By the same token, it is not in the interest of the contented moral defective to have our ideal of virtue, which he doesn't share, imposed on him, unless, of course, we speak of thrift, prudence, diligence, etc., all of which could improve his chances of satisfying his other ulterior wants. But if he is clever enough to make a "good thing" in material terms out of dishonesty and unscrupulousness, even while he is cold-hearted, mean, vulgar, greedy, and vain, then it can hardly be in his interest to become warm, sensitive, cultivated, and generous, much less witty, perceptive, tactful, disinterested, and wise. We would not trade places with him to be sure, for it would not be in *our* interests to do so insofar as we have a stake, through the investment of our wants, in excellent character. We think, and rightly so in most cases, that we could only lose by becoming worse persons, and that the change itself would constitute a loss, whatever further losses or gains it caused to our other interests.

Partisans of the ideal-regarding theory often rest their case on the example of child-raising. Surely, it is said, we do not educate our children simply to become good want-fulfillers; rather we wish them to have the right wants in the first place, and to acquire the traits of character from which right wants emerge. Thus Stanley Benn claims that we are promoting the interests of the child when, at a time before he has achieved a good character, we commence with "educating him to be a person of a certain sort." "His desires are beside the point," Benn writes, "for it is often a question of whether he is to be encouraged to have desires of some approved sort instead of undesirable ones. It might be in the child's interests to deny him satisfaction of some of his desires to save him from becoming the sort of person who habitually desires the wrong thing."[6] Benn's example supports an important point, but not the one he claims to be making. The point of moral education at the time it is undertaken is not simply to serve the child's interests either as they are or as they might one day become; not simply to promote his gain, profit, or advantage, his happiness or well-being. The aim is rather to lead the child, through creating new wants in him, to seek his happiness *by* pursuing personal excellence: to give him a *stake* in having a good character. The parent who values good character will want to give the child his own interest in it, so that the child's pursuit of his own interests will necessarily involve seeking and preserving virtues of character. The effect of making goodness one of a person's ulterior interests is to make the achievement of happiness impossible without attention to it. So, far from showing that a good character is in a person's interest even if it does not promote want-fulfillment, Benn's example shows instead that good character can be something that is directly in a person's interest only when the person has a want-based interest in *it*.

One of the advantages of the want-regarding theory is that it enables us all the more forcibly to praise personal excellence. Good character would be a good thing to have even if it didn't advance a person's self-interest. Self-interest, after all, isn't everything. It is no aid to clarity to insist that everything that is good *in* a person must be good *for* the person. Nor does it help to say that the evil in a person must be harmful to him. The contented moral defective is an ineligible model for emulation even though his faults cause no harm to himself. He is both evil and well off, and his evil character does not detract from his well-offness. Epictetus's "pity" for him then is ill placed. Vice is its own punishment, just as virtue is its own reward, only to the person who has a stake in being good.

It is not merely useful but morally important to preserve in this way the distinction between being good and being well off, for it saves us from speaking as if and perhaps really believing that well-offness is the sole good. It is important to be a good person and not merely a happy or fulfilled one. That is why we train children to seek their happiness in part through seeking their goodness. In that way we ensure that they will not be completely happy unless they are good.

Morally corrupting a person, that is, causing him to be a worse person than he would otherwise be, can *harm* him, therefore, only if he has an antecedent interest in being good. (It may in fact harm no one to corrupt him if he is corrupted in a way that does not make him dangerous to others.) The moral corruption or neglect of an unformed child, then, is not direct harm to him, provided that he has the resources to pursue his own interests effectively anyway, but it can be a very real harm to his parents if *they* have a powerful stake in the child's moral development.

2. Other-regarding interests and vicarious harms

This brings us by a natural route to the subject of our wants for others and the unselfish interests they sometimes underwrite. There are two ways in which one person can have an interest in the well-being of another. In the one case, A may be dependent upon the help of B for the advancement of his own (A's) interests, so that if B's fortunes should decline, B would be less likely to help A. What promotes B's interest, in this case, indirectly promotes that of his dependent A as well. It is therefore in A's interest that B's interest be advanced. In the extreme version of this case, where A is *wholly* dependent on B's help, and so long as B's personal interest flourishes the help is sure to continue, B's good is, in effect, one of A's welfare interests, the advancement of which (like his own health) promotes the whole economy of his ulterior interests and is absolutely essential to his well-being, whatever his ulterior interests happen to be.

In the second kind of case, C has "invested" a desire so strong, durable, and stable in D's well-being, that he comes to have a personal stake in it himself. It becomes, therefore, one of his ulterior interests or focal aims. This should be contrasted with the more common phenomenon of spontaneous sympathy, pity, or compassion which can be directed at total strangers. It may make A very unhappy to see B (a stranger) suffer, and A may do what he can to help B, from genuinely disinterested, compassionate motives. But the harm that has been done to B, say by a hit-and-run motorist who knocked him down, is not *also* harm done to *A*. The interests of *A* have not been invaded by the harm done *B;* he has only suffered some vicarious unhappiness on *B*'s behalf which will leave his own personal interests largely unaffected. In the case of the genuinely other-regarding interest that I have in mind, *C* has an abiding interest of his own in *D*'s well-being which is not merely an episodic "passing desire." Further, he desires *D*'s good not simply as a means to the promotion of the other ulterior aims that are components of his own good, but quite sincerely as an end in itself. Such cases are, of course, rare, but no rarer than disinterested love. Indeed, there is one sense of "love" (that which the New Testament writers called *agape*) which is well defined by the presence of purely other-regarding interest. Ralph Barton Perry once defined "love" in this sense as an interest in the advancement of someone else's interests.[7] When *C* has a loving interest in *D*'s personal interest, then anything that harms *D* directly *ipso facto* harms *C* indirectly. Can anyone doubt that one harms a loving parent by maiming his or her child (or as in the previous example, by corrupting his or her child) or that one harms a loving husband or wife by causing a disappointment that plunges his or her spouse into despair?

The separation of the two kinds of cases distinguished in the preceding paragraphs is somewhat artificial. The distinction is clearly enough conceived, but in real life psychological elements rarely separate so neatly. Most of the things we desire for their own sakes we *also* desire as means to other things. Harm to a child may itself be harm to its loving parent in that it directly violates the parent's "purely" other-regarding interest, but it may also be instrumentally damaging to various self-regarding interests of the parents, in that it creates a drain on their funds, a burden on their time and energy, and a strain on their emotional stability. Similarly, when one spouse sinks into despair, this not only harms the other person's wholly other-regarding interest in the ailing mate's well-being; it also deprives him or her of the myriad services and pleasures that a cheerful partner would contribute.

Loving interests are so commonly intertwined with, and reinforced by, instrumental, essentially self-regarding interests, that many observers are led to discount the former, or even deny altogether their existence in given cases. Others have embraced the apparently cynical view that there are no purely other-regarding interests at all, that human nature being what it is, no one "really cares" about the well-being of other persons, except insofar as it affects his own self-regarding interests. All interests in the well-being of others, on this view, are of the first type distinguished above. This extreme form of psychological egoism rules out not only disinterested love, but episodic sympathy and compassion as well. Egoism of this sort can never be persuasive to those who are deeply impressed by the genuine purity of their own love for others, so its advocates must posit a good deal of self-deception in their opponents. Since the purity of people's motives is not readily subject to careful scrutiny, the egoistic theory, as a matter of empirical psychology, is not easily refuted, though the stronger philosophical arguments *for* the view are invariably muddled.

Some types of apparently other-regarding interests are so familiar, however, that the burden of explaining them away should be placed on the egoist. One common example is the case of pooled interest, where, either through design or accident, separate persons are so related that they share a common lot. Such common interests, "all for one and one for all," are found wherever parties are led (or forced) by circumstances to act in concert and share the risk of common failure or the fruits of an indivisible success.[8] Whatever the ultimate truth of the matter, common sense reports that persons with pooled or interdependent interests are sometimes drawn even closer by bonds of sentiment directed toward common objects or reciprocal affection (of an *apparently* disinterested kind) between the parties. And when this happens, as it sometimes seems to in marriages and family groups, each has a genuine stake of a not merely instrumental kind in the well-being of the others, a stable ulterior goal, or focal aim, that the others flourish, partly as an end in itself, partly as a means to a great diversity of other ends.

Despite the familiarity of these observations, some very able philosophers have chosen to exclude purely other-regarding wants altogether from their otherwise want-regarding analyses of interest. The writers in question do not necessarily deny that there are purely other-regarding wants. Brian Barry, for example, admits that some of us, some of the time, genuinely want other persons as well as ourselves to enjoy increased opportunities to satisfy ulterior wants. Indeed, he concedes that some persons, some of the time, even voluntarily suffer a diminution of their opportunities for want-satisfaction in order to increase the opportunities of other persons to satisfy *their* wants. But the latter cases, Barry insists, are best described as cases where our *principles* are allowed to override our interests.[9] Barry is right about the cases he seems to be considering, where persons voluntarily sacrifice their own interests for others out of a sense of justice, or for ideal-regarding reasons, or for charity. But he doesn't even consider cases of the kind discussed above where help to others is not thought to be a *sacrifice* at all, but a direct promotion of one's own other-regarding interest in the advancement of the interests of another party.

I think the theoretical motives of writers who exclude other-regarding wants from their analyses of self-interest are clear enough, and worthy of respect. They are simply taking the easiest way out of a kind of linguistic muddle. They are afraid that inclusion of purely other-regarding aims as eligible constituents of a person's own self-interest would commit them to saying various odd-sounding things. They fear that we would have to say when Jones gives his last cent to promote the cause of his favorite political party, or to finance his child's education, or to secure the very best doctor for his sick wife, that he is advancing his own interest *merely* (treacherous word, "merely"). Hence, we must think of his act as "selfish," since it was done in his own self-interest, after all. The less paradoxical alternative, they think, is to deny that the act is in the actor's own interest at all, and to say instead that Jones was acting from conscience, or out of principle, or for charity, and against his own interest. After all, how could his act be at once disinterested and self-interested, unselfish yet self-advancing?

There is, however, a more satisfactory, if less direct, way out of the muddle. That is simply to consider very carefully what it means to call an act "unselfish" and "disinterested," and to come by this route to appreciate how unselfish and disinterested conduct, without affecting any of the actor's interests other than those he has in the well-being of others, can nevertheless be in his own personal interest. A person who has such a stake in the happiness of other people that his own well-being depends on the advancement of their interests is not the proper model of a selfish person. A selfish person is one who pays insufficient attention to the interests of other people, and thus comes to pursue his own self-regarding interests at the expense of, or in disregard of, the interests of others. That is quite another thing than pursuing one's own interest in *promoting* the interests of others. The loving parent or spouse and the public-spirited zealot can make no distinction between their own interests and that of their children, or spouse, or party. Far from indicating their selfishness, that identity of interests shows how unselfish they probably are. They might yet be blamably selfish, however, if they pursue those of their own interests which include the interests of *some* other people (for example, a daughter and a son) at the expense of still *other* people (for example, their neighbors' children). It is in fact an advantage of our analysis (as opposed to Barry's) that it enables us to explain why conduct of the latter kind is selfish. On Barry's analysis, neither want—that for the well-being of my children or that for the well-being of my neighbor's children—is one of my own interests. Hence, when I promote the interests of some of these parties at the expense of those of the others, I am acting neither for nor against my own interests. I can be acting oddly or wrongly in that case, but not specifically selfishly. That judgment, however, seems plainly false. It surely *is* selfish wrongly to benefit one's own loved ones at the expense of others.

The best way, it seems to me, to conceive of the relation between self-

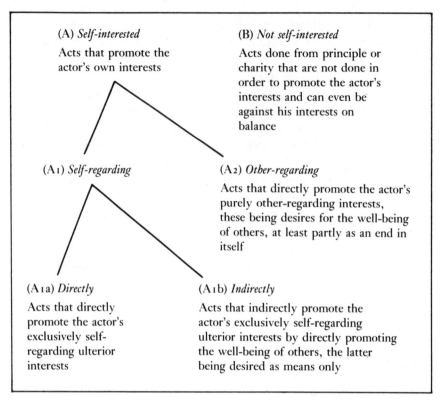

(A) *Self-interested*
Acts that promote the
actor's own interests

(B) *Not self-interested*
Acts done from principle or
charity that are not done in
order to promote the actor's
interests and can even be
against his interests on
balance

(A1) *Self-regarding*

(A2) *Other-regarding*
Acts that directly promote the actor's
purely other-regarding interests,
these being desires for the well-being
of others, at least partly as an end in
itself

(A1a) *Directly*
Acts that directly
promote the actor's
exclusively self-
regarding ulterior
interests

(A1b) *Indirectly*
Acts that indirectly promote the
actor's exclusively self-regarding
ulterior interests by directly promoting
the well-being of others, the latter
being desired as means only

Diagram 1

interested, selfish, unselfish, and disinterested acts is that indicated in a
chart with two genera, one of which is further subdivided (see Diagram 1).

The generic distinction in the chart is that on the top line between
self-interested acts and acts that are not self-interested, particularly those
that concern Barry, namely, conscientious or charitable acts that are not
predominantly in the actor's interest. Self-interested acts are then divided
into self-regarding and other-regarding species. Depending on our purposes, of course, we would classify the acts in this motley category in
various alternative ways, but it is especially useful for our present purposes
to divide them into these mutually exclusive and jointly exhaustive categories. The self-regarding class is then further divided into directly and indirectly self-regarding subclasses. For an example of directly self-regarding
activity (A1a) consider an unmarried homeowner's labor at improving his
property so that he can get more enjoyment and pride from it, impress
those in a position to help him, and disproportionately increase its resale
value in a rising market. Such a person is promoting his own purely self-

regarding ulterior interests in material possession, career advancement, and capital accumulation. An example of indirectly self-regarding activity (A1b) is found in the story of the gambler, A, who bets B $50,000 that C will recover from a serious illness. Thus C's health is in A's interest, and A has a stake (in a literal sense) in C's recovery. To protect that stake he works hard to promote C's recovery, providing at his own expense the best medical and nursing care that he can find. He thus promotes the well-being of another as ardently as a lover or a saint would, though the other's well-being, his immediate goal, is desired only as a means to the advancement of his own self-regarding interest.

In contrast, acts in the genuinely other-regarding species of the self-interested genus (A2) aim at the promotion of another's good at least partly as an end in itself. An example would be that of a parent whose stake in the well-being of his child is derived from his love for the child simply, and not from any incidental service to his other (self-regarding) interests that the child might contribute. If such a parent depletes his own life savings to advance or protect his child, his act would fall in the other-regarding species of the self-interested genus. This is the species which is thought to be empty, for quite different reasons, by psychological egoists and Brian Barry. The egoists deny that any acts are genuinely other-regarding (that is, motivated by a desire to promote or retard the good of another as an end in itself), while Barry denies that any other-regarding acts are self-interested. But if any person ever does "really care" whether another person is harmed or benefited, and not simply as a means to his own gain but at least in part for the other's own sake, then the egoists are wrong. And if any person ever does have a genuine stake in the happiness of another person—an independent ulterior interest not wholly derived from its service to other ulterior interests—such that he himself gains or loses directly depending on the condition of the other person, then the view suggested by Barry is wrong.

The chart enables us to distinguish several senses of "disinterested action" and also two kinds of selfish action. A disinterested act can be defined in a first approximation as one not done simply to advance the actor's interests.[10] One class of disinterested actions, then, consists of those in the chart's second genus: those not done to advance *any* of the actor's interests, self-regarding or other-regarding. These are actions done from conscience, or out of a sense of justice, or from charity, or from a spontaneous benevolent impulse, often with the conscious expectation that they will be against the actor's own interest. A second kind of disinterested action is one which meets a stricter test; it is done neither to promote the actor's own interest nor to favor the interests of any second parties unfairly at the expense of third parties when the actor's own interests simply aren't involved one way or the other. Thus, a judge's decision is disinterested when it is unbiased and impartial. These related senses of the word "disinterested" are well established in usage. A third sense (one which is suggested by our chart) is not so clearly established and may in fact be somewhat extended beyond what is recognized in ordinary usage. I am not sure. Still, it stands for an important category that deserves to be distinguished from the others, whatever name it bears. I refer to actions in the other-regarding species of the self-interested genus (A2), acts done out of the perfectly genuine desire to help another whose well-being is actually a constituent of the actor's own good. When a person promotes the well-being of a loved one in a self-sacrificing or otherwise "selfless" way, it may be misleading to call his act disinterested since he does have a personal stake, even a predominant ulterior interest, in the outcome. But it can be equally misleading to deny that his act is disinterested since apart from the well-being of the loved one that is his goal, there may be no "personal advantage" in his action, and no trace of self-interest in his motivation. In an extreme case, he might even sacrifice all his other interests for the good of another person or cause in which he has "invested" everything. The least misleading thing to say about such conduct is that it is not disinterested in one very familiar sense of the term, but that it is disinterested in another, less familiar, sense. In any event, extreme psychological egoists are likely to deny that there are disinterested acts of either kind, and sometimes put that view by saying that all voluntary actions are "selfish."

Now a selfish act, whatever else it may be, is one that is morally defective. A person acts selfishly when he pursues his own interests (or the satisfaction of transitory desires and appetites) *wrongly* at the expense of others. Sometimes, of course, there is nothing blamable in the pursuit of self-interest at the expense of others, as for example, in legitimately or unavoidably competitive contexts. An act is selfish only when its pursuit of self-interest is somehow in excess of what is right or reasonable in the situation.

The more familiar kind of selfish act is a defective specimen of those in the self-regarding species of self-interested actions (A1a and b). The father who refuses to spend money on his children for anything beyond their minimal needs, and uses his surplus instead to buy fine clothes and wines for himself, is selfish in this way. But as we have seen, defective specimens of acts in the other-regarding species of the self-interested genus (A2) can also be selfish, as when a parent with a genuinely independent stake in his own children's advancement (an "other-regarding interest") pursues that interest wrongly at the expense of his neighbor's children. We would be reluctant, I think, to call the latter actions "disinterested" in *any* sense, since it would be intolerably odd to think of an act as both disinterested and selfish. Hence I am forced to qualify the account given above of the self-interested acts that can also be, in an "unfamiliar sense," disinterested, as follows: an act is disinterested in that third sense provided that (1) it is done in order to advance the good of another party, but (2) not merely as a means to the advancement of the actor's own self-regarding interests, *and* (3) it is not done to promote the actor's other-regarding interest in the well-being of one party wrongly at the expense of still another party. (This third condition amends the definition, in effect, by requiring that a disinterested act not be a selfish act of the second kind.)

Selfish actions, then, can be defined as those which pursue the actor's self-interest *wrongly* at the expense of, or in disregard of, other people, and the two main types of selfish actions are those which are appropriately defective instances of category A1 on the chart, and those which are appropriately defective instances of A2. (Morally defective instances of *B*, as we shall see, are not called "selfish.") It is best, I think, to define "selfish" and "unselfish" as logical contraries rather than contradictories, in recognition of a large and motley class of actions that are neither selfish nor unselfish. An unselfish act then can be defined as one which pursues the interests of others (or the fulfillment of their transitory wants or appetites) *rightly* at the expense of, or in praiseworthy disregard of, the actor's own interests (or wants and appetites).[11] Voluntary actions in the middle group that qualify neither as selfish nor as unselfish include those which pursue the actor's own self-regarding wants or interests (A1) in a nondefective way (not wrong or blamable, not deficient in concern for others) as well as those whose motivation does not include concern for self-interest one way or the other, as in the case of the judge in a controversy between two persons who are strangers to him.

There are blamably defective specimens of acts even in the nonselfinterested genus (B on the chart), but these characteristically bear names other than "selfish." Acting entirely out of principle, for example, a person might be rigid, cruel, or intolerant. A person might, in another case, act honestly in accord with a dictate of his own mistaken or confused conscience. Another person might act unjustly or imprudently out of spontaneous compassion. All of these morally defective acts can be against the actor's interest and known to be such, yet deliberately chosen anyway. They may be blamable, but they are not selfish.

According to our previous definition of "harm," a setback to an interest in any of the categories in the chart is a harm to its possessor. Any action, omission, or rule that interferes with a person's self-interested action, thus thwarting his interest, causes him harm. But does it follow from the defini-

tion that interferences with voluntary acts in the nonselfinterested genus (B)
are *not* harms? That would seem at first sight to be the case. Since acting
out of conscience or benevolence is not acting to advance one's own interest,
interference with such action does not violate one's interest, and therefore is
not, by definition, a harm to one. Moreover, such interference, when it
prevents a person from acting contrary to his own interest, actually *serves*
his interest, and would seem therefore to be beneficial to him. Any interference, however, with a voluntary action, even with a nonselfinterested one,
is an invasion of a person's interest in *liberty*, and is thus harmful to him to
that extent. If that seems too trivial a harm in the case at hand to be the
basis of a powerful claim to noninterference, the liberal will have to retreat
from the harm principle and seek a stronger defensive position. I develop
such a position in Volume 3, basing it on the principle, discussed with
sympathy there, that infringements of an actor's *autonomy* (see Chap. 18,
§5, and Chap. 19) are serious wrongs to him even when they do him, at
most, only trivial harm, and indeed even when on balance they *advance* his
interests. That development in the argument, as we shall see, will mark a
liberal departure (though a small one) from the wholly unsupplemented
harm principle as it is defined here. The mature liberal view is that the state
might interfere with A's treatment of B either to prevent wrongful harm to
B, *or*, in certain rare cases of harmless wrongs (for example, where A
interferes with B's voluntary but self-sacrificing act of service to C), to
prevent A from violating B's right of autonomy.

Further problems for this analysis of vicarious harms are raised by the
possibility of an infinite regress. Suppose that A and B love each other. C
harms A which *ipso facto* sets back B's other-regarding interest in A. That in
turn affects A's other-regarding interest in B, and he is further harmed,
occasioning still further harm to B, *etc. ad infinitum*.[12] This largely accurate
account of the matter would stagger the understanding if each new harm it
mentions (the whole infinitude of them!) were fresh and of equal or greater
magnitude than the earlier one. In fact, however, the reverberating effect is
more like that of an ever-receding series of echos generated by a single
original, or like the infinite series of mirrored images within mirrored images in certain puzzling drawings of human figures looking into glass mirrors and seeing their images looking into mirrors, or of artists painting
themselves painting themselves, etc. When C harms A, that *does* harm B,
though not *all* of B's interests, but only her interest in A's well-being. That
subsequent harm to B is not as great as the original harm to A unless B's
interest in A's good is her own entire good, her single predominant ulterior
interest, or even an indispensable welfare interest. Even if B is harmed as
much as A by the direct harm to A, that derivative harm to A's interest in B

is not as great a harm to *A* as the original harm to his whole interest network, since it sets back only one of his ulterior interests, strong as it might be. And that secondary reenforcing harm to *A*, in turn, would indeed be a reenforcing harm to *B*, but not of the same magnitude as her original. The receding echoes have already begun. After several more reverberating reenforcements, the diminishing increments will be so small, that for all practical purposes they vanish entirely.[13]

There will be a genuine paradox, however, if *A*'s *entire* well-being is invested in *B*'s well-being and *B*'s *entire* well-being is invested in *A*'s well-being. (This is similar to the paradox of ethical altruism when self-sacrifice for the sake of others is made morally mandatory for everyone!) In that case, harm to *A* will be *ipso facto* equal harm to *B*, and that in turn will be a fresh harm of undiminished magnitude to *A*, and that in turn to *B*, etc. The paradox is brought out in another way when we consider that the only way *A* can be harmed in the first place is by harm to *B*, but the only way harm can come to *B* is by harm to *A*, and so on. It would seem to follow that harm could never come to either! These are indeed absurd consequences. But they bring out the incoherence of total, reciprocal, exclusively other-regarding self-interest, not the incoherence of the concept of vicarious harm itself.

3. Death and posthumous harms

Can a person be harmed by his own death? On the one hand, we are inclined to answer unhesitatingly, "of course." To murder a person, we think, is to inflict on him what is in general the most serious harm a person can suffer. On the other hand, a moment's reflection makes us hesitate. In order to be harmed, common sense reminds us, a person must be in existence at the time, but death (real total death of the person, not the mere "apparent death" of theological teachings) is the cessation of one's existence, the first moment of a state of nonbeing, which is beyond harm or gain. Thus there is another tendency, opposite to the first, to suppose that death is *not* a harm. Ordinary usage gives support to both these tendencies, and philosophers line up on both sides with reenforcing arguments. If their disagreements are over their descriptions of pretheoretical ordinary thinking (or "common sense"), then it may never be resolved, for the issue may be inherently indeterminate.[14] In that case our task will be to propose a further refinement of ordinary thinking in the interest of our emerging general theory of harm, and to support that proposal with the best reasons we can find.

First, consider the case against classifying death as a harm. Even ordinary language gives it some backing. If a murderer is asked whether he has harmed his victim, he might well reply: "Harmed him? Hell no; I killed him outright!" The victim's mourners too might feel that it is something of an understatement to describe the death of their loved one as a harm (to him). The death of the victim, it would seem, is not a mere "harmed condition" he is put in, and certainly not a "harmful" one; it is no "condition" of him at all, but rather his total extinction. Ordinary language, to be sure, is not univocal, but the main case against calling death a harm is not based on ordinary language, but rather on a very simple and powerful argument: there cannot be harm without a subject to be harmed, and when death occurs it obliterates the subject, and thus excludes the possibility of harm. Even this way of speaking is misleading, the argument goes, for it suggests that death *does something* to the subject and that therefore there is a period of time during which they are both coexistent. Actually, death is defined simply as the first moment of the subject's nonexistence,[15] so it is not something that ever coexists with the dying person for the time required for it to have a directly harmful effect on him.

Consider the purest possible hypothetical case of the infliction of death, where all extraneous and distracting harms have been excluded from the example. A woman in the prime of her life, with many ongoing projects and enterprises, but with no dependents or friends close enough to mourn her, is shot in the head by an unseen assailant, while she is asleep. Without ever being aware that she was even in danger, much less that she has been fatally wounded, she dies instantly. Right up to the very instant she was shot she was unharmed, then at that very moment, perhaps one second after the killer squeezed the trigger, she was dead. At the very most, she was in a "harmed condition" for the one-half second or so before she died. As for death itself, one might agree with the ancient Epicureans: "Where she was, death was not, and where death was, she was not."

This powerful argument against classifying death as a harm is indeed a problem for the position on the other side, a difficulty commonly called "the problem of the subject." Like a rock withstanding the lashings of a storm it stands resistant to all counterarguments, maintaining and reiterating that there cannot be a harm without a subject to be harmed.[16] Indeed, if the argument has any weakness at first sight, it consists in its tendency to prove too much. The ancient Epicureans, after all, were not quibbling over the word "harm." They used the problem of the subject to argue more sweepingly that death is not *any kind of evil* to the one who dies, and therefore nothing to be feared or regretted, a conclusion generally thought to be paradoxical.[17]

The case in favor of classifying death as a harm can be put almost equally quickly. To begin with, ordinary language lends some support to this side of the controversy too. It is so natural, almost unavoidable, to speak in idioms that seem to imply this view, that there must be some point in it (at least points of analogy). For example, we sometimes say of a person who has been killed that "he was deprived of his life," or of years of happiness he might otherwise have enjoyed. Incurably ill persons, on the other hand, are said to "seek release" and when they find it, to be "better off dead," since their "lives were of no further use to them." People killed in accidents are often characterized in the language of loss: "Hundreds lost their lives in the storm." We can, of course, avoid these idioms and talk only of the destruction of the person, not harm or benefit to the person, as the evil or good in question, because there is no survivor to be the proper subject of harm or benefit. But this linguistic strictness would deprive us of metaphors of striking aptness and utility.

The main support for the view of death as harm, however, comes not from ordinary language, but from whatever support has already been mustered for the analysis of harm as set-back interest, which, given the universal interest in not dying, implies that death is a harm. The continuance of our lives for most of us, at most moments in our lives, is something manifestly in our interests, and that being so, the sudden extinction of life would, as a thwarting of that interest, be a harm. (The skeptical question, harm to whom? must for the moment be put aside.) Consider again the sleeping victim of a murder who dies instantaneously. One second before the trigger was pulled, it was true of the victim (as it is now true of both the author and reader of these words) that continued life was something in her *interest*. Indeed, there is nothing a normal person (in reasonable health and tolerable circumstances) dreads more than his own death, and that dread, in the vast majority of cases, is as rational as it is unavoidable, for unless we continue alive, we have no chance whatever of achieving those goals that are the ground of our ultimate interest. Some of these goals, perhaps, might be achieved for us by others after our deaths, publicly oriented and other-regarding goals in particular. But most of our interests require not simply that some result be brought about, but rather that it be brought about *by* us, or if not by us, then *for* us. My interest in producing an excellent book, or a beautiful art object, is not fully satisfied by another person's creation of such objects. My interest was not simply that such objects exist, but that *I* bring them into existence. Similarly my aim to build a dream house, or to achieve leisure in security, is not satisfied when such a house or such leisure comes into existence, but only when I am present to enjoy and use it. Our interest in avoiding death is a supreme welfare interest, an indispensable condition for the advancement of most, if not all, of the ulterior interests that constitute our good. There is something bare minimal about it on the one hand, yet something supremely important on the other. Apart from the interests it serves, it has no value in itself; yet unless it is protected, hardly any of a person's ulterior interests will be advanced. To extinguish a person's life is, at one stroke, to defeat almost all of his self-regarding interests: to ensure that his ongoing projects and enterprises, his long-range goals, and his most earnest hopes for his own achievement and personal enjoyment, must all be dashed.

If the prior interests set back by death justify our characterization of death as a harm (even without a subject), then equally some of them warrant our speaking of certain later events as posthumous harms. On the other hand, if the absence of a subject (even given prior interests whose targets postdate death) prevents us from speaking of death as a harm, then it equally precludes talk of posthumous harms. Death and developments after death are alike in coming into existence during a period when there is no longer a subject. If the absence of a subject precludes our speaking of posthumous harms, then equally it precludes our speaking of death as a harm (a rather harder pill to swallow) since both death and posthumous events are postpersonal. Either death and posthumous events both alike can be harms or neither can.[18] (I discuss posthumous harms in more detail below).

There is a case then for saying both that death is not (ever) a harm and that it is (often) a thwarting of the antecedent interest in staying alive. That makes death a very hard case indeed for the analysis of harm as set-back or thwarted interest. The writer who has strong theoretical incentives for saving the set-back interest theory of harm has only two alternative moves at this point. He might simply stipulate an admittedly extended sense of "harm" broad enough to include death as a harm, or he might search for a way to solve "the problem of the subject" by explaining how a person can be harmed by events that occur subsequent to his own existence. Failing both of these moves, he must revise or supplement the harm principle so as to make it more adequate as a liberal principle of liberty-limitation. He could do that by a simple amendment to his formulation of that principle so that it certifies as a relevant reason for the restriction of liberty that it is necessary to prevent *harm or death* to others (implying that they are not the same thing). The cost of this amendment, clearly, would be the abandonment of the analysis of a harm (which has been so useful thus far) as any setback to interest, for there *is* an interest in avoiding death, yet the amendment implies that death is not a harm.

Stipulating a new sense of "harm" broad enough to include death would be but a minor and quite excusable departure from the conventions of ordinary language for the sake of theoretical economy, similar perhaps to the restriction of the sense of "fish" to exclude whales and seals, which were once commonly and properly called "fish." Still it would make things tidier all around if we could show that first appearance to the contrary, there *is* a plausible subject for harmful deaths and posthumous events. Although a whiff of paradox may still attach to it, there is a way of conceiving death, even without the assumption of survival or immortality, that lends plausibility to the description of death as sometimes harmful to the one who dies. That is all that can be claimed for the theory suggested in sections 5 and 6 below.

To be sure, death is not always and necessarily a harm to the one who dies. To the person in hopeless, painful illness, who has already "withdrawn his investments" in all ulterior interests, there may be nothing to lose, and cessation of agony or boredom to be "gained," in which case death is a blessing. For the retired nonagenarian, death may not exactly be ardently desired, but still it will be a nontragedy. Those who mourn his death will not think of themselves as mourning *for him*, but rather for his dependents and loved ones, if any, or simply in virtue of the capacity of any *memento mori* to evoke sadness. In contrast, when a young vigorous person dies, we think of *him* as chief among those who suffered loss. The strength of that conviction provides much of the motivation for the search for a solution to the problem of the subject.

4. *Surviving interests*

I would like to suggest that we can think of some of a person's interests as surviving his death, just as some of the debts and claims of his estate do, and that in virtue of the defeat of these interests, either by death itself or by subsequent events, we can think of the person who was, as harmed. I no longer wish to say that these interests themselves are the "true subjects of harm,"[19] because that suggests a bizarre ontological reification, as if each interest were a little person in its own right. Ernest Partridge is understandably impatient with this view and quite right when he says, "But surely by 'interests themselves' he [Feinberg] cannot mean interests of no one."[20] All interests are the interest of some persons or other, and a person's surviving interests are simply the ones that we identify by naming *him*, the person whose interests they were. He is of course at this moment dead, but that does not prevent us from referring now, in the present tense, to his interests, if they are still capable of being blocked or fulfilled, just as we refer to his outstanding debts or claims, if they are still capable of being paid. The final tally book on a person's life is not closed until some time after his death.

Even Partridge finds himself obliged, when speaking of a hypothetical violation of the will of Alfred Nobel, to use the idiom "contrary to the wishes of the late Alfred Nobel,"[21] implying that what is done *now* can affect ("be contrary to") what was wished *then*. There *are* such wishes, in a kind of timeless propositional sense, rendered, by grammatical convention merely, in the present tense, even though there is no longer an Alfred Nobel. The conditions of the will "exist" and are binding now, and they give present expression to the wishes that Nobel had *then*. That does not imply a peculiar metaphysical status for the wishes as being still consciously experienced in some universal mind, or in the head of a decaying corpse, or whatever. Similar comments can be made about surviving interests. In this section I shall try to explain more fully what it is for interests to survive before tackling head-on, in section 5, the problem of the subject.

What then does it mean to say that a "surviving interest" has been set back or defeated? Our answer to this question will depend on which of two conceptions of interest enhancement and impairment we adopt. As we have seen, interests are "stakes" that are derived from and linked to wants, in the case of ulterior interests to more ulterior goals or focal aims. Now we can apply to these wants W. D. Ross's distinction between want-fulfillment and want-satisfaction.[22] The *fulfillment* of a want is simply the coming into existence of that which is desired. The *satisfaction* of a want is the pleasant experience of contentment or gratification that normally occurs in the mind of the desirer when he believes that his desire has been fulfilled. When the object of a want does not come into existence, we can say that the want has been *unfulfilled* or *thwarted;* the experience in the mind of the desirer when he believes that his desire has been thwarted is called *frustration* or *disappointment*. Notoriously, fulfillment of desire can fail to give satisfaction. There is no more melancholy state than the disillusionment that comes from getting what we wanted and finding it disappointing. Such disillusionment can usually be explained as the consequence of a rash or ill-considered desire and unrealistic expectations. On other occasions, the original desire will bear up under retrospective scrutiny, and yet its fulfillment gives no pleasure. Indeed, the occurrence of subjective satisfaction is a highly contingent and unreliable phenomenon. Sometimes when our goals are achieved, we don't experience much joy, but only fatigue and sadness, or an affective blankness. Some persons, perhaps, are disposed by temperament normally to receive their achievements in this unthrilled fashion. Still, even in these cases, reexamination of the goal whose fulfillment failed to satisfy may disclose no hidden defects, no reasons for regret, in a word, no disillusionment. Not only can one have fulfillment without satisfaction; one can also have satisfaction of a want in the absence of its actual fulfillment, provided only that one is led to believe, falsely, that one's want has been fulfilled. Similarly, pleasant states of mind resembling "satisfaction" can be induced by drugs, hypnosis, and other forms of manipulation that have no relation whatever to prior wants.

Similarly, one's wants can be thwarted without causing frustration, or disappointment, and one can be quite discontented even when one's wants have in fact been fulfilled. These negative cases are perfectly parallel with the positive ones. Nonfulfillment of a want yields no disappointment when the want was ill-advised in the first place. In such a case, the want can happily be renounced after rational reassessment. Disillusionment, however, is often not involved. A perfectly genuine and well-considered goal may be thwarted without causing mental pain when the desirer has a placid temperament or a stoic philosophy. And discontent does not presuppose thwarting of desire any more than satisfaction presupposes fulfillment. One can have feelings of frustration and disappointment caused by false beliefs that one's wants have been thwarted, or by drugs and other manipulative techniques.

For these reasons, harm to an interest is better defined in terms of the objective blocking of goals and thwarting of desires than in subjective terms; and the enhancement or advancing of an interest is likewise best defined in terms of the objective fulfillment of well-considered wants rather than in terms of subjective states of pleasure. Most persons will agree, I think, that the important thing is to get what they want, even if that causes no joy.[23] The pleasure that normally attends want-fulfillment is a welcome dividend, but the object of our efforts is to fulfill our wants in the external world, not to bring about states of our own minds. Indeed, if this were not the case, there would be no way to account for the pleasure of satisfaction when it does come; we are satisfied only because we think that our desires are fulfilled. If the object of our desires were valuable to us only as a means to our pleasant inner states, those glows could never come.

The object of a focal aim that is the basis of an interest, then, like the object of any want, is not simply satisfaction or contentment, and the defeat of an interest is not to be identified with disappointment or frustration. Hence, death can be a thwarting of the interests of the person who dies, and must be the total defeat of most of his self-regarding interests, even though, as a dead man, he can feel no pain.

This account helps explain, I think, why we grieve for a young, vigorous "victim of death" himself, and not *only* for those who loved him and depended on him. We grieve for him in virtue of his unfulfilled interests. We think of him as one who has invested all his energies and hopes in the world, and then has lost everything. We think of his life as a whole as not as good a thing as it might have been had he lived on. In some special circumstances, death not only does its harm in this wholly "negative" way, preventing the flowering of the interests in which a person's lifetime good consists, it also does direct and "positive" harm to a person by undoing or setting back important interests that were already prospering. Death, in these cases, leads to the harming of surviving interests that might otherwise have been prevented.[24]

Because the objects of a person's interests are usually wanted or aimed-at events that occur outside his immediate experience and at some future time, the area of a person's good or harm is necessarily wider than his subjective experience and longer than his biological life. The moment of death is the terminating boundary of one's biological life, but it is itself an important event within the life of one's future-oriented interests. When death thwarts an interest, the harm can be ascribed to the person who is no more, charged as it were to his "moral estate."

The interests that die with a person are those that can no longer be helped or harmed by posthumous events. These include most of his self-regarding interests, those based, for example, on desires for personal achievement and personal enjoyment, and those based on "self-confined" wants that a person could have "if he were the only person that had ever existed,"[25] for example, the desire to be a self of a certain kind, or the desire for self-respect. Other self-regarding wants, in contrast, seem more like other-regarding and publicly oriented wants, in that they can be fulfilled or thwarted after the death of the person whose wants they are. I refer to some of a person's desires to stand in certain relations to other people where "the concern is primarily with the self . . . and with others only as objects or as other terms in a relation to me."[26] These desires can be called "self-centered," and include as a class such wants as the desire to assert or display oneself before others, to be the object of affection or esteem of others, and so on. In particular, the desire to maintain a good reputation, like the desire that some social or political cause triumph, or the desire that one's loved ones flourish, can be the basis of interests that survive their owner's death, in a manner of speaking, and can be promoted or harmed by events subsequent to that death. Fulfillment and thwarting of interest, after all, may still be possible, even when it is too late for satisfaction or disappointment.

The above account might still contain elements of paradox, but it can be defended against one objection that is sure to be made. How can a person be harmed, it might be asked, by what he can't know? Dead men are permanently unconscious; hence they cannot be aware of events as they occur; hence (it will be said) they can have no stake one way or the other in such events. That this argument employs a false premise can be shown by a consideration of various interests of *living* persons that can be violated without their ever becoming aware of it. Many of these are "possessory interests" whose rationality can be doubted, for example, a landowner's interest in the *exclusive* possession and enjoyment of his land—an interest that can be invaded by an otherwise harmless trespasser who takes one unobserved step inside the entrance gates; or the legally recognized "interest in domestic relations" which is invaded when one's spouse engages in secret adulterous activity with a lover. The latter is an interest in being the exclusive object of one's spouse's love, and has been criticized by some as implying property in another's affections. But there is no criticizing on such grounds the interest every person has in his own reputation, which is perhaps the best example for our present purposes from the purely self-regarding category. If someone spreads a libelous description of me among a group whose good opinion I covet and cherish, altogether without my knowledge, I have been injured in virtue of the harm done my interest in a good reputation, even though I *never* learn what has happened. That is because I have an interest, so I believe, in having a good reputation *as such*, in addition to my interest in avoiding hurt feelings, embarrassment, and economic injury. And *that* interest can be seriously harmed without my ever learning of it.

How is the situation changed in any relevant way by the death of the person defamed? If knowledge is not a necessary condition of harm before one's death why should it be necessary afterward? Suppose that after my death, an enemy cleverly forges documents to "prove" very convincingly that I was a philanderer, an adulterer, and a plagiarist, and communicates this "information" to the general public that includes my widow, children, and former colleagues and friends. Can there be any doubt that I have been harmed by such libels? The "self-centered" interest I had at my death in the continued high regard of my fellows, in this example, was not thwarted by my death itself, but by events that occurred afterward. Similarly, my other-regarding interest in the well-being of my children could be defeated or harmed after my death by other parties overturning my will, or by thieves and swindlers who cheat my heirs of their inheritance. None of these events will embarrass or distress me, since dead men can have no feelings; but all of them can harm my interests by forcing nonfulfillment of goals in which I had placed a great stake.

This liability, to which we are all subject, to drastic changes in our fortune both before and after death was well understood by the Greeks. Aristotle devotes a chapter of his *Nicomachean Ethics* to a saying already ancient in his time, and attributed by some to Solon, that we can "call no man fortunate before his death."[27] On one interpretation, this dark saying means that "only when he is dead is it safe to call a man . . . beyond the arrows of outrageous fortune." On the day before he dies, his interests can be totally smashed and his life thus ruined. But as Aristotle shrewdly observes (attributing the point to the general popular wisdom), some of a person's interests are not made safe even by his death, and we cannot call him fortunate with perfect confidence until several more decades have passed; "For a dead man is popularly believed to be capable of having both good and ill fortune—honor and dishonor and prosperity and the loss of it among his children and descendants generally—in exactly the same way as if he were alive but unaware or unobservant of what was happening."[28]

Three hypothetical cases can illustrate the "popular belief" mentioned by Aristotle, and a part of the case for posthumous harm can rest with them.

Case A. A woman devotes thirty years of her life to the furtherance of certain ideals and ambitions in the form of one vast undertaking. She founds an institution dedicated to these ends and works single-mindedly for its advancement, both for the sake of the social good she believes it to promote, and for the sake of her own glory. One month before she dies, the "empire of her hopes" collapses utterly as the establishment into which she has poured her life's energies crumbles into ruin, and she is personally disgraced. She never learns the unhappy truth, however, as her friends, eager to save her from disappointment, conceal or misrepresent the facts. She dies contented.

Case B. The facts are the same as in Case A, except that the institution in which the woman had so great an interest remains healthy, growing and flourishing, until her death. But it begins to founder a month later, and within a year, it collapses utterly, while at the same time, the woman and her life's work are totally discredited.

Case C. The facts are the same as in Case B, except for an additional surmise about the cause of the decline and collapse of the woman's fortune after her death. In the present case, a group of malevolent conspirators, having made solemn promises to the woman before her death, deliberately violate them after she has died. From motives of vengeance, malice, and envy, they spread damaging lies about her and her institution, reveal secret plans, and otherwise betray her trust in order to bring about the ruin of her interests.

It would not be very controversial to say that the woman in Case A had suffered grievous harm to her interests although she never learned the bad news. Those very same interests are harmed in Case B to exactly the same extent, and again the woman does not learn the bad news, in this case because she is dead, and dead people hear no news at all. There seems no relevant difference between Case A and Case B except that in Case B there might seem to be no subject of the harm, the woman being dead at the specific moment when the harm occurred. (But see §5 below.) We have seen, however, that there is a sense in which some of her interests survive her, and that these, like all interests, are harmed by thwarting or nonfulfillment rather than by subjective disappointment. But if that point is not convincing, the argument must depend on its reinforcement by Case C. In that example, the woman is not *merely* harmed (if she is harmed at all); rather she is exploited, betrayed, and wronged. When a promise is broken, someone is wronged, and who if not the promisee? When a confidence is revealed, someone is betrayed, and who, if not the person whose confidence it was? When a reputation is falsely blackened, someone is defamed, and who, if not the person lied about? If there is no "problem of the subject" when we speak of wronging the dead, why should there be when we speak of harming them, especially when the harm is an essential ingredient of the wrong?

5. The proper subject of surviving interests

The motivation for thinking of death and some posthumous events as harms should now be clear, but the central puzzle still remains. The surviving interests, like the interests instantly squelched by death itself, must be the interests of someone or other. If they are the interests of the person who is now dead, then we are faced with the impossible problem of explaining how a mere physical thing—a decaying body six feet underground—can have any want-based interests. If the interests are those of the living person who is no more, then the problem is to explain how his lot can be made better or worse, as it were *retroactively*. If, on the contrary, the detached interests themselves are the only proper subjects of the harm, then either they are nobody's interests at all (the view Partridge derides) or they are the interests of some Absolute Mind, a metaphysical assumption that is uneconomical, to put it mildly.

The view I would like to defend is that the interests harmed by events that occur at or after the moment a person's nonexistence commences are interests of the living person who no longer is with us, not the interests of the decaying body he left behind. (The latter attribution of course is utterly absurd.) As George Pitcher points out (in an important article[29] from which I shall now proceed to borrow heavily), a dead person can be described in two different ways: (1) "as he was at some stage of his life—i.e. as a living person" or (2) "as he is now, in death—mouldering, perhaps, in a grave." Pitcher calls the first "a description of an *ante*-mortem person after his death" and the second "a description of a *post*-mortem person after his death."[30] All antemortem persons are subject not only to being described, but also to being wronged after their deaths, by betrayals, broken promises, defamatory lies, and the like, but no "postmortem person" can be wronged at all. (How could one break a promise to a corpse, or wrong the corpse by misdescribing it?) Postmortem persons cannot be *harmed* either, for as we have seen (Chap. 1, §1) no "mere thing" can be harmed directly in its own right, but only in a "derivative sense." The only troublesome category is that of acts after death that harm the antemortem person. As Pitcher puts it, the question is whether it is possible "for something to happen after a person's death that harms the living person he was before he died."[31] The main obstacle to an affirmative answer is its apparent implication that "posthumous harms" are *retroactive*, "that when an unfortunate post-mortem event happens, then *for the first time* the ante-mortem person is harmed,"[32] though he was unharmed when he died. Pitcher wisely rejects this apparent implication.

Retroactivity is as puzzling and paradoxical a concept, or worse, than the concepts it is meant to clarify, and we are well advised to follow Pitcher in disowning it. We especially should avoid that version of the retroactivity thesis which interprets posthumously harmful events as standing in the relation of *backward causation* to the earlier harms they are said to inflict on the antemortem person. It is probably not possible to conceive of posthumous harms in this way and fortunately not necessary to do so. When the malevolent A destroys B's life's work six months after B's death, he does not *cause* something to happen to the living B six months earlier. The posthumous harm thesis, according to Pitcher, does not entail this misleading picture any more than a spatially distant harmful event (like the death of one's beloved son in an airplane crash in Australia, halfway around the world) entails the scientifically unacceptable thesis of instantaneous causation at a distance (as Pitcher puts it, "the plane crash sending out infinitely rapid waves of horror, as it were, diminishing [the father's] metaphysical condition").[33] At the moment his son was killed, the father's other-regarding interest in his son's well-being was totally and irrevocably defeated, and he was *ipso facto* in a harmed condition though he did not yet know it. But the accident did not reach out, as it were, and instantaneously smite the father in defiance of the known laws of physics. The reason why that unacceptable consequence does not follow is that the relation between the crash and the vicarious harm is not a relation of physical causation at all. Similarly, posthumous harms do not entail backward causation because they too do not entail physical causation at all.

Once we reject the model of physical causation, moreover, there is no reason to suppose that either vicarious or posthumous harms involve any notion of retroactivity that is offensive to common sense. The occurrence of the harmful posthumous event, in Pitcher's language, *makes it true* that the antemortem person is harmed, and that occurrence is in a sense *responsible* for the antemortem harm. But Pitcher quickly points out that the relevant senses of "make true" and "responsible" neither imply retroactivity nor are they in any way mysterious. The antemortem person was harmed in being the subject of interests that were going to be defeated whether he knew it or not. It does not become "retroactively true" that as the subject of doomed interests he is in a harmed state; rather it was true all along. Our *pity* for the harmed person, of course, can be unparadoxically retroactive. If we had known at the time before his death that the cause to which he had devoted his life was doomed all along, we would have been sorry for him then, as we feel sorry for him *now*, "in retrospect." But whatever causation *is* involved in the narrative is not retroactive. An event occurs after Smith's death that causes something to happen at that time. So far, so good; no paradox. Now, in virtue of the thing that was caused to happen at that time it is true that Smith was in a harmed condition before he died. It does not suddenly "become true" that the antemortem Smith was harmed. Rather it becomes apparent to us for the first time that it was true all along—that from the time Smith invested enough in his cause to make it one of his interests, he was playing a losing game. Pitcher provides his own example of the "unmysterious" character of the senses of "make true" and "responsible for" that are employed here: "If the world should be blasted to smithereens during the next presidency after Ronald Reagan's, this would make it true (be responsible for the fact) that even now, during Reagan's term, he is the penultimate president of the United States."[34] Similarly, the financial collapse of the life-insurance company through which I have protected my loved dependents, occurring, let us imagine, five minutes after my death, several years in the future, makes it true that my present interest in my children's security is harmed, and therefore, that *I* am harmed too, though I know it not. When that time comes, my friends might feel sorry not only for my children but for me too, though I am dead. If the present account is correct, there is no more paradox in this than in my feeling sorry for a living friend whose wife I know to be unfaithful and unloving though he has invested much of his own well-being in the marriage, or for another friend whose beloved daughter, unknown to him, must soon die of a rare disease.[35]

6. Doomed interest and the dating of harm

How does the theory of posthumous harms lightly sketched above account for the harmfulness of death itself? The puzzles and doubts that remain, for the most part, have to do with the dating of harms, and we would be well advised not to seek more precision in answer to such questions than the subject matter permits. Consider first how we have already chosen to date "posthumous harms." Exactly when did the harmed state of the antemortem person, for which the posthumous event is "responsible," begin? I think the best answer is: "at the point, well before his death, when the person had invested so much in some postdated outcome that it became one of his interests." From that point on (we now know) he was playing a losing game, betting a substantial component of his own good on a doomed cause. Of course, the harm in question may not have been a *net harm*, since other equally important interests perhaps were flourishing, and many fulfillments were in store for him before death. But insofar as this one important interest was going to be defeated (that is, was actually doomed), he was in a harmed state.

Applying this model to the dating problems associated with the harm of death itself is a trickier matter. We should now say that it is the living person antemortem who is (usually) harmed directly by his own death. When then did his harmed condition begin? Presumably not at the moment of death itself, because that is when *he* ceased to be. Let us say then, still following the model of harmful posthumous events, that the harmed condition began at the moment he first acquired the interests that death defeats. Chief among these of course is the paramount welfare interest in remaining alive. But that interest is presupposed by most of his other interests, so he must have "acquired" it from the moment he acquired any others. It would follow that if it was going to happen that he would die at time t, he must have been in a harmed condition for almost all of his life before t—a conclusion that does not at first sight carry much conviction.

I think that the distinction between partial harm and net harm (or harm on balance) is the key to this and similar dating riddles. If John is going to be the victim of a fatal accident on his thirtieth birthday, then he is in at least a partially harmed condition from the time (many years earlier) when he acquires any interests at all. More specifically, he is in a partially harmed state from the time he acquires interests which themselves need more than thirty years to be fulfilled or satisfactorily advanced. But he has thirty years worth of other interests that will be advanced, promoted, and fulfilled, to his continual and repeated benefit. He is benefited in having the means to fulfill *them*, but harmed in lacking the means (as it turns out) of fulfilling those other interests that require more years of life. The degree of harmfulness of a person's premature death thus depends on *how* premature it is, given the interests that defined his own particular good. We now have at our disposal also an interpretation of the commonsense observation that "all life is tragic." Almost everyone will die with some interests that will be defeated by his death. And because of the inevitability of death, all of us are, while alive, in at least a partially harmed condition in that *those* interests are doomed (see note 13, p. 249), and thus generative of harm, from the time they are first acquired. But the person who will die at thirty is in a condition of greater harm on balance between ages of one and thirty than the person who will die at eighty is between ages of one and eighty. That is because death defeats fewer interests, and especially fewer important interests, of the latter than of the former. Hence, we have an interpretation of still another commonsense maxim, that "Young deaths are more tragic than old ones." Other things being equal, a long life is more beneficial (less harmful) than a short one.

It is time now to summarize our conclusions in this and the previous sections about the harmfulness of death and certain posthumous events. Death can be a harm to the person who dies in virtue of the interests he had antemortem that are totally and irrevocably defeated by his death. The subject of the harm in death is the living person antemortem, whose interests are squelched. The fact of a person's death "makes it true" that some of his antemortem interests were going to be defeated and to that extent the antemortem person was harmed too, though his impending death was still unknown to him. Only the person who no longer has an interest in any goal that can be set back by his death is unharmed by death, and indeed such a person may even be the antemortem beneficiary on balance of his own death. The interests of a person that can be said to have "survived" his death are those ulterior interests that can still be thwarted or promoted by subsequent events. These include his publicly oriented and other-regarding interests, and also his "self-centered" interests in being thought of in certain ways by others. Posthumous harm occurs when one of the deceased's surviving interests is thwarted after his death. The subject of a surviving interest and of the harm or benefit that can accrue to it after a person's death is the living person antemortem whose interest it was. Events after death do not retroactively produce effects at an earlier time, but their occurrence can lead us to revise our estimates of an earlier person's well-being, and correct the record before closing the book on his life.

7. A note on posthumous wrongs

Ernest Partridge denies not only that the dead can be harmed but also that they can be wronged, betrayed, or treated unfairly, on the grounds that they do not exist, and nonexistent beings are beyond all wronging. Nevertheless, he insists,[36] it is wrong to defame, cheat, or break promises to the dead; we may not simply do as we please with them. But the correct explanation of our duties toward persons now dead, he argues, does not imply that they have rights against us that we can violate. Rather there are general practices—making wills, insurance contracts, promises, truth-telling, among others—which most people, including *us now*, have an interest in preserving, and in the absence of rules imposing duties on us in respect to the dead, those useful practices would collapse, to our great collective loss. What would be the point of cherishing a person's memory, if he could be defamed with moral impunity by anyone? Those of us who care what memories of ourselves are left behind would feel insecure indeed while alive, if people generally did not accept the duty of truth-telling about the dead. There would be no point whatever in buying life insurance policies if the vendors could not be trusted to keep their promise made to the deceased when he was alive to pay his beneficiary at the appropriate time. Life insurance companies, in the absence of such trust, would be forced out of business, and all of us who *care* about our dependents would be left insecure and the dependents themselves highly vulnerable. If there were no acknowledged obligation to distribute a person's estate in accordance with the testimonial directions he left for us before his death, then there would be no point in making wills ourselves, and we would be deprived of something we value. We behave in certain appropriate ways toward the dead then because it is our duty to do so, and that duty is imposed by the rules that define certain practices that are highly useful to living people. The tendency of acts that are derelictions of these duties is to cause harm—not to people already dead (that, says Partridge, is impossible)—but rather to cause public harm, that is harm that consists in weakening the capacity of public practices to serve the interests of living people.

Rule-utilitarian arguments of this familiar kind[37] do indeed give the truth about our duties toward the dead, and nothing but the truth, but they do not give the whole truth. The very rules that impose duties on us as promisors, speakers, insurers, and testimonial instruction receivers confer, by the same token, *rights* on the living persons who are the corresponding promisees, parties talked about, insurance buyers, and testimonial instruction givers. These are the rights that can be violated after the right-holder's death by the wrongful behavior of those who violate their own duties. The duties in question are not without their corresponding claimants; a promise, for example, imposes a duty *to* the promisee, quite distinct from the more dilute and general duty toward all the rest of us who have an interest in protecting the general trust in promises. Its violation creates a quite distinct and powerful grievance in the right-holder (or his spokesman) which cannot wholly be derived from the more diffuse grievance the rest of us may have that "our practice" has been weakened or threatened. And indeed in some cases, where the violation is kept secret, there may be no such general consequences at all, yet the wrong to the party now deceased is clear and pointed. The practice may or may not be endangered; but only the right-holder has been betrayed.

It is absurd to think that once a promisee has died, the status of a broken promise made to him while he was still alive suddenly ceases to be that of a serious injustice to a victim, and becomes instead a mere diffuse public harm. Once we recall that the betrayed party is the person now dead as he was in his trusting state antemortem, all temptation to give this distorted account of the matter ceases. We no longer need embrace one absurdity to avoid an even greater one, namely that the wronged party is a corpse mouldering in the ground or a detached interest floating in the air.

8. Birth and prenatal harms

There is no doubt that there can be harms to persons caused after their births, between conception and birth, and even before conception. Whether giving birth to a baby itself can be a harm to it is more difficult, and whether the sexual congress that causes conception can be a harm to the being who is so conceived is the hardest of all. Let us begin with the easier cases and work toward the trickier ones.

Fetuses and contingent harms. Let us assume, if only for the sake of expository convenience, that human personhood begins at birth. Then we can pose our first question about prenatal harms as follows: can a being be harmed by events that occur between the moment of its biological conception and the moment of its birth (the start of its personal existence)? To many readers it will seem highly implausible to date the start of personhood at so late a point in biological development, but those readers may substitute for "birth" in our question their own idea of the starting point of personhood in the prenatal period. They might, for example, follow L. W. Summer's "moderate theory" and locate the commencement of personhood at the presumed onset of sentience some time in the second trimester of pregnancy,[38] or more "conservative" theories that locate it earlier still. Such readers should substitute for "birth" in the formulation of our question "moment at which personhood commences." Our question for these readers then is whether the developing embryo or fetus can be harmed by events that occur before *that point* in their biological development. If the reader holds the view that personhood begins at the very moment of conception, then the period about which we raise our question has been narrowed to the vanishing point for him, and he can move on to the next question with the assurance in his mind that the fetus, being a person at *every* stage of its existence, is clearly subject to harm at every stage. I will take no stand here at all on the complicated question of the point of onset of personhood for it would require an unrewarding digression to do so, but I must confess that the view that newly fertilized eggs are already people strikes me as extremely implausible.[39]

Harm can be caused to a person before his birth, or before the commencement of personhood in pregnancy, in virtue of the later interests of the child that can already be anticipated. A prepersonal fetus, however, presumably has no actual interests, from which it follows that no actual harm can be done to it while it is in that state. But on the assumption that the fetus will be born (or evolve before that into a person), we can ascribe to it certain "future interests," as the law calls them, and these can be damaged by actions done before the potential person even becomes an actual person.[40] A negligent motorist who runs over a pregnant woman may cause damage to the fetus that causes it later to be born deformed or chronically ill. Sometime after birth that infant will have an actual welfare interest in self-locomotion or health that may be harmed (doomed to defeat) right from the beginning. The child comes into existence in a harmed state caused by the earlier negligence of a motorist whose act initiated the causal sequence, at a point before actual personhood, that later resulted in the harm. The motorist's negligent driving made the actual person who came into existence months later worse off than she would otherwise have been. If the motorist had not been negligent, the child would have been born undamaged.

It is important to notice, however, that in all cases of harm to potential interests, the child does eventually emerge from the womb. Death to a fetus before it has any actual interests, on the other hand, is no harm to it. The aborted fetal preperson has no actual interests that can be harmed, and since it dies before any "potential interests" can become actual, no harm can be done to these either. A "potential interest" cannot be thought of as predating the person in a way parallel to that in which some interests can be thought of as surviving him, for a prenatal "potential interest" is at no time before birth (or personhood) actual, whereas a dead person's interest was real, and continues so for a period after death. One can grieve for an interest that might have been fulfilled, but was not; but that is quite another thing than grieving for a nonexistent interest that might have become real, but never did.

Harms produced before conception. Imagine if you can a criminal so wicked that he wishes to blow up a schoolhouse to kill or mutilate pupils. He conceals a powerful bomb in a closet of the kindergarten room and sets a timing device to go off in six years' time. Six years later the bomb explodes, killing or mutilating dozens of five-year-old children. The children obviously have been harmed by the explosion, and equally obviously (it seems to me) it was the evil action of the wicked criminal six years earlier, *before they were even conceived*, that harmed them. If the criminal denies that he caused harm to the children on the grounds that they didn't exist when he performed the act that allegedly caused the harm, we can reply that he set in motion the causal sequence that led to the harm and did it with the deliberate intention that the harm ensue, and that common sense requires no more for an act to be the cause of a harm. Examples of harm caused to children by actions that took place before they were conceived are by no means unknown to the law. A pharmaceutical manufacturer who carelessly prepares medicine six months before an infant's conception will be answerable to a child fifteen months later, if the medicine taken by the mother damaged the embryo, and the fetus nonetheless survived until birth. Or consider the case where a blood transfusion to a mother gives her syphilis. One year later she conceives, and her child is subsequently born syphilitic. In an actual West German case the infant was able to recover damages from the hospital for its negligence in administering the blood transfusion to his mother almost two years before *he* was even born.[41]

"Harmful life." Giving birth is not itself a voluntary act of commission under the control of a pregnant woman who at the last minute is free to change her mind. At most it can be thought of as the consequence of voluntary acts of omission at earlier stages insofar as the parents had the opportunity to abort and deliberately refrained from doing so. If the failure to abort can be thought of as a cause of the harm that ensues to the newborn (see Chap. 4, §7), in what can that harm consist?

The past twenty years have seen a worldwide upsurgence of legal suits by newborn infants for compensation for harms allegedly caused by their births, hence the name of this new cause of action—"Wrongful Life." These suits have been more often unsuccessful than successful, but their numbers continue to increase in a period when parental responsibility toward children is under increasing judicial scrutiny and abortion is now legally permissible. The harm allegedly caused by birth itself is the coming into existence under severe handicap, sometimes physical (congenital disease or genetic deformity and impairment), sometimes social (illegitimacy). There is relatively little difficulty in conceiving of these states as harmful. The puzzles for law and public policy have to do more with the questions of imputability and causation than with the nature of the resultant condition. Granted that the infants in question appear to be in a condition properly called "harmed" or (more clearly) "harmful," the question is whether the actions and omissions of others can be said to have done the harming. For the present, however, let us linger a bit longer with the nature of the harmed condition itself.

To be born with defective sight, hearing, speech, and mental capacities is indeed to be born with certain handicaps that will in time be harmful to the emergent interests of the child. In some times and places illegitimacy has been a severe legal and social handicap. Suppose that a child is born out of wedlock (thus with a social handicap) of a mother who had contracted German measles (rubella) in the first month of pregnancy. The child's biological parents, let us suppose, were fully informed of the likelihood of these handicaps, and had every opportunity for a safe and legal abortion, yet they permitted the pregnancy to go to term, with the result that the infant is born with severe physical and social impairments. The only alternative the parents might have procured for their child by opting for abortion was nonexistence. So the question of whether their decision made the child worse off than he would otherwise have been reduces to the question of whether the child would have been "better off had he never been born," a question which has seemed to many, including some leading judges, to make no sense.

If the "damage" caused by birth is relatively minor, say a clubfoot or a harelip, it might yet be a handicap, but hardly a harm on balance, and no rational person would prefer nonexistence to it. The question before us then seems to be whether an inherited condition can be so severe a handicap that, when compared with nonexistence as the exclusive alternative, it can be judged a *net* harm, or harm on balance. There can be no doubt in many cases that the condition of the infant at birth amounts to a *dooming* of his future interests to total defeat, so that when he comes into existence he already is in what we would normally call a state of harm (See Chap. 1, §5). But the question remains: how severe must the harm be to be a "worse-off condition" than nonexistence?

The doomed interests must be basic ones, including welfare interests in the possession of those unimpaired faculties that are essential to the existence and advancement of any ulterior interests. The advance dooming of these interests deprives the child of what can be called his birth-rights. (But note the new interpretation of the idea of a birth-right suggested by this point: if you cannot have that to which you have a birth-right then you are wronged if you are brought to birth.) Thus, if the conditions for the eventual fulfillment of the child's future interests are destroyed before he is born, the child can claim, after he has been born, that his *rights* (his present rights) have been violated. Moreover, if before the child has been born, we *know* that the conditions for the fulfillment of his most basic interests have already been destroyed, and we permit him nevertheless to be born, we become a party to the violation of his rights. It bears repeating that not all interests of the newborn child should or can qualify for prenatal legal protection, but only those very basic ones whose satisfaction is known to be indispensable to a decent life. The state cannot insure all or even many of its citizens against bad luck in the lottery of life. As a skeptical appelate court put it: "Being born under one set of circumstances rather than another or to one pair of parents rather than another is not a suable wrong that is cognizable in court."[42] On the other hand, to be dealt severe mental retardation, congenital syphillis, blindness, deafness, advanced heroin addiction, permanent paralysis or incontinence, guaranteed malnutrition, and economic deprivation so far below a reasonable minimum as to be inescapably degrading and sordid, is not merely to have "bad luck." It is to be dealt a card from a stacked deck in a transaction that is not a "game" so much as a swindle.

We can conclude tentatively that there are some inherited handicaps that are so severe that they doom a child's most basic future interests to defeat. A child born with such handicaps is in a condition that we would not hesitate to call "harmed" if it were not for the fact that it is not, like standard harms, a worsening of some prior condition, being itself the *initial* condition of the person who is born. Whether or not we can call him harmed and impute the harming to his parents or others for not aborting the fetus from which he grew (a matter to which we shall turn below), there is good reason to claim that he has been *wronged* to be brought into existence in such a state. (The state is a *harmful* one, even if it is not strictly speaking a "harmed" one.) It is, of course, possible to be wronged without being harmed (see Chap. 1, §1, for examples of quite different kinds), and it is possible to blame A for bringing B into existence in an initially harmful condition, but that is still another thing than A harming B, which as we have seen (Chap. 1, §5) requires worsening a person's prior condition, or at least making it worse than it would otherwise have been. If A had aborted B, B would not have been better off, for B would not have *been*, at all. Nonexistence would not have been a better condition for B to be in, for it would have been no condition of *B* at all. It would seem then that *A* did not harm *B* even though he wronged him by bringing him into existence in an already harmful—severely and irrevocably harmful—condition. The "problem of the subject" for harmful births and conceptions that has driven us to this conclusion is dramatically illustrated in the next section by the civil case of *Williams v. State of New York.*[43]

"Wrongful conception." Although there is another legal form of action with this name, a kind of wrongful conception is what is implied by "wrongful life" wherever abortion is illegal, as it was in 1965 when an infant girl sued the State of New York for damages resulting from the state's negligent operation of a mental hospital. The infant's mother, a mentally deficient patient in the state institution, was sexually assaulted by an attendant, as a result of which the plaintiff was born out of wedlock to an incompetent mother. The suit, which charged the state with negligence in failing to protect the mother from the rape, met with success in the trial court, but was overturned on appeal. It was part of the plaintiff's pleading at the trial court that she had been "deprived of property rights; deprived of a normal childhood and home life; deprived of proper parental care, support and rearing; caused to bear the stigma of illegitimacy and has otherwise been greatly injured all to her damage in the sum of $100,000." From the philosophical point of view this bill of injuries would have been more interesting still had it included inherited mental retardation, genetically transmitted from the mother, and also an inherited tendency to some chronically painful and incurable condition. In that (fictitious) case, the attorney for the plaintiff might have been in a stronger position to counter the argument that the new type of lawsuit would encourage suits by infants against their parents for any and all kinds of inherited disadvantages.[44]

The only reservations of the trial judge in allowing the case to be tried were that there was at the time no clear precedent for that kind of suit and that there was something approaching paradox in the idea that a tort can "be inflicted upon a being simultaneously with its conception."[45] He took neither of these misgivings seriously, but the second one proved to be the plaintiff's undoing at the appellate level. The Court of Appeals in its majority opinion held that the infant had no right to recover, "rejecting the idea that there could be an obligation of the State to a person not yet conceived." If my sketch of an argument above is correct, however, the court was too hasty. The obligation of the State, in my view, was not owed to some shadowy creature waiting in its metaphysical limbo to be born. Rather it was an obligation to its patient to protect her from assault, and as a consequence of its breach of duty to her, the rights of another human being, her daughter, which like most prenatal rights are contingent upon later birth, were violated. Or perhaps the duty of the state can be characterized more felicitously still as a duty of care owed to anybody likely to be affected by its conduct, on analogy with the duty of a producer of canned baby food toward *all* eventual consumers of its product including some children yet unborn or even unconceived.

In a separate concurring opinion, Judge Kenneth Keating found another ground for ruling against the infant:

> Damages are awarded in tort cases on the basis of a comparison between the position the plaintiff would have been in, had the defendant not committed the acts causing injury, and the position in which the plaintiff presently finds herself. The damages sought by the plaintiff in the case at bar involve a determination as to whether nonexistence or nonlife is preferable to life as an illegitimate with all the hardship attendant thereon. It is impossible to make that choice.[46]

Now, it is perhaps true as a matter of law that assessments of damages in tort cases (or at any rate, in all *other* kinds of tort cases) rest upon a hypothetical comparison of the plaintiff's condition after his injury with what his condition would have been had the defendant not affected it by his intentional or negligent wrongdoing; and of course that kind of comparison cannot be made when the alleged injury occurs at the very moment of conception, for it would have us consider the "condition" the plaintiff would have been in had he never been conceived, which is a contradiction in terms. In this kind of case, then, assessments of damages would have to be made in some other way; but even if assessments were made on *admittedly arbitrary* grounds, they might better serve justice than if no damages are awarded at all. In any case, the question of damages aside, the grounds for charging that a wrongdoer has violated another's right not to be born do not include reference to a strange never-never land from which phantom beings are dragged struggling and kicking into their mother's wombs and thence into existence as persons in the real world. Talk of a "right not to be born" is a compendious way of referring to the plausible moral requirement that no child be brought into the world unless certain very minimal conditions of well-being are assured, and certain basic "future interests" are protected in advance, at least in the sense that the possibility of his fulfilling those interests is kept open. When a child is brought into existence even though those requirements have not been observed, he has been wronged thereby; and that is not to say that any metaphysical interpretation, or any sense at all, can be given to the statement that he would have been better off had he never been born.

How then, in summary, should we characterize the state of those unfortunate infants whose impaired condition is the consequence of the very act that produced their conception, when that act was grossly negligent or otherwise wrongful? I have come, with varying degrees of confidence, to the following conclusions:

1. In wrongfully conceiving the child despite the known risk of genetic deformity (say), A and/or C (the biological parents) do not harm B (the resultant infant), even if B comes into existence in a state that makes a "life worth living" impossible. B has been born in a condition extremely *harmful* to it, but strictly speaking, that is not a *harmed* condition, not the effect of a prior act of harming. To be harmed is to be put in a worse condition than one would otherwise be in (to be made "worse off"), but if the negligent act had not occurred, B would not have existed at all. The creation of an initial condition is not the worsening of a prior condition; therefore it is not an act of harming, no matter how harmful it is.

2. Nevertheless, the wrongful act of A and/or C can wrong B even though, strictly speaking, it does not harm B, provided its consequences for B are so severe as to render his life not worth living. In that case B comes into existence with his most basic "birth-rights" already violated, and he has a genuine moral grievance against his parent(s). To the parent's defense that the only alternative to so harmful an existence was the nonexistence that would have followed their abstinence, the infant can make the re-joinder that nonexistence was the preferred alternative, even though it would not have been a "better off" condition of B. Any rational being, he might add, would prefer not to exist than to exist in his state.

The harm principle does not permit criminal liability for "wrongful conception" since the act causing the conception does not cause harm in the special narrow sense that requires both set-back interests and violated rights. (Although there can be criminal liability for the sexual act insofar as it harms and wrongs the sexual partner or third parties.) But since infant-rights are violated in the case where inherited impairment is severe, there is no reason why the wrongful progenitors (or other wrongful facilitators—doctors,[47] pharmaceutical companies, earlier partners transmitting venereal disease, etc.) should not be held civilly liable to pay damages to the child. So long as the infant's spokesman can make a convincing case that nonexistence would have been preferable to such radically handicapped existence, the child has a moral grievance against those responsible for his coming into existence, even though admittedly they did not harm him by making some prior condition of his worse. One can wish that one had never been born without claiming that one would have been *literally* "better off unborn."

We have not yet considered, however, the most puzzling test case for the application of the concept of harm, the case in which a grossly negligent act of intercourse leads to the birth of an only moderately handicapped child, whose impairment sets back an interest but does not impair his net personal interest to anywhere near the point where he could prefer nonexistence. In this case, as Derek Parfit was the first to point out,[48] the child has no grievance against his parent(s); he has neither been harmed nor wronged by them, even though they are, in a clear sense, responsible for his handicapped condition.

Parfit's famous example has us imagine a woman who is warned by her doctor to take a certain medicine and abstain from sexual intercourse for a month until she is cured of a condition which would cause any child she conceives to be born with a physical abnormality (say a withered arm). Nevertheless, either through willful perversity or negligence, she ignores the doctor's orders and consequently conceives a child who is born with the abnormality. At this point, Parfit asks us to make the reasonable assumption that the inherited disability of the child, while of course a bad thing, is not so severe as to render his life not worth living. He never ever regrets that he was born, but only that he was born with a withered arm. Now if the child, grown older, complains to his mother that her outrageous behavior harmed him, or wronged him, or was unjust to him, she can undermine his grievance by replying in the following way: "I had two options in respect to your birth. One was to do what I did, which led to your being born with a withered arm. The other was to obey the doctor, which would have led to your never having existed at all. You admit that you are glad to have been born. Therefore you ought to be pleased (if not exactly grateful) that I did what I did." I submit that the mother's reply, while not relieving her of blame, does show that her child was not harmed by her wrongful conduct, for to be harmed one must be put in a worse state than one would otherwise have been in, and in this case, that condition is not fulfilled. The child's arm is a handicap to him, and its withered condition an indubitably evil state of affairs. But the child has no personal grievance against anyone. The wrongdoer in the example must be blamed for wantonly introducing a certain evil into the world, not for inflicting harm on a person.

The facts of the Parfit case would not warrant a civil suit by the child, since his rights were not violated by the morally wrongful act that produced his handicapped existence but neither harmed nor wronged him. Nor will the harm principle warrant statutes under which the parent can be prosecuted. Such a statute could only be morally legitimate in virtue of its certification as such by the principle of legal moralism. If this result strikes

the liberal reader as counterintuitive, his best recourse is to modify the
harm principle so that it accepts as a reason for criminal prohibitions not
only the need to prevent people from wrongfully harming other persons,
but also the need to prevent people from wrongfully bringing other persons
into existence in an initially harmful (handicapped) condition. After careful
consideration, however, the need for such a revision is not apparent to me.

3

Harming as Wronging

1. The verbal forms: to harm and to wrong

Up to this point, we have examined the notion of harm as it is expressed in language by the nominative "a harm," because we have been interested primarily in a condition or state of a person to which the noun "harm" refers, namely the state that results when one's interests are affected adversely by events. The condition of set-back interest, however, is only one of the components of harm in the special narrow sense employed by the harm principle. In that sense, as we have seen (Chap. 1, § 1), a harm is a *wrongfully* set-back interest, and the adverb modifies an adjective that is itself a past participle of a verb. Harm, in this special sense, is produced by *acts* of setting back, thwarting, impairing, defeating, and so on, when those acts are wrongful. Hence our full paradigm of (wrongful) harm will include a person who acts on a victim, and the *act of harming* that produces the setback to the victim's interest. Henceforth then, when we speak of "harm" we shall refer to the effect on a person B when another person, A, harms B by setting back his interest. In the sense to be analyzed, A harms B when:

1. A acts (perhaps in a sense of "act" broad enough to include acts of omission, but this question can be left open until Chapter 4)
2. in a manner which is defective or faulty in respect to the risks it creates to B, that is, with the intention of producing the consequences for B that follow, or similarly adverse ones, or with negligence or recklessness in respect to those consequences; and

3. A's acting in that manner is morally indefensible, that is, neither excusable nor justifiable; and
4. A's action is the cause of a setback to B's interests, which is also
5. a violation of B's right.

In short, A *wrongs* B (defined by conditions 1, 2, 3, and 5) and harms his interests (condition 4).

2. Harming and injuring

Harming in the relevant sense is sometimes contrasted and sometimes identified with injuring, but this confusion is easily eliminable. We are apt to think of injury as specific damage done to the body—broken bones, lacerations, "internal injuries." So conceived, injury is one kind of harm. In ordinary speech, persons are not said to be injured by inflictions of harm to interests other than that in physical health and bodily integrity, except by analogy. Psychological shock, for example, is a kind of harm analogous to physical traumas, and can be called an "injury," though not without some linguistic strain. (A physician attending a dazed soldier might find it more natural to say that "he has not been injured, only shocked.") The more distant the analogy to physical wounds, the less appropriate is the term "injury."[1] A person may be harmed (in his economic interest) by a theft, but we would not normally say that he is injured by a loss of money. Even more distant from the physical paradigm, failure to be promoted at one's work, or to win an election, or to have a manuscript accepted by a publisher, while clearly harmful to a person's interests, is not an injury that a person suffers.

The authors of the American Law Institute's *Restatement of the Law of Torts*[2] understood the distinction between harm and injury well, but unaccountably reversed the terms in their definitions. In the following quotation, I have substituted the word "harm" wherever they used the word "injury," and the word "injury" wherever they used the word "harm." The result, I think, makes good sense:

> The word "harm" is used throughout the Restatement . . . to denote the fact that there has been an invasion of a legally protected interest. . . . It differs from the word "injury" in this: "injury" implies the existence of a tangible and material detriment. The most usual form of harm is tangible injury; but there may be a harm although no injury is done. Thus, any intrusion upon the land in possession of another is a harm and, if unprivileged, gives rise to a cause of action even though the intrusion is beneficial or so transitory that it constitutes no tangible interference with the beneficial enjoyment of the land.[3]

The authors of the *Restatement* make no claim to be reporting accurately on ordinary usage. They are not dictionary makers. Still, their stipulations of meanings for "injury" and "harm" would be more useful and less likely to generate misunderstandings if they had not got the terms exactly backwards. Their example of trespass to land is a very helpful one. A trespasser invades the landowner's interest in "the exclusive enjoyment and possession of his land." Technically that interest is violated when the trespasser takes one quiet and unobserved step on the other's land; in the somewhat special sense of harm we have been developing, such a violation sets back an interest, and to that extent therefore harms the interest's owner, even though it does not harm any other interest, and may even be beneficial on balance. In no ordinary sense is such a harm an "injury" to anyone.

There is a clue, however, to the peculiar inverted usage of the *Restatement* to be found in the history of the usage of the word "injury" in modern English. Unlike the word "harm," which for many centuries has meant damage, impairment, or loss, "injury" originally and for many centuries meant a wrong, or a violation of one's rights, or an injustice. ("Injury" derives from the Latin *injuria*, which meant "unjust" or "wrongful.") In the senses that these terms have borne through many centuries of political and legal theory, it is quite possible for a person to suffer a harm that is not an injury, for example, an unforeseeable accident, an unlucky business investment, such privileged contacts as punches in a legal boxing match, and legal punishment.[4] Injuries were thus understood to be one class of harms. In the traditional jurisprudential usage, now archaic, an injury is the violation of a right, whose normal consequence is criminal or civil liability, or at the very least, that the right-holder is "morally entitled to complain." The distinction between "injury" in its older sense and "mere harm" is even more important than the modern distinction, which cuts across it, between specific damage to the body or to health, and general setback to interest. For that reason the distinction should be preserved and put in modern dress: we can contrast policies, actions, and omissions that harm a person without *wronging* him, with those that not only harm him but wrong him too. We can now examine this distinction with care, and leave the word "injury" to do other work.

3. Moral indefensibility

One person, A, can be said to *wrong* another, B, when he treats him unjustly. More precisely the injustice occurs when A's act or omission has as its intention to produce an adverse effect on B's interests, or is negligent or reckless in respect to the risk of such an effect; and A's conduct is morally indefensible; and *B*'s set-back interest is one that he has a *right* to have respected. There is no point in adding further analysis here to the great volume of discussion in works of analytic jurisprudence and philosophical psychology of the concepts of action, intention, *mens rea*, negligence, and recklessness,[5] and we can postpone until the next section our discussion of the role of the victim's rights. Our immediate task is to explain the requirement that the harmer's action or omission be blameworthy, that is "morally indefensible."

I use the phrase "indefensible conduct" as the most generic term for actions and omissions that have no adequate justification or excuse. The distinction between justification and excuse comes from commentaries on the criminal law where it is used to mark two general categories of legal defense that can exonerate a defendant (or mitigate his culpability) even though the accused concedes that his conduct was of the sort proscribed by law and in fact violated the right, or invaded a protected interest, of some victim. To plead an excuse is in effect to admit that one's action "wasn't a good thing to have done, but to argue that it is not quite fair or correct to say *baldly*,"[6] or without qualification, that one did the thing at all, that it was one's *action*. This is to deny responsibility for an admittedly unfortunate episode. It is done by means of a variety of qualifying adverbs or adverbial phrases, and their corresponding legal defenses. I did it, but accidentally, or by mistake, inadvertently, under duress, in innocent ignorance, while a mere infant, while insane or temporarily out of my mind with rage, or innocently under the influence of drugs or hypnosis, or while sleep-walking or in an epileptic seizure, etc. To plead a justification, on the other hand, is to admit responsibility for an act, but to argue that it was "a good thing, or the right or sensible thing, or a permissible thing to do, either in general or at least in the special circumstances of the occasion."[7] "I did it all right," one might say, "but I had to do it to defend myself, or my family, or my property from threatened harm, or in order to rush a critically ill person to the hospital in an emergency, or as the least of all the evils I might have done or permitted to happen. In the unhappy circumstances that obtained, somebody's interests had to be harmed; I tried to choose as reasonably as possible."

We needn't linger over the nature of acceptable legal defenses and their informal analogues in everyday life. Our purpose here is to formulate principles for determining when legal interference with a citizen's liberty is morally legitimate. Whichever principles we adopt for deciding what may rightly be forbidden by law under threat of punishment, it will go without saying that only people who, without good reason, voluntarily break the law—only those whose harmful conduct was unexcused and unjustified—

should be convicted and punished. These are the only people of whom it can truly be said that the harm is "their fault," the only persons who are "to blame for it," the only persons without exculpating "defense." Excused or justified wrongdoing is not wrongdoing at all, and without wrongdoing there is no "harming," however severe the harm that might have resulted.

A more difficult question concerns another element that is always present when one person wrongs another, namely the violated right of the victim. We have qualified the harm principle so that the only harmful acts whose prevention can justify legal coercion are wrongful acts.[8] This restriction would still not make the prevention of wrongs a sufficient ground for justified coercion, since the state might yet refrain from using the criminal law to prevent wrongs that are relatively harmless or luckily beneficial, but it would remove from the realm of coercive protection altogether harms that are not wrongs. This reformulation of the harm principle gets us nowhere, however, until we have an account of which interests a person has a *right* not to have invaded by another. And the notion of a right is notoriously obscure and ambiguous.

4. Harming as right-violating

Speaking generally, a right is a valid claim which an individual can make in either or both of two directions. On the one hand, some of a person's rights are claims he can make against specific individuals for assistance, repayment of debts, compensation for losses, and so on, or against *all* other individuals—the "world at large"—to noninterference in his private affairs. On the other hand, an individual citizen also can make claims against the state, not only for specific services and promised repayments, and noninterference in his private affairs (claims analogous to those he has against other individuals), but also claims to the legal *enforcement* of the valid claims he has against other private citizens. All enforcement claims against the state, of course, are associated with the prior claims against individuals that the state is bound to enforce, but not all claims against individuals are backed up by enforcement claims against the state. My right not to be treated rudely, for example, cannot be legally enforced. Many or most of my rights, however, give rise to double claims, both against other individuals and against the state to force performance from others of what is my due, or to protect me, by threat of punishment, from unwarranted interference from other individuals. My legal right not to be punched in the nose has this double character: it is a claim against all other citizens to their noninterference and a claim against the state to its protection. So indeed do some of my claims against the state; for example, my claim against the Internal Revenue Service for the refund of my overpaid income taxes is also a valid claim against the courts for enforcement. All such double-barreled claims are *legal rights*. Reason-backed claims against other individuals, for example not to be treated rudely, or against the state, for example not to be victimized by the passage into law of invidious legislation, that are *not* at the same time legally valid claims against the state for enforcement, are often called *moral rights merely*. A moral right is a claim backed by valid reasons and addressed to the conscience of the claimee or to public opinion. When such claims are also enforcible by law, they are at once *both moral and legal rights*. When legally enforcible claims are arbitrary and supported by no reasons (for example, a slaveowner's right to beat and starve his slave), they are *legal rights merely*.

As we shall see in the sequel, there are some special contexts in which moral rights seem to be derivative from, rather than prior to, legal determinations of one sort or another. The state, for example, authoritatively endorses a particular convention of coordination like the rule for driving on the right, and in virtue of that official decision, each motorist has a moral as well as a legal right that other motorists not drive on the left. Sometimes legislatures must balance conflicting interests of private individuals and then rank them in importance. Only then can *A*'s setting back of *B*'s "more important interest" in protecting *A*'s own "less important interest" be meaningfully judged to be a wronging of *B*, a violation of *B*'s moral right. (See Chap. 5, § 6.) Similarly, it is only against the background of a legally established system of resource allocations, defining "fair shares" for prospective industrial emitters, that judgments can be made that *A* has violated *B*'s moral right to unpolluted air. (See Chap. 6, § 4.) In more typical contexts for criminal prohibitions, however, we can know that a person has been wronged quite independently of any status that has been conferred upon him by the law. Even in the exceptional cases mentioned above, the moral-right-creating determinations of the law are not straightforward criminal prohibitions. The determinations in question do not come from the criminal law; rather they provide background for subsequent criminal legislation. It would be especially misleading to interpret these official determinations as declarations of *legal rights;* rather they are legal judgments that make possible findings of moral and legal rights alike.

Having qualified the harm principle so that legal coercion is justified by it only when necessary to prevent that subclass of harms that are wrongs, we must take care not to identify wrongs, *simpliciter*, with violated *legal* rights, for then we would fall into the vicious circle spelled out in the following propositions:

1. We cannot know which harms may properly be prevented by the criminal law until we know which harms when inflicted indefensibly are wrongs.
2. We cannot know which harms are wrongs until we know which harms people have a *legal right* not to have inflicted upon them, or what amounts to the same thing, which of their interests people have a *legal right* not to have invaded. [This is the mistaken premise.]
3. But since a legal right is a valid claim both against one's fellow citizens *and* against the state for its protection, we cannot know which harms people have a legal right not to have inflicted on them until we know which interests they can validly claim protection for from the state (*via* the criminal law).

But that brings us right back to step (1) and closes the circle, for our original inquiry was to learn which interests can validly be protected by the criminal law, and what we have learned is that we cannot know which harms can properly be prevented by legal coercion until we know which harms can properly be prevented by legal coercion. We cannot start our task until we have completed it!

If we are to substitute "wrong" for "harm," then, in our formulation of the harm principle, we shall have to think of a wrong as a violation of a *moral right merely*, that is a claim directed against one's fellow citizens prior to and independent of any claim of enforcement against the state. In this way our analysis can avoid a vicious circle, but it is not free of other difficulties. First of all, it is now committed to a theory of "moral rights" that are independent of and antecedent to law, a conception strongly reminiscent of the doctrine of "natural rights" which many philosophers have found incoherent.[9] And even if that is no difficulty (and many *other* philosophers are untroubled by it), it places on us the burden, if we are to avoid vacuity, of distinguishing those of our interests that ground morally valid claims to respect and noninterference from our fellows, from those of our interests that do not. That task, in turn, would seem to presuppose a rather complete moral system.

Nothing as elaborate as all that, however, is required. Certain kinds of morally disreputable interests can be ruled out, straightaway, as possible grounds for valid moral claims. If there are any interests in causing pain and suffering for their own sakes, for example, such interests cannot be the grounds of claims against others. Cruel and sadistic interests, morbid interests, wicked and sick interests, if there are such things, can be peremptorily ruled out of court, and put aside. No one has a moral right to the protection of such "interests," if, indeed, such things exist at all. Then it is a quite simple move to declare that *any interest at all* (apart from the sick and wicked ones) is the basis of a valid claim against others for their respect and noninterference. Then it will follow that *any* indefensible invasion of another's interest (excepting of course the sick and wicked ones) is a wrong committed against him as well as a harm.

As we have seen (Chap. 1, § 7), most ulterior interests are only indirectly invadable. The usual way of harming one of another person's ulterior interests is by invading one of the welfare interests whose maintenance at a minimal level is a necessary condition for the advancement of any other interests at all. Welfare interests most certainly are grounds for moral claims against others if any interests are. If we can speak of moral rights at all, then, each of us has a moral right to life, minimal health, economic sufficiency, political liberty, and so on. But if a given ulterior interest is such that it can be invaded directly, and another person does indeed do so indefensibly, then that would be a wrong too. At least one class of ulterior interests *are* directly vulnerable: those that consist of the extension of welfare interests to transminimal levels. The rich man is wronged by indefensible acts of theft just as the poor man is, though he will not be harmed as much.

The welfare interests then are the grounds for valid claims against others (moral rights) *par excellence.* They are reasonable interests reasonably ascribed, if not to every person in the world without exception, at least to the standard person that must always be before the legislator's eye. There may be mystic ascetics who have no interest whatever in bodily health as we normally understand it; there may be happy vagabonds and vagrants, or mendicant gurus, who have no interest in financial sufficiency as ordinarily understood; there may be indoctrinated submissives with no stake in political liberty. And there are even persons in hospitals, human warehouses, and elsewhere who have no remaining interest in continued life. But the presumption in respect to possession of any given welfare interest in any given case is overwhelmingly strong, and the law, which must be phrased in general and not overly complicated terms, must therefore protect even hoboes from theft and depressives from murder. In making basic criminal prohibitions universal, moreover, the law increases the protection given to the overwhelming majority who have the protected welfare interests without harming the occasional eccentrics who do not, for it would make us all less secure if our fellows were given legal discretion to decide whether a given welfare interest is present in a given case before acting in a manner that would invade that interest if it were present. The criminal law would encourage the commission of wrongs if it prohibited assault and battery except against mystics who have no stake in health, larceny except against vagabonds with no stake in wealth, and murder except of depressives who have nothing more to gain from life. But the most important consideration of all in favor of presuming welfare interests even where they are absent is that the welfare interest in *freedom of choice*, while no more universal than any of the others, is normally present even when another welfare interest is dead. To murder the depressive, for example, is to deprive him of the right to decide, insofar as it is within his power, when and how he shall die, and similarly in the other examples the bully and the thief deprive their eccentric victims of the right to choose for themselves, within the limits of the circumstances, how they shall shape and pursue their own interests, and at every new moment, whether to ratify or reject their own life policies.

A problem about the relation between right-invasion and moral indefensibility is posed by situations of conflicting interests (to be discussed in more detail in Chaps. 5, §6, and 6, §1). If Abel invades *any* nonmorbid, nonwicked interest of Baker's *indefensibly*, he has thereby wronged Baker. But suppose the circumstances are such that if Abel does not harm Baker's interest in X, his own interest in Y will itself be harmed. If interests of type Y are more important than interests of type X, then Abel may understandably feel morally justified in reluctantly invading Baker's interest in X, and if he is in fact justified, then he has not acted indefensibly, and Baker has been harmed but not wronged by him. The result is the same if Abel violates Baker's interest in Y in order to protect Charley's more important interest in Z. It is obvious then that if legislators are to be guided by our harm principle reinterpreted so that only harms that are wrongs count, they must find some way of ranking distinct sorts of interest in an order of importance. (We will return to this problem in Chapter 5.)

Abel and Baker may be pursuing interests of quite the same type and importance, however, and still find themselves in circumstances such that the fulfillment of each person's interest is possible only at the cost of the thwarting of the other's. They may both be so much in love with Camelia that marriage to her is a paramount focal aim in each of their interest networks; yet only one can marry her. Similarly, they may both apply for a job that only one can fill, and the rejected applicant may sink into poverty and despair. The winner in these unavoidable competitions is benefited at the expense of the loser who is harmed; yet he cannot be said to have *wronged* the other, unless he cheated, or achieved his goal by means of an indefensible attack on a welfare interest of his rival. Here again, the modified harm principle must be supplemented by rules for distinguishing legitimate from pernicious forms of competition, and justified from unjustified tactics within legitimate contests. (See Chap. 6, §1.) The subject is too large to be treated summarily, but one rule, at least, is immediately evident. No "contestant" can attempt to defeat his rival by directly wounding him in one of his welfare interests. There may be a point to the maxim that "all's fair in love and war," but it cannot be a "fair way" of courting a lady to kick one's rival in the groin and thereby put him out of the running. In a fair contest a loser may be unavoidably harmed, but when he is harmed by means of an attack on his welfare interests, he is not only harmed but doubly wronged: the indefensible infliction of harm on his welfare interest wronged him, and the defeat of his more ultimate interest (say in fair Camelia's hand) by foul means also wronged, as well as harmed, him.

5. Harm and consent: the Volenti maxim

There is no doubt that a person can be harmed both by fully voluntary, self-regarding actions of his own and by conduct of others to which he fully consents. A person may even desire to be harmed, and consent to another's conduct precisely because he believes that it will be harmful to himself. (Imagine, for example, a guilt-stricken person in the grip of self-hatred seeking expiation through self-punishment.) One may doubt, of course, whether any normal or sane person could have such a desire, and hold that the wish to be harmed, being symptomatic of illness, invalidates consent by rendering it less than fully voluntary. There are many other more convincing examples, however, of persons voluntarily consenting to behavior (including their own) which they know to carry a very high *risk* (in some cases a risk approaching certainty) of harm to themselves. Women who consent to advances sometimes become pregnant; cigarette smokers often incur lung cancer; slot-machine players and other overhandicapped gamblers usually go broke.

The more interesting question is whether a person can ever be *wronged* by conduct to which he has fully consented. There is a principle of law which emphatically answers this question in the negative: *Volenti non fit injuria* ("To one who has consented no wrong is done"). This ancient maxim is found in the Roman Law and has a central place in all modern legal systems.[10] Perhaps the earliest arguments for it are found in Aristotle's *Nicomachean Ethics*.[11] One person wrongs another, according to Aristotle, when he inflicts harm on him voluntarily, and a harmful infliction is voluntary when it is not the result of compulsion, and is performed in full awareness of all the relevant circumstances including the fact that the action is contrary to the wish of the person acted upon. Therefore it is impossible for a person to consent to being treated unjustly (wronged) by another, for this would be to consent to being-treated-contrary-to-one's-wishes, which is absurd.[12]

The maxim *Volenti no fit injuria* finds ample support in common sense. We don't normally take seriously the person who gives us permission to do something and later complains, in wounded or indignant tones, that we did it. "He cannot waive his right and then complain of its infringement."[13] To give one's consent to an action is to be, in some sense, a party to it, so that any subsequent complaint must at least in part be directed at oneself. It may seem that I maintain a moral right, in some circumstances, to complain of another's harmful conduct even when I had in fact consented to it. The other person may have had more experience or knowledge than I, and in soliciting my consent in the first place, he may have taken advantage of me. Normally, however, this is a risk that free individuals are expected to shoulder for themselves. If I am foolish enough, for example, to make a wager on an outcome with a person who is far better informed than I, my complaints, when I lose, are more properly directly to myself for my folly than to him for his opportunism. (But see Chap. 31 on exploitation.)

There are other circumstances, however, in which even a responsible person may feel strongly inclined to complain of another's harmful but consented-to conduct. I may have been "taken advantage of" by a person who had information not remotely accessible to me—knowledge I could be presumed by him not to have, and which I could not reasonably be expected to have. Examples of this kind, however, are not usually allowed to count against the *Volenti* maxim. Instead they are taken to throw into doubt the genuineness or validity of the "consent." The more strongly we hold to the *Volenti* principle, the higher must be the standards we employ for determining the voluntariness of consent. *Volenti* is most plausible when it denies title to complain only to him whose consent was *fully voluntary*, and a person's consent is fully voluntary only when he is a competent and unimpaired adult who has not been threatened, misled, or lied to about relevant facts, nor manipulated by subtle forms of conditioning. It is worth giving emphasis here to two points: that both force and fraud can invalidate consent, and that "force" can be very subtle indeed.

Mill left no doubt about how his harm principle was to be interpreted on this question. (See Chap. 19, §5.) Only the prevention of harm can justify coercion, he held, and what a person consents to is not "harm" in the requisite sense. It follows from these premises that no one can rightly intervene to prevent a responsible adult from voluntarily doing something that will harm only himself (for such a harm is not a "wrong"), and also that one person cannot properly be prevented from doing something that will harm another when the latter has voluntarily assumed the risk of harm himself through his free and informed consent. Of course, when the consented-to behavior seems so patently harmful that no sane person could ever consent to it, we may properly assume that the consenter is *not* sane and that his consent was therefore not valid. This would permit us to interfere with his liberty in a way permitted by the harm principle as supplemented by the *Volenti* maxim. But if our *sole* evidence of insanity or other invalidating nonresponsibility is the patently harmful character of the agreed-to conduct itself, and the consenter fails to satisfy any of the other independent criteria of nonresponsibility and nonvoluntariness, then we cannot invalidate the consent without reasoning in a circle. If we say, in these circumstances, that "he must have been mad to agree to such a thing," we will be inferring the madness of the person from the character of the agreement in order to infer the madness of the agreement from the "established" mad condition of the person. This would be to treat a person as nonresponsible when there is no good reason to do so. And if we defend our coercive interference nevertheless, on the grounds that sometimes even responsible adults must be protected from the consequences of their own folly (whether they like it or not), then we have abandoned the harm principle as I have interpreted it here, that is, as applying only to those harms that are also wrongs. In arguing in this way for our intervention, we imply that the relation between us and the person that we are constraining is in some important way analogous to that between a parent (who "knows best") and a child. Hence, this mode of argument, which Mill detested, has come to be known by the not altogether neutral name "paternalism." I shall consider in detail the cases for and against legal paternalism in Volume 3.

6. The concept of a victim

The English word "victim" derives from the Latin *victima*, "a person or animal killed as a sacrifice to a god in a religious rite."[14] The sense the word bears in the phrase "sacrificial victim," then, is the original from which the others have evolved. It is not clear whether it was thought in ancient times that persons offered as sacrifices to the gods were necessarily wronged or even harmed by their selection for that role. Indeed, among the Aztecs only the bravest warriors and most beautiful maidens were considered suitable for the propitiation of the deities, so that to be selected as a sacrificial victim must have been thought a high honor. (But for the honor of the thing, some of them must have thought, it would be better to go on living.)

According to the *Oxford English Dictionary*, "The Rhemish translators of the Bible were the first to make free use of the word as English, and its general currency dates only from the latter part of the seventeenth century." Before long the word had evolved two other senses, or groups of senses. It can refer to a person who suffers any kind of serious misfortune (and not just death or physical injury), whether through cruel or oppressive treatment by other persons, or from any kind of hard circumstances. Thus we refer to victims of the Nazis and Communists, but also to victims of earthquakes, wars, depressions, and plagues, even to victims of changing tastes, styles, and movements of thought. And we are no longer speaking colorfully or ironically when we speak of persons who are "victims" of their own folly, ignorance, or zeal. In this very general usage, a victim is one who suffers any kind of harm from any kind of cause, and there is suggestion neither of propitiatory offering (and the "honor" derived therefrom) nor of indefensible agency (and the "wrong" produced thereby).

Most dictionaries, however, list as an independent third sense, "a person who suffers harm by being swindled; a dupe." In this sense, the harm suffered by a "victim" is always a wrong done to him, and a wrong of a special kind, namely, a fraud. To be "victimized" (in the related phrase) is to be deceived, cheated, misused, in short, to be wronged. It is in this sense that one cannot be a victim of one's own mischief (that is, one cannot "victimize" oneself) and one cannot be victimized by actions of another to which one has fully consented.

Now that the senses of the word "victim" have been clearly laid out on display, there is no point in further discussion of the fruitless quibbles over whether certain crimes are "victimless" or not, except insofar as those controversies rest on genuine disagreements over the empirical facts. In the first sense, all crimes *except* the killing of living things (animals or people) as sacrificial offerings to a deity are "victimless." In the second sense, only those disapproved actions which harm no one at all are victimless. Thus if private, unobserved acts of masturbation were made criminal, they would be victimless crimes (unless, what is unlikely, it turns out to be a medical fact that masturbation causes harm directly to the perpetrator). In this second sense of "victim," a person can be his own victim; so a criminal act which harms only the perpetrator is *not* a victimless crime. Similarly, in this second sense, a person can be the victim of (that is, can suffer harm from) an action of another to which he has fully consented. Thus, if two persons voluntarily and illegally make a wager and one loses, the crime of which they are both guilty is *not*, in this sense, victimless. In the third sense, however, a crime which only harms its own perpetrator, and a crime which only harms a person who has fully consented to the risk, are quite genuinely victimless crimes, for although someone was harmed in each case, no one was duped. In the third sense of "victim," a person cannot be a victim unless he has been *wronged*. Unless otherwise indicated, this sense of "victim," expanded to refer to *any* kind of unconsented-to harm to interest and not *only* "duping," is the one that will be used throughout this work.[15]

7. The "causal component" in harming

In explaining what harm in the special narrow sense is, we have had to list qualifying characteristics of a harmer (action, fault, indefensibility) and of a victim (set-back interest), but to complete our analysis we need some account of the connection between them. The requisite linkage can be called "causal" provided we take care to mean no more by the language of cause and effect than what is meant in ordinary practical discourse by such phrases as: "*B*'s harm occurred because of *A*'s action," "*B*'s harm was due to *A*'s action," "As a consequence of *A*'s action *B* was harmed," "As a result of what *A* did, *B* was harmed," etc. It can be very difficult to explain what these roughly equivalent terms mean, and there are some notorious "puzzling cases" for the application of such language. For the most part, however, legislators have used these everyday causal idioms in the formulation of criminal statutes and have left it to the courts, and the legal commentators who influence the courts, to apply them to the puzzling cases. It would be ill-advised, therefore, if in this work, directed at the dilemmas of legislators rather than courts, still another attempt were made to analyze the causal idioms that are used in the law. There is a distinction, after all, between the question "What conduct should the law forbid?" (our question) and "How can we tell whether an accused person is liable for breaking the law?" The latter question, but not the former, can call for an investigation of the causal relations between an action and subsequent harm. Even in court hearings, inquiries into causal relations are less likely to be required in criminal cases than in civil ones, since an accused can often be held criminally liable for faulty conduct as such, intended or attempted harm, extreme recklessness, and the like, even in the absence of actual harm, whereas in the law of torts liability means payment of compensation, and where no actual harm has been caused, there is nothing to compensate.

We shall not be drawn into a deep discussion of the riddles of legal causation, therefore, except where necessary to settle such general questions (of interest even to legislators) as whether acts of omission can *ever* be the causes of harm (Chap. 4, §§7, 8), and whether acts that merely serve as models to suggestible second parties can *ever* be said to be the causes of the harm produced by the second parties to their victims (Chap. 6, §5). Apart from these general questions, our account of causal linkage can be restricted to a survey of the main riddles of legal causation and the main ways that have been proposed for dealing with them.

"When it is clear that there has been both harm and wrongdoing, the law must frequently decide whether or not the harm is attributable to the wrongdoing."[16] Traditional formulas have provided two tests. The wrongdoing must have been a genuine causal factor (condition, element) in the production of the harm, and it must be an especially substantial (important, direct, crucial) causal contributor. In the traditional language of the courts, the act must be both a "cause in fact" and "the proximate cause" of the harm. I have expressed a preference for speaking of "a causal factor" in the production of the harm (no matter how minor a contributor), on the one hand, and that particular causal factor that can be selected as *the* cause of the resultant harm, on the other.[17] Often legal writers have identified a causal factor with *any* earlier causally necessary condition of the harm, calling it a *conditio sine qua non* of the harm or a "but for cause," that is a condition *but for* which the harm would not have occurred. This facile identification leads to difficulties immediately, since it seems to permit judges and assigners of responsibility to search among the entire infinitude of past events "but for" which the harm would not have occurred, allowing even the actions of the defendant's grandparents to have relevance, at least, to the final selection of *the* cause of the harm.

There are even worse difficulties for the identification of causally relevant factors with necessary conditions. Where there are simultaneous or concurrent causes, for example, neither is a necessary condition of the resulting harm because the other alone would have been sufficient in the circumstances, yet clearly both are "causal factors." Thus, "Two men may simultaneously fire and lodge a bullet in their victim's brain, or may simultaneously approach escaping gas with a lighted candle . . . . the identification of cause with a necessary condition would entail that neither action could be ranked even as *a* cause" (much less *the* cause of the resultant harm).[18] There is a similar problem with subsequent additional causes as when "a beach house, momentarily about to topple into the sea, is destroyed by a fire [set by an arsonist]" or where "*A* pushes *B* off a building to a certain death below [and] as *B* is falling *C* shoots and kills him."[19] The arsonist's act was not necessary to the destruction of the house, let us suppose, because it would have collapsed anyway five minutes later, and the killer's shot was not necessary for *B*'s death because he would have died anyway, let us suppose five seconds later. Yet clearly both were at least causally relevant factors in the production of the harm. A more difficult problem still for the necessary-condition theory is that of additional neutralizing causes, a problem amusingly illustrated by a hypothetical example from J. A. McLaughlin[20] which I paraphrase as follows:

> *C* is preparing for a trip across the Sahara Desert. *A*, who hates him, on the night before his departure puts poison in his water containers with the intention of causing his death. Quite independently, *B*, who also hates *C*, then quietly pours out all the water, with the intention of causing *C* to die of thirst. *C* undertakes the trip and dies of thirst. Whose act caused the harm?

Insofar as it comes to any judgment at all, common sense would presumably be prepared to cite either or both actions as the cause of death, but the necessary-condition theory would entail that neither was even a causally relevant factor since the other would have been sufficient in any case, and *a fortiori* both *A* and *B* can deny that their acts were *the cause* of the harm to poor old *C* (though each could be convicted of making the attempt to kill him).

No doubt the "but for cause" theory of causal relevance can be saved by sufficient *ad hoc* emendation. In the simultaneous-causation case, we could allow an event to be a causal factor in the production of a harm "either if it is a necessary condition or would have been necessary if no other conditions sufficient to produce the effect had been present."[21] And in the additional-cause cases we can specify that one of the events in question was indeed necessary for the harm when the harm is described and dated *exactly* (e.g. dying of thirst at time *t* instead of dying of poison at time *t-n*). But Hart and Honoré find it less adventitious to replace the theory altogether with an account of causal relevancy in terms of membership in a set of coexisting jointly sufficient conditions. I find their suggestion quite persuasive, but there is no point in pursuing the matter here.

The more thoroughly debated issue among jurisprudential writers is how we are to distinguish *the* cause of a harm from the welter of events that are acknowledged causal factors. Put from the opposite vantage point, the question is how we are to identify the consequences[22] of a given act of wrongdoing. A given act can have effects radiating out to great distances in space and echoing through the corridors of time for centuries. There may be an infinite number of ways in which the world will be different because this act was done and not another. Yet clearly not all of these future effects can be charged to the act in question as its consequences, no more than the act itself is the consequence of every prior event but for which it would not have been done. The making of singular causal judgments in the interest of such practical purposes as imputations of responsibility obviously requires that infinite causal chains, both past and future, be severed abruptly. The causal component in acts of harming is a finite one: *In jure non remota causa sed proxima spectatur* ("In law, not the remote but the near (proximate) cause is sought for.")

The problem of "proximate cause" for the law is to select *the* cause of a given harm from among the countless candidates among earlier events that are genuine causal factors (many but not necessarily all of which were themselves "but for causes"), or, from the other direction, to select from among the infinitude of effects of a given wrongful act those only that can be attributed to it as its consequences. The problem very commonly presents itself to a court in this form: "whether a certain harm is a consequence of a certain wrongful act, *given the presence of a third factor.*"[23] The third factor is often an unsuspected underlying condition or an intervening event, or a subsequent wrongful action by a third party. The following puzzles do not frequently confront courts, but are typical of the hypothetical examples that fill legal treatises:

1. "*A* strikes *B* with intent to kill, but only dislocates *B*'s jaw. The ambulance carrying *B* to the hospital is struck by lightning and *B* is killed. Has *A* caused *B*'s death? [Put alternatively: Is *B*'s death a consequence of *A*'s wrongdoing?]

2. "*A* strikes *B* without intent to kill. Owing however to *B*'s hemophilia, which is unknown to his assailant, *B* bleeds to death from the wound. Has *A* caused *B*'s death? [Alternatively: Is *B*'s death a consequence of *A*'s wrongdoing?]

3. "*A* shoots *B* with intent to kill. *B* is not mortally wounded but anesthesia is negligently administered to him in the hospital and he dies. Has *A* caused his death? [Alternatively: Is *B*'s death a consequence of *A*'s wrongdoing?]"[24]

4. A train conductor negligently lets a passenger off a train a half-mile beyond the station. She is then raped and killed by hoboes in the woods near the track (in a notorious high-crime area). Did the railroad's negligence cause her death? Alternatively, is her death a consequence of the conductor's negligent act?[25]

Quite obviously, *A*'s action in each of the first three examples, and the conductor's action in the fourth, are genuine causal factors in the production of the harm to *B*. Indeed each is a necessary condition or "but for cause" of that harm. Yet in each case a "third factor" intervened in a manner that was itself a critically necessary condition for the precise harm that resulted. The problem for the courts is to decide under what conditions *A*'s causal contribution is substantial enough for the harm to be attributed to it as its consequence, despite the contribution of the underlying condition or the intervening party (also genuine causal factors and "but for conditions"), and under what conditions the intervening factor becomes "the cause," relieving *A* of causal responsibility for the outcome. The history of legal approaches to these questions goes through several stages. In the beginning there is reliance on obscure metaphysical talk about the relative "potency" of different causal contributions, with only the more powerful among them qualifying as *the* cause or the proximate cause. Then there is a skeptical reaction to the metaphysics, and writers speak of the choice among the qualified causal factors (usually thought of as "but for causes") as a "policy decision disguised as a factual discovery."[26] *The* cause, for legal purposes, is that one event among the infinitude of conditions but for which the harm would not have occurred, upon which it is desirable to exert public pressure. Put more bluntly, it is the causally contributory action of the person it would be best to punish or force to pay compensation.

Then another reaction sets in, and writers abandon the skeptical theory for "commonsense principles" implied by the everyday concept of causation itself. Hart and Honoré do not deny that policy considerations play a role, but they do so within narrow limits imposed by the concept of causation as it is ordinarily understood. Two principles stand out particularly in their analysis: (a) singular causal judgments attribute the status of *the* cause to deviations from the normal course of events, and (b) when an intervening cause is a free and deliberate (fully voluntary) human action then it cancels the causal connection that would otherwise hold between an earlier causal factor and the harm. A more elegant theory explains the selection of causes by means of the single concept of *risk:* X is the consequence of A's wrongful (negligent or intentional) act if and only if it is a result that falls within the risk (or corresponds to the intention) by virtue of which A's act is judged to be blameworthy. Thus, in example (2), A wrongfully created a risk of routine physical injury to B, and causing that injury also was his intention. Perhaps also he negligently created the risk of more serious physical injury than he actually intended, for example a broken jaw or a concussion. But bleeding to death was not a result within that risk. Therefore A's wrongdoing was not its cause. Obviously the application of this principle to the other hypothetical examples will require more distinction-making, and some guide to the way one determines, after the fact, exactly what risk was created by a given careless or malicious act, that is what dangers might have been "foreseen." It is interesting to note in passing that Hart and Honoré's voluntary intervention principle would make the death of the passenger in example (4) the exclusive consequence of the wrongdoing of the hoboes, whereas the risk or foreseeability theory would allow its attribution (also?) to the negligence of the railroad.

One cannot help but suspect that all the leading theories of proximate cause "pick out elements," as Herbert Morris suggests, "all of which are relevant in determining cause in some cases but none of which is common to all cases."[27] Be that as it may, we shall make no effort here to evaluate these theories of legal causation. My intention has been only to sketch the problems with which they are meant to deal, and the general way they proceed. For our purposes one of the main lessons to be learned from this survey is how grossly misleading the "billiard ball" conception of cause and effect is when used as a model for those attributions of given harms to given wrongful acts that are made in law courts and in ordinary practical judgments. When the white ball strikes the stationary red ball on the billiard table, it transmits its motion to it through the impact of the collision and "forces" it to move in a given direction at a given velocity. "The cause" of the red ball's motion is an *event* (the collision) that occurred just before, or simultaneously with, the effect. We know that the red ball's motion was *propter hoc* (because of the first event) and not merely *post hoc* (after the first event) because of various experiments that confirm generalizations about the invariant connection between events of these types. Inductive methods have a role in attributive inquiries too, but they establish only that one condition was a genuine causal factor in the production of some further condition, not that it is, for our practical purposes, *the* crucial factor. Selection of one causal factor from out of many to be denominated *the* cause of a harm, or one causal result of an act to be denominated *the* consequence of that act, involves us in such matters as (depending on one's theory) the justice or efficiency of public policies, the nature of the wrongdoer's fault, foreseeability, the scope of risks, normal patterns and abnormal deviations, the voluntariness of human interventions, and more. None of these additional concerns need trouble the scientist when he attempts a "causal explanation" of some normal course of events, like the variations of the tides, in terms of various natural laws. The scientist's work, therefore, is a poor model for understanding the specific attributive judgments connecting acts and consequences.

For these reasons we must reject such dogmas as that only events can be causes, that causes must occur just prior to their effects or simultaneously with them, that they are ultimately bodies in motion transmitting their force to effects, and so on. Once we have established by observation and the usual inductive methods that a given act was a causally relevant factor in the production of some harm, then our task is to determine whether it satisfies further conditions of "importance" imposed either by our practical purposes or by "commonsense causal principles." As William Dray puts it, the inductive inquiry establishes the "importance of a condition to the event," whereas its citation as *the* cause indicates its "importance to the inquirer."[28] And the inquirer's purposes may well lead him to single out as *the* cause an event, a motion, an underlying condition, an omission, or an action, either just prior to the consequence, or substantially earlier. As Hart and Honoré put it,

> . . . for common sense, as for the law, causes are not restricted to what may ordinarily be called events. A cause may be an action, an event, a state, a failure to act, the nonoccurrence of a condition. . . . [E.g.:] "The cause of the fire was the dropping of a lighted cigarette into the wastepaper basket" [act]. "The cause of the workman's injury was the fall of the lead pipe" [event]. "The cause of the accident was the icy state of the road" [state]. "The cause of the accident was the signalman's failure to pull the signal" [failure to act]. "The cause of the famine in India was the lack of rain" [nonoccurrence of a condition]. "The cause of the famine in India was the failure of the government to build up adequate reserves" [failure of actions to achieve goals].[29]

There may be reasons which I have been unable to appreciate for giving a privileged status to the billiard-ball model and refusing to give the title of cause and effect to conditions that deviate rather drastically from it. In that case we should drop all reference to cause and effect in discussing "the causal component in harming," and speak instead of "attributing consequences to actions" (or to faults, failures, nonhappenings, states, omissions, etc.). Reference to actions as *the* causes of harms, however, is so well established in practical discourse that it need not be jettisoned here. We can pay whatever homage is required to the billiard-ball model by speaking of cause and consequence, rather than cause and effect. It is the *consequences* of our actions, after all, and not mere random effects, that we must "face up to."

4

Failures to Prevent Harm

1. Easy rescue and the bad samaritan

In the biblical parable,[1] the good Samaritan was a person who chanced upon the victim of a violent crime, a total stranger to him, lying "half dead" on the side of the road. Instead of passing him by on the other side, as a priest and a Levite had done earlier, and thus staying "uninvolved," he bound up the stranger's wounds, transported him to an inn, prepaid his bill, and otherwise offered him aid and succor. We can speak in contrast of the "bad samaritan," referring to any person who is a stranger to a given endangered person, and who, like the priest and the Levite in the biblical story, fails to come to that person's aid. More exactly, the bad samaritan is—

1. a stranger standing in no "special relationship" to the endangered party
2. who omits to do something—warn of unperceived peril, undertake rescue, seek aid, notify police, protect against further injury, etc.—for the endangered party,
3. which he could have done without unreasonable cost or risk to himself or others,
4. as a result of which the other party suffers harm, or an increased degree of harm,
5. and for these reasons the omitter is "bad" (morally blameworthy).

Among the many questions for legal policy raised by the bad samaritan, the central one for our purposes is whether statutes may legitimately be enacted threatening him with criminal liability for his failure to prevent harm to others.

Among European nations, Portugal was the first to enact a bad samaritan criminal statute in the mid nineteenth century. One hundred years later, a legal duty to undertake "easy rescue" had been recognized by the criminal codes of fifteen European nations.[2] In striking contrast, the English-speaking countries have remained apart from the European consensus. Their common law has never imposed liability either in tort or in criminal law for failures to rescue (except where there exist *special* duties to rescue, as for example those of a paid lifeguard toward the specific persons who bathe on his stretch of beach), and with few exceptions, the statutory law of Great Britain, the United States, Canada, and Australia has also treated the bad samaritan with grudging tolerance. Until joined recently by Minnesota, the only American state to enact a criminal bad samaritan statute of the European type was Vermont, whose criminal code now provides that "A person who knows that another is exposed to grave physical harm shall, to the extent that it can be rendered without danger or peril to himself or without interference with important duties owed to others, give reasonable assistance to the exposed person unless that assistance or care is being provided by others."[3] Even the Vermont law only slaps the wrist of the bad samaritan, creating a mere misdemeanor and imposing only a $100 fine, in contrast to the French law, for example, which provides imprisonment up to five years for violations.[4]

The common-law tradition has left unpunished even harmful omissions of an immoral kind—malicious failures to warn a blind man of an open manhole, to lift the head of a sleeping drunk out of a puddle of water, to throw a rope from a bridge to a drowning swimmer, to rescue or even report the discovery of a small child wandering lost in a wood, and so on. Not only negligent but wicked samaritans have escaped answerability to the law, which in English-speaking countries has not only declined to punish them, but has not even made them liable for damages to those they have failed to aid.

Our concern in this chapter is twofold. On the one hand, we must decide which legal policy, that of the fifteen or more European countries which impose a legal duty to rescue or that of the common-law countries which do not, makes the better moral sense. On the other hand, we must decide what the implications of the harm principle are in respect to failures to prevent harm. The two questions are intimately interconnected. We wish to formulate the harm principle in such a way that it accurately summarizes our spontaneous and basic convictions about moral legitimacy (Introduction, §6), a project that would seem to require us to make up our minds about the moral legitimacy of bad samaritan statutes, and use our judgment on that question as a guide to our understanding and more precise formulation of the harm principle. But the order of procedure can just as well go in the other direction. Having already developed confidence in the harm principle as so far formulated and tested, we might apply it directly to the problem of wrongful omissions to rescue, and follow its dictates on that question whatever they should happen to be.

Our preliminary formulation of the harm principle in the Introduction is comfortably vague and expansive. It endorses "harm-prevention" as a legitimate purpose of criminalization, apparently putting its stamp of approval both on statutes that forbid people from (actively) causing harm to others and statutes that require people to prevent harm to others, since the point of both sorts of statutes is "to prevent harm" to persons other than the person addressed. So interpreted, the harm principle is easily reconciled with bad samaritan statutes. In Chapter 3, however, a "full paradigm" of wrongful harming was spelled out that implies that the harm with which the harm principle is concerned is only that which is the product of a wrongful *act*. In that case legitimate statutes are precisely those that forbid people from *harming* or *causing harm* to others. If it is true, as many philosophers have claimed, that failure to rescue another person from harm is not as such to harm, or cause harm to, that person, then either we must leave bad samaritan statutes unsupported by any liberty-limiting principle other than legal moralism, and hence without liberal credentials, or else we shall have to supplement the harm principle with an additional liberty-limiting provision, holding now that it is a good reason for a criminal statute that it is needed to prevent persons *either* from harming one another *or* (what is different) from allowing harm to others that they could prevent. The additional provision would legitimize affirmative duties to rescue on pain of penalty even if it should turn out, after conceptual analysis, that the non-performance of such duties does not *cause*, but only allows, harm to occur. If we take the latter course, adding the new liberty-limiting provision, then we can argue for the moral legitimacy of bad samaritan statutes; not, however, on grounds of the strictly formulated harm principle of Chapter 3, but rather, in effect, on the basis of a newly expanded principle that *might* lead us, on other issues, where we are sure we have no right to go.

My own intuition is that bad samaritan statutes *are* morally legitimate in principle, though there may be some practical difficulties in their implementation. Therefore, if the harm principle does not place its stamp of certification on them, we shall have to amend that principle (or what amounts to the same thing, endorse an additional liberty-limiting principle) so that preventing as well as not-doing harm may be required by the criminal law. In either case, allowing as well as causing harm could rightly be punished.

We have not decided yet whether the amendment is necessary. That will depend on whether allowing harm can itself, in some circumstances, be a way of doing or causing harm (§§6–8). If an omission to prevent harm *is* the cause of the ensuing harm, then it already is rightly prohibitable under the strictly formulated harm principle, and no amendment is needed to legitimize bad samaritan statutes. If allowing harm, on the other hand, cannot be reduced to doing or causing harm, then a special provision is required if the state is properly to legislate against it.

At first sight, at least, the amendment to include allowing (not-preventing) harm within the scope of the harm principle, if that should prove necessary, raises no problems for our moral judgments. Preventing people from causing harm is noncontroversially a legitimate function of criminal law, and prohibiting people from allowing harm has precisely the same point, namely *to prevent harms*. Surely this common aim creates a presumption of moral legitimacy for bad samaritan statutes, whether that be expressed in the simple or the amended harm principle. As a matter of methodology, we should make this presumption until or unless we find an overriding reason against it. The overriding consideration would be some allegedly crucial moral difference between wrongfully causing and wrongfully not-preventing. If there is such a difference, one important enough to bear all of the moral weight that would have to be put on it, we would expect to find it cited and explained in the works of the writers who have defended the common-law tradition of tolerance toward bad samaritans. What reasons then have these writers advanced and why have they been so adamant?

Unsurprisingly, the arguments against bad samaritan statutes invoke the liberal ideals of individualism and liberty that infuse the Anglo-American common law generally. There is thus common ground between the leading opponents of a legal duty to rescue and their liberal critics, raising hopes that their internecine disagreement can be rationally resolved. There are at least four standard arguments commonly used against bad samaritan statutes:

1. *The enforced benevolence argument.* Bad samaritan statutes enforce a benevolent morality, making charity mandatory, and erasing the distinctions between harm and nonbenefit, and between duty and supererogation.
2. *The line-drawing argument.* If a general duty to rescue in some circumstances may be imposed on the public then there will be no principled way of drawing the line between aid in unanticipated emergencies near at hand, and aid to starving paupers or the distant needy who cannot be saved without extreme inconvenience, unfair sacrifice, or unreasonable risk.
3. *The argument from undue interference with liberty.* Affirmative legal duties

to render assistance are, in the very nature of the case, more serious interferences with liberty than negative legal duties not to harm others.

4. *The argument from causation.*

    a. *The restricted causation claim:* there is a clear conceptual distinction between causing and merely allowing harm, such that only active doings can cause harm whereas nondoings at most allow harm to happen, and

    b. *the moral significance thesis:* there is a special moral stringency in the requirement that people be held responsible only for the harms they *cause.*

None of these arguments seems convincing to me despite my strong allegiance to the values of liberty and autonomy affirmed in their premises. We shall now examine them in turn.

2. The confusion of active aid with gratuitous benefit

The first argument identifies active aid as such with gratuitous benefit, a mistake (as it seems to me) which is made with remarkable frequency. It matters not to the writers who argue in this fashion that a given instance of active aid required hardly any effort or danger to the actor, or that it was necessary to the very survival of the imperiled party. Insofar as it is *active*, no matter what other characteristics it may have, these writers insist, it confers a mere gratuitous benefit, and therefore cannot have been required by duty, not even by moral duty. This confusion takes a variety of interrelated forms, all of which derive from the uncritical acceptance of the apparent truism that a failure to prevent harm is "merely a *failure to benefit* the victim."[5] Thus Jeffrie G. Murphy (to select one of many possible examples) writes:

> I can be highly morally lacking even in cases where I violate no one's rights. For example, I am sitting in a lounge chair next to a swimming pool. A child (not mine) is drowning in the pool a few inches from where I am sitting. I notice him and realize that all I would have to do to save him is put down my drink, reach down, grab him by the trunks, and pull him out (he is so light I could do it with one hand without even getting out of my seat). *If I do not save him I violate no rights (strangers do not have a right to be saved by me)* but would still reveal myself as a piece of moral slime properly to be shunned by all decent people.[6]

These remarks are very puzzling to me, for the more natural view, I should think, is that the child in Murphy's example has a moral claim against the lounger, that in ignoring it the lounger violates the child's right to be saved, that the child's parents therefore not only have justification for reviling the lounger, for assigning him low moral grades, and for shunning him; they also have a legitimate personal *grievance* against him, both on their child's behalf and on their own.

In the passage quoted, Murphy gives no arguments for his surprising interpretation of the drowning-child example. But insofar as he fits into the tradition of writers with his view, the unstated assumptions are that apart from special moral relationships, our moral claim against others is only to be let alone, that is, not harmed; that any active help we get from others is a positive "benefit," and benefits, as opposed to nonharms, cannot be claimed against strangers as a matter of right. In Murphy's example, that which would have to be classified as "a mere benefit" is the child's very life.

There are, of course, cases in which one person may behave badly toward another, and thus show himself to be morally defective, without violating the other's rights, but the clearest instances of these make poor models for Murphy's example. If a casual acquaintance asks me to spend a day helping him to paint his house (I have the skills and lots of leisure time, being a retired house painter, and what can he lose by asking?), and I dismiss him immediately with a gruff and self-righteous refusal, I may reveal myself as something less than a moral paragon, and the requester (although he is also something less than a paragon) may join the rest of mankind in making that judgment of me, but he cannot voice a personal grievance against me, since he had no right to my assistance. What he requested of me, in effect, was that I confer a large gratuitous benefit on him. The child in the pool, however, does not seek a "large gratuitous benefit" from the lounger; he seeks only to avoid utter disaster.

Perhaps Murphy and others are misled by the fact that persons in desperate straits characteristically *implore* others for their help rather than claim or demand it, and after rescue express their gratitude, and even offer rewards. These facts have independent explanations, however, that are quite compatible with a right to be assisted. A person is in no mood to be morally high and mighty, and make righteous demands, when he is drowning. Pleading for help is the natural animal response to imminent peril, as is warm appreciation and the impulse to reciprocate after the fact. Rights are rarely in the forefront of attention through the typical salvation episode; they become more visible when they are infringed.

Murphy's judgment of bad samaritans is supported by Lance K. Stell, who claims that defenders of a right to be rescued have confused the requirements of justice with those of benevolence:

In the parable of the "Good Samaritan" the injustice (= violation of right) done to the man on the road to Jericho occurred at the hands of the thieves who beat, robbed, and left him for dead. The priest and the Levite who passed him by definitely did something immoral, but their immorality did not constitute a violation of the wounded man's *rights*. Their moral defect was to fail in kindness or benevolence (which one should expect from those who make their living preaching the love of God). Similarly, the wounded man did not have a right to the Good Samaritan's aid. That aid reflected the true spirit of brotherly love—the disposition to respond with compassion to human need even though justice does not require it. (Recall that the parable was occasioned by the question "Who is my neighbor?" not "What does it mean to respect the rights of others?") The point I am trying to make is well expressed by John Stuart Mill, who distinguishes between perfect and imperfect obligation. "Duties of perfect obligation are those duties in virtue of which a correlative *right* resides in some person or persons; duties of imperfect obligation are those moral obligations which do not give birth to any right. I think it will be found that this distinction exactly coincides with that which exists between justice and the other obligations of morality."[7]

In my defense of what I take to be the more natural account of the matter, I could concede to Stell that the moral defect that led the priest and the Levite to pass the victim by was a failure in kindness, benevolence, compassion, and brotherly love. But whatever character flaw *explains* their omission, it can remain true that it was their *duty* that they failed to do, and the victim's *rights* that were violated. If the recovered victim, months later, were to encounter the priest or Levite (having learned of their conduct toward him), he could indignantly voice a grievance against them, accusing them of having done him wrong. When wrongdoers knowingly violate the rights of others, their conduct, whether active or omissive, normally manifests the character flaw of injustice (lack of conscientiousness or dutifulness), but frequently such conduct is morally overdetermined, manifesting also a failure of sensitivity, sympathy, or benevolence. When the latter virtues are conspicuously missing, we may well choose to emphasize their absence in our subsequent account of the actor's wrongdoing. But it can remain true nonetheless that a victim's rights were violated, that a blamably coldhearted person, precisely because of his lack of benevolence, has committed an *injustice*.

There is an alternative to Stell's way of interpreting the point of the parable of the good Samaritan (though I lack the scholarship to claim any authority for it). The reason why a *lawyer* might ask Jesus "Who is my neighbor?" may be that a neighbor, in the ordinary narrow sense of the term, is a person with whom one has a somewhat special moral relationship, if only in virtue of his constant proximity and shared interests. Special relationships often generate special duties and reciprocal expectations.

When my friends and next-door neighbors of twenty years move away, I may owe them a farewell party, but I do not owe a farewell party to all persons everywhere who change their place of residence. Such gracious gestures will be the proper job of *their* neighbors. Similarly, I should be happy to comply when my neighbor comes to my door to borrow a cup of sugar, but I surely need not convert my house into a sugar warehouse in order to provision householders everywhere who happen to run out of sugar at inopportune times. Loaning sugar and throwing parties are examples of duties I have only to my "neighbor" in the strict and narrow sense. They are plausibly derived from a general duty of neighborliness that requires a willingness to be friendly, cooperative, and helpful with those who share one's area of residency.

Jesus therefore puzzles the lawyer by framing his most basic moral teaching in terms of one's "neighbor." "Love thy neighbor as thyself" is a rule universal in scope, taking the model of the neighbor relationship as somehow a guide to one's conduct towards *everybody*. Hence, the naturalness of the lawyer's question. In what respects, he wonders, can everybody be his "neighbor"? One way of interpreting Jesus' parable as a response to that question is that in certain basic respects the "special relationship duties" of neighbors in the strict sense find parallels in the moral relationships that exist between any pair of human beings whose life paths happen to cross in a time of crisis for one. When it comes to *aiding the imperiled*, all people who happen to find themselves in a position to help—all who have by chance wandered into the vicinity, or "portable neighborhood," of the imperiled party—are his "neighbors," with reciprocal dependencies, expectations, duties, and claims. (In contrast, if in the course of my travels in a distant city, I come across a family moving out of their home, I do not suddenly acquire the duty to throw a farewell party for them then and there.)

The biblical Samaritan, of course, was more than merely "neighborly." He did his duty and then some. The victim would have had no complaint against him if he had done a good deal less. Rights tend to be rather minimal claims. But to have done nothing at all, in the manner of the priest and the Levite, would have been to fall well below the required minimum. As Judith Thomson has pointed out, there are minimally decent samaritans, good samaritans, very good samaritans, and splendid samaritans.[8] The biblical Samaritan was a splendid samaritan indeed. Justice required only that he be "minimally decent." A surplus of benevolence prompted him to be more.

The reference to Mill's doctrine of imperfect obligation adds a further and independent confusion to Stell's discussion of the good samaritan. It is clear that Mill's model of a "duty of imperfect obligation" is our duty to contribute to charitable causes, since that is the first and only example he gives of the genre. Indeed, he defines "duties of imperfect obligation" (in a sentence just preceding that quoted by Stell) in terms of the very features that are peculiar to the duty to make charitable contributions: as "those in which, though the act is obligatory, the particular occasions of performing it are left to our choice, as in the case of charity or beneficence, which we are indeed bound to practice but not toward any definite person, nor at any prescribed time."[9] If there are more deserving needy people than I can help, and more worthy causes than I have funds to support, then a duty to be charitable can only require me to contribute a reasonable net amount, allocated as I see fit, among the eligible recipients. In the very nature of the case, some must do without help from me, deserving though they may be.[10] It follows from their equal worthiness and my inadequate capacity to serve them all, that *none* of them have a right to my help, even though I have a duty to help as many of them as I can. In short, the reason why my duty is "imperfect," lacking determinate recipients with correlative claims against me, is entirely a logistic one, a problem of coordination, that could be solved, if at all, by a cooperative scheme among similarly situated donors, defined by set rules. Nothing like this is involved in either Murphy's drowning child example or the parable of the good Samaritan, where the emergency is clear and present, and the aid can be given to one victim without being withheld from another. There is no reason to think of the rescuer's duty as merely to select from among the equally needy those he can afford to help, for there is no other need so near and pressing as that which commands his attention and demands his help right now. His act is not a "contribution to charity," and there can be no other reason for thinking of it as "imperfect" in Mill's sense.

Holding before our minds such examples of minimally decent samaritanism as that of Murphy's pool lounger had he pulled in the child, and the biblical Samaritan had he merely comforted the victim and reported his injuries to the authorities (or "called an ambulance" as would be required in our time), let us, in summary fashion, consider critically the overlapping descriptions that have been given of these actions by various writers (not always the same writers) in the common-law tradition, namely: (a) as "mere" conferrals of benefits, (b) as gratuitous favors, (c) as fulfillments of the general imperfect duty to be charitable, (d) as performance of a specific duty toward *this* person, but one without a correlative right in the beneficiary, (e) as an act of supererogation. I think that all of these descriptions are mistaken accounts of minimally decent samaritan interventions, but perhaps the root mistake is the first one, in the application of the concept of benefiting, and the tricky distinctions between harming and mere nonbenefiting, and benefiting and mere nonharming.

Conferrals of benefit. When *A* is in a position to affect *B*'s interests at a given time for better or worse, he may passively refrain from acting or he may actively intervene to produce the effect on *B* that he desires. Defenders of the common law have frequently taken these distinctions (active-passive and effect–no effect) to be coextensive: *A* harms or benefits *B* by actively intervening, but if he passively refrains, he can have no effect on *B*'s interests one way or the other. In passing up his opportunity to affect *B*'s interests then and there for the better, he merely *fails to benefit B*. (It goes without saying that he fails to harm him also.) If *B*'s interests suffer a setback that *A* could have prevented, then *A* can be charged only with the failure to benefit (where "benefit" is a generic term for affecting the other's interests at the time favorably *either* by advancing them or preventing their setback). In the opportunity-to-rescue situation, then, action coincides with benefit and nonaction with mere nonbenefit. *A* cannot harm *B* unless he actively does something (like hold his head under water). Speaking of an example similar to Murphy's pool lounger, James Barr Ames (writing in 1908) reports the orthodox view:

> . . . however revolting the conduct of the man who declined to interfere, he was in no way responsible for the perilous situation; he did not increase the jeopardy; *he simply failed to confer a benefit upon a stranger.* As the law stands today, there would be no legal liability, either civilly or criminally, in . . . these cases. *The law does not compel active benevolence* between man and man. It is left to one's conscience whether he shall be the good Samaritan or not.[11]

A major source for this argument is Thomas Babington Macaulay, who wrote in 1837:

> It is indeed most highly desirable that men should not merely abstain from doing harm to their neighbors, but should render active services to their neighbors. In general, however, the penal law must content itself with keeping men from doing positive harm, and must leave to public opinion, and to the teachers of morality and religion, the office of furnishing men with motives for doing positive good.[12]

Whether or not *A*, the samaritan, intervenes in these cases determines whether *B*'s interest remains as it was in the *status quo ante* (before the onset of his peril) or is disastrously set back. Yet Ames contends that the intervention positively benefits *B*, implying that it advances his interests to a condition superior to that of the *status quo ante*, so that *B* receives a kind of net windfall profit, all because of *A*'s munificent generosity. It is in this respect much as if *A* walked up to a stranger on the street and handed him a $100 bill! Similarly, Macaulay thinks of the rescue as an "active service" and a "positive good," implying that actively intervening to save another's interest, in virtue simply of being *active*, is therefore a "service," presumably as a gift out of the blue would be, helping to promote the other's interest to a condition superior to its normal one.

Something has gone wrong here, and the cause must be the concept of *benefiting* someone, which evidently has more than one sense. The legal writers who have defended the common law seem often to use the term in a generic sense to refer to any and all ways of affecting another party's interest for the better: advancing it beyond its present condition, advancing it beyond its normal condition, preventing it from getting worse than it is at the moment, preventing it from remaining worse than it normally is, and so on. Correspondingly, *harming* in the generic sense is any way of adversely affecting a party's interest-condition, including preventing its improvement, and setting it back either from its immediate state or its normal one. All of these conceptions involve the metaphor of the computational ledger and the starting point or "baseline" for measurement. (See Chap. 1, §5.) To save a drowning person is indeed to "benefit" him in the generic sense, for it is to affect his interest in a favorable as opposed to an adverse or neutral way. It is to prevent his interest-curve from taking a sharp decline from the baseline of its normal condition, as well as from the alternative measuring point of its immediately present condition.

The trouble with this generic usage is that it creates an especially tempting danger of equivocation. When it is so very obvious that the generic notion of "benefit" is applicable, it is easy to slide into one of the specific senses of "benefit" whose applicability is by no means evident. It does not follow from the fact that a rescuer affects the endangered party's interests favorably that he "benefits" him in the sense of elevating his interest-curve to a point on the graph *above* the baseline of his condition before he fell into the water. It is only the latter sense of "benefiting" that would support further descriptions of the rescue as benevolent generosity, "active service," "positive good," and so on, or the effect on the rescued party as "profit," "gain," or "advantage." Benefiting another, in this latter sense, is often to go beyond duty in a manner approved by our moral ideals but not required by moral rules. The liberal advocate of a bad samaritan statute can agree with Macaulay that in this precise sense of "benefit," governmental coercion can never be used to force one person to benefit another. But he should insist that easy rescue of a drowning child is not a "mere benefiting" in this sense. It is a benefit only in the generic sense of affecting the child's interest favorably, specifically by preventing a drastic decline in his fortunes from a normal baseline. That is quite another thing than conferring a windfall profit on him.

The subtle distinctions among the various senses of "harm" and "benefit," and their relations to the other distinctions with which they are

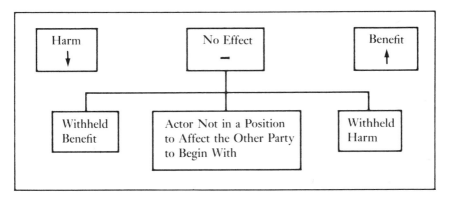

Diagram 1. Gross distinction of possible effects of one person's conduct on another person's interests. Downward arrow indicates adverse effect. Upward arrow indicates favorable effect.

frequently intertwined, can be illustrated by a series of diagrams of increasing complexity. Diagrams 1 and 2 distinguish among the things meant by "benefit" and "harm" when they refer simply to the state or condition of the person affected. Diagram 3 distinguishes senses of the verbs "to benefit" and "to harm" insofar as they correspond to the conditions produced in the affected party relative to some baseline or comparison point. Diagram 4 distinguishes further senses of "to benefit" and "to harm" that are based not only on changes produced in the condition of the affected party, but also on the prior presence or absence of a duty to produce those changes.

Diagram 1 represents a crude initial approach to the concepts of benefit and harm that encourages the view that effective doings can harm or benefit, whereas any nondoing (mere "withholding") will have no effect of its own on another party's interests. If A is in a position to benefit B yet withholds his benefiting action, he cannot have harmed B. Rather the only possible category for his inaction is that of "no effect." The three categories distinguished in Diagram 1 are intended to be mutually exclusive and jointly exhaustive. "Benefit" and "harm" are both used in what we have already called their generic senses, referring to *any* favorable or adverse effect of the conduct of one person on the interests of another. It follows that whatever the one person does, the effect on the other will be either harmful, beneficial, or neutral.

Diagram 2 complicates the picture by introducing other sources of favorable or adverse effects on the second party and their possible prevention by the intervening conduct of the actor. The effect of the intervening behavior is to leave the second party's interests exactly where they were to begin

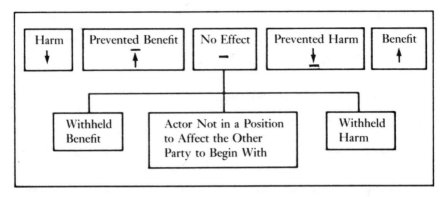

Diagram 2. Continuum of possible effects of one person's conduct on another person's interests. The downward arrow indicates adverse effect. The line blocking the upward arrow indicates the prevention of a rise in the second party's interest-curve that would otherwise come from other sources. The line blocking the downward arrow indicates the first party's prevention of a decline in the second party's interest-curve threatened by other causes. The upward arrow indicates favorable effect.

with by blocking, intercepting, or diverting the events (or conduct of a third party) that would otherwise have advanced them or set them back. There is a sense, as we shall see in Diagram 3, in which the benefit-preventing intervention is harmful and the harm-preventing intervention is beneficial even though both leave the second party's interest-curve at exactly the same point, neither higher nor lower, than it was at the start.

Now we introduce the notion of a "normal baseline," the point on the interest-graph where a person's interest-line usually is, or at any rate where it was during the period before the present episode began. Diagram 3 makes more refined and useful distinctions than Diagrams 1 or 2. One basic mistake of many writers in the common-law tradition, as we have seen, is to infer from the fact that a rescue attempt would be an effort to benefit$_G$ the imperiled party that it would therefore be an effort to benefit$_2$ him. Requiring the rescue under threat of punishment, therefore, would be to force people to confer windfall profit (so to speak) on others, which would be absurd. Actually, the specific mode of benefit in an easy rescue would be benefit$_1$, and to require it would not be to force people to be so extravagantly generous. To escape with one's life is not to become better off than one was before one's life was imperiled.

Gratuitous favors. Those who say that easy rescues are mere conferrals of benefits sometimes also say that minimally decent samaritans have no moral duty to be even minimally decent, and their easy rescues are indeed gratuitous services like favors or gifts. The two mistakes are independent, however, and not all writers who make the one make the other. Still those who do make both claims often use the second as a reason for the first, and it will be instructive to see how that is so. The distinction between harm and nonbenefit is clear enough in the extreme cases. To be robbed is to suffer a harm; not to be given a gift or to be given a worthless trifle is a mere nonbenefit. When we get away from these examples, however, the distinction can become very troublesome, and one kind of factor that can contribute complications is the nature of the relationship between the actor and

---

The Generic Sense of "To Benefit" Another

To benefit$_G$ = To produce any kind of favorable effect on another's interest, including those of benefiting$_1$ and benefiting$_2$, and also that of preventing harm threatened from another source.

Specific Senses of "To Benefit" Another

To benefit$_1$ = To advance another's declining interest back up to or toward his normal baseline (i.e. back to some *status quo ante*) or to prevent it from falling below that baseline.

To benefit$_2$ = To advance another's interest to a point beyond his normal baseline (i.e. above its point at some *status quo ante*). This would be to produce a benefit for him in the sense of net gain, profit, advantage, etc.

The Generic Sense of "To Harm" Another

To harm$_G$ = To produce any kind of adverse effect on another's interests, including those of harming$_1$ and harming$_2$, and also that of preventing a benefit (i.e. by thwarting, intercepting, or diverting) that would otherwise accrue from another source.

Specific Senses of "To Harm" Another

To harm$_1$ = To set back another's advancing interest to or toward a normal baseline (i.e. back to some *status quo ante*) or to prevent it from rising above that baseline.

To harm$_2$ = To set back another's interest to a point below his normal baseline (i.e. below its point at some *status quo ante*). This would be to produce a harm to him in the sense of net loss.

Diagram 3. Senses of "to benefit" and "to harm" corresponding to the type and degree of effect of the actor's conduct on the other party's interest-graph.

the person whose interests he affects. In particular, one question is crucial: whether the relations between the two parties are the ground of moral rights and duties between them.

It is now generally believed that no two human beings are so widely separated by interest and circumstance that there are no moral relations between them, although "all men are brothers," even as a metaphor, is probably an exaggeration. Even soldiers in opposing armies, bent on destroying each other, must nevertheless show some respect for the humanity of their enemies. There is a duty, even in such an extreme situation, not to be wanton, or cruel, for example. For the most part, however, duties and obligations toward others derive from certain special relations and prior agreements. The duty of a debtor to his creditor is not a duty he has toward everyone; and similarly the moral relations that hold between parents and children, husbands and wives, employers and employees, governors and the governed, are not the same as those that hold between any two random strangers.

These special and general moral relations have a strong influence on our conceptions of harm and benefit. If the argument of this section is right, the good swimmer on the bridge who watches a stranger drown in the water below has inflicted a harm, and a grievous one, by his omission (the common law notwithstanding); and this is so not only because death is the sort of thing we regard as harm whatever its cause, but also because the victim has a right to the assistance of the stranger, and the stranger had a correlative duty to save him. Merely being a fellow human being is enough to ground a duty when the threatened harm is that severe.

Now consider a second example, that of a condemned murderer whose last-minute appeal for clemency is denied by the governor. Here it is plausible to say that the governor merely "withheld a benefit" by his omission. The cause of the "harm" to the prisoner was his own crime and subsequent conviction, not any action or omission of the governor. At least part of the reason why this is so is that the governor had no duty to save the prisoner and the prisoner had no right to demand clemency. Clemency is something given freely, something "beyond duty," like a favor or a gift. We now have a third specific sense of "benefit." One person benefits another either (1) by restoring his interest to or maintaining it at a normal condition, or (2) by advancing his interests beyond a properly selected baseline (in this sense benefit is gain or profit), or (3) by any favorable effect on his interests (any generic benefit) that is *gratuitous* (like an act of grace or clemency).

To benefit₃ =	To produce gratuitously any favorable effect, including the prevention and withholding of harm, on another's interest (e.g. executive clemency, divine grace, forgiven debts, gifts, favors). Withheld harm is a benefit₃ when the withholding person had a right, which he freely decided not to exercise, to inflict or permit the harm.
To harm₃ =	To produce gratuitously any adverse effect, including the prevention and withholding of benefit, on another's interest (e.g. unprovoked blows, thefts).

Diagram 4. Senses of "to benefit" and "to harm" corresponding to gratuitous conduct.

Diagram 4, we should note, suggests an apparent asymmetry between harm and benefit. The governor who exempted the convicted murderer from capital punishment had a right to send the murderer to his death. He freely chose not to exercise that right, and that was a way of benefiting the murderer in this third sense of benefit. But had the governor chosen instead to withhold this benefit, which was also his right, that would *not* have been to harm the prisoner, but only to leave the course of his interest-curve unaffected.

Bestowing executive clemency then *is* a good example of benefiting a person by preventing his interest-curve from sinking even lower. Moreover, withholding the clemency in the same circumstances would not be to harm (further) the prisoner. These are precisely the two characteristics attributed by opponents of bad samaritan laws to the easy rescue of drowning swimmers. The withholding of executive clemency can hardly be a model, however, for interpreting the bad samaritan's failure to make an easy rescue of another party from imminent and severe peril. Doing a favor and making a gift are equally unpersuasive models (except to the person who is already convinced that there is no moral duty to attempt easy rescue). As we gradually change the examples, however, to weaken the severity or probability of the threatened harm, the model of the gratuity begins to take on plausibility. One stranger has a clear moral duty to make easy rescue of another threatened with death, or to notify police or an ambulance when he perceives another under attack (as in the famous Kitty Genovese case), but he has a less stringent duty, or no duty at all, to walk to the corner drugstore to buy a Band-Aid for a stranger who has just cut his finger and finds the interruption of his activities inconvenient. (Still, as Thomson would say, it would be a splendidly decent thing to do.) And such nonphysical harms as economic loss, when suffered by strangers, are even less plausible grounds for a duty to render assistance. It may break one's heart to see the distress on the face of a losing bettor at a racetrack, and it would be a marvelously generous thing to make good the stranger's losses, but hardly a duty to discharge, and hardly a right (on his part) to demand. When one does good anyway, even without duty, then the service is a gratuity—a gift or a favor. And in *that* sense, it is also a mere conferral of a benefit, even though without it, the beneficiary would remain in a severely harmed condition.

The distinction between gratuitous benefiting and nongratuitous benefiting cuts across the other distinctions we have made. One may benefit another party when in the absence of a duty to do so, one either benefits$_1$ him or benefits$_2$ him. If I give $100 to a stranger on the street who was not in need, I benefit$_3$ him by benefiting$_2$ him. My gift advances his interest above the appropriate initial comparison point. When I give the distraught stranger the money he has just lost at the racetrack, I benefit$_3$ him by benefiting$_1$ him. My gift merely restored his interest to its condition at the appropriate initial comparison point, without further profit to him. If I have a duty, however, to pay the sum in question to either of these persons, then my payment is no longer a gift but rather the repayment of a debt, the discharge of a promise, or the like, and it is no mere benefit$_3$ to them at all, though it may conceivably be a benefit$_2$ (my duty is to pay him what he has just won on the lottery ticket I sold him), or a benefit$_1$ (my duty was to repay a loan, bringing his assets just back to the point where they were when he made the loan).

Philosophers who distrust glib talk of "different senses" of puzzle-generating words could incorporate these distinctions into a unitary account of benefits and harms. In this alternative way of talking, we could say that there are two kinds of factors that determine whether A's conduct toward B harms or benefits B: (1) the effects of the conduct on B's interest curve and (2) whether or not A had a duty to B to act as he did. The important point concerns how factor (2) affects the way factor (1) is determined. When there is no duty to aid, we use a different baseline to measure benefits and harms. In my alternative terminology of "senses," we use a different method of distinguishing between benefits$_1$ and benefits$_2$, and between harms$_1$ and harms$_2$, depending on whether or not A's act was gratuitous. (In the unitary account benefits$_1$ would not be genuine benefits, and harms$_1$ would not be genuine harms.)

How then does the presence or absence of a duty determine which baseline we use for deciding whether the favorable effect on the assisted party's interest is a benefit$_1$ merely or a benefit$_2$ (or, in the unitary account, for determining whether or not it is a genuine benefit, that is a *gain*)? Gratuitous assistance is a benefit$_2$ when its favorable effect on interest is measured, as it should be, from the baseline of the interest-condition *at the moment the assistance is proffered.* The benevolent stranger's gift to the distraught bettor then might be regarded as a "sheer gain" for him, indeed a windfall profit, even though it only brings him back to the break-even point at which he began the day. It does bring him above the point where his benefactor found him, however, and in this case, because the act was gratuitous, *that* is the appropriate measuring point. If there had been a duty to contribute that very assistance, however, then the appropriate baseline would be the interest condition of the beneficiary at some earlier "normal" point (say before the races began, or, in our earlier example, before B fell in the water). Then we would say that A benefited$_2$ B only if he elevated B's interest curve *above* that earlier normal point, so that by merely bringing him back to that point, he neither harms$_2$ nor benefits$_2$ him.

Where there is a duty to aid B, then failure to assist B back to the *status quo ante* would be to harm$_2$ him. If Governor A commutes B's death sentence, then since he had no duty to do so, we measure B's improved interest-condition from its state at the moment the governor's rescue is effected. Formerly, death impended; now it does not—a clear improvement. Alternatively, we can say that the commutation of sentence did not improve the convict's condition; it only prevented it from getting worse. The point, however, is that the governor, by preventing the convict's condition from deteriorating, *when he had no duty to do so,* conferred upon him a benefit$_2$. But A's easy rescue of the drowning swimmer B, given A's duty to do so, does not advance B's condition beyond the normal baseline. Instead it simply *restores* it to its condition at that baseline. It is therefore not a "sheer gain"—not a net profit—for B. Rather B is "benefited" only in the somewhat strained sense that harm to him has been prevented.

Imperfect duties. There is no need to repeat here our earlier discussion of the strange thesis that minimally decent samaritan rescues are performances only of "imperfect duties" that lack correlative rights, but a brief application of the thesis to the Murphy pool lounger case will show how utterly inadequate it is. An imperfect duty in Mill's sense is a duty toward no one in particular, but rather toward the disjunction of the whole class of eligible (worthy and needy) receipients. My duty is to give *either* to these, *or* to those, *or* to those, etc. The pool lounger's duty to rescue the drowning baby, however, is not a plausible analogue of a general duty to be charitable. It is not as if he has a small lifeboat on the ocean and a general duty to pick up as many overboard passengers as he can from a sinking liner, a general duty to save drowning people—either this one, or that one, or the other one, but not necessarily *this* one here and now. A duty becomes indeterminate, or "imperfect" in Mill's sense, only when there are more persons to be assisted than there are personal resources effectively to aid them, and that condition is explicitly ruled out in the Murphy example, as it is in all the cases that would be covered by bad samaritan statutes.

We encounter a more serious problem, however, when we modify Murphy's example by adding more imperiled parties. Suppose that there are two drowning babies in the pool, one twenty meters to the lounger's right and the other twenty meters to his left, and that the circumstances make it clear that the lounger, by taking a few steps in either direction, can easily scoop up one baby, but that there is insufficient time to rescue both. (We can suppose that the lounger is unable himself to swim or stay afloat in the water.) Now the lounger's duty begins to resemble the "imperfect duty" to contribute to charitable agencies. Since the lounger can save one but not both babies, neither baby, it will be said, can claim as a matter of right that *he* be the one who is saved. If the lounger is the same scoundrel as in Murphy's original example, he will be no more inclined to rescue one of two imperiled babies than he was to rescue the solitary baby, and he will let them *both* die. If he is philosophically clever, he will say in his own defense afterward that while of course he deserves low moral grades for his heart-lessness and for his failure to discharge a duty of imperfect obligation, nevertheless he violated no one's rights; no one was wronged; no one has a legitimate grievance against him. And for that reason, he will add, he cannot rightly be punished in this case, even on the assumption that he could have been punished in the earlier example where he neglected only a single drowning child. To compound the paradox, the greater the number of hypothetical imperiled babies we throw into the fictitious pool, the more plausible will the lounger's case seem to become, that *none* of them had a right to his assistance.

These results are intolerably paradoxical in their own terms, but they are particularly unsettling to the liberal, for they seem to force him to embrace an inconsistent triad of propositions:

1. Criminal prohibitions are legitimate only when they protect individual rights, that is, there should be no victimless crimes;
2. Murphy's lounger in the two-or-more-drowning-baby cases should be criminally liable;
3. but Murphy's lounger in those cases violates no one's rights.

I cannot escape this trap by giving up proposition (1), for that would be utterly to abandon either the liberalism that it is the aim of this book to defend, or else the analysis of harm as right-violating setback to interest. Proposition (2) is hardly any easier to abandon. Since I would argue that the lounger should be criminally liable in the case where there is only one party in peril, I cannot, in all consistency, argue for his immunity when there are two or more in peril and it is easy for him to rescue one. The statute imposing that liability could have some legitimacy, I suppose, on the ground that it functions to diminish setbacks to interest, in this case to prevent the loss of salvageable human life, but that legitimacy would tend to be undermined by the bad samaritan's claim that his crime lacked a determinate victim since neither drowned child had a moral right against him to be saved (proposition [3]). The reply to this claim must be that in fact at least one of the babies did have rights that were violated by the lounger's deliberate omission to act. Now the problem becomes that of giving a plausible account of those rights.

One possibility is to say that each child had a right against the lounger that he save as many of them as he could without unreasonable risk to himself. In this case that would be a right that each baby has that the lounger save one or another of them. It would follow that by failing to act at all, the lounger violated the rights of both babies, even though by hypothesis it would have been impossible to save one of them. A somewhat odd consequence of this view of the matter is that if the lounger had rescued one of the babies then he would have entirely fulfilled the moral right of the other, and his duty to the one baby would be entirely discharged by his rescue of the other.

Another interpretation is that each baby had a right, not to a rescue attempt from the lounger, but rather to equal consideration, and that by rescuing neither he violated that right. There are some difficulties with this view too. In giving neither imperiled party *any* consideration, the lounger treated them with perfect equality. Moreover, if one baby had been a boy and the other a girl, or one a black and the other a white, and a different hypothetical lounger, able to save only one but not both, chose on the basis of his bigoted racial or sexual preferences, it is not clear that the neglected party's rights would be thereby violated, especially if we add to the example that *this* pool lounger would have saved both had he been able to do so. It is part of the conception of a duty of imperfect obligation that the obligated party must save as many as he reasonably can, but that it be left up to his own free choice which ones are selected for rescue. In any case, the moral charge against our original lounger is not that he gave the babies unequal chances, but that he gave neither of them any chance at all. And for that reason, it might be thought that each of them has, equally, a grievance against him.

A final interpretation of the babies' violated rights does not conceive of them as rights that each held equally against the lounger. Rather, on this view we would say that only one of the babies was wronged by the lounger's omission, but that it is impossible to say which one. This view avoids the odd consequence of the joint-right theory that the lounger, had he rescued one baby, would thereby have fulfilled his obligation toward the other. Now we can say instead that had he rescued one baby he would have satisfied that baby's right against him without violating *or* fulfilling any right of the other baby, since the other baby is the one (we now know) who had no right against the lounger, and to whom the lounger had no duty. This third interpretation of the rights and duties of the parties in the two-baby case has some advantages, but like the others, it raises some daunting difficulties. One obvious drawback is that we cannot say who the bad samaritan's wronged victim is when the number who perished is greater than he could have saved, even though we can say that he was responsible for at least one of the deaths.

In some ways, however, this "drawback" has the advantage of congruing with the way we think of the grievances of the unrescued when the numbers of those imperiled are vastly greater than the resources for rescuing them. When 1,000 overboard passengers are imperiled, and only one can be saved (there is room for only one more in a tiny rescue craft), but the boatman chooses to rescue no one, the grievances of the 1,000 (or their surviving loved ones) are greatly diluted. On the theory considered here, only one of the 1,000 had a right against the boatman to be rescued, namely the one the boatman would have selected had he been willing to rescue anyone at all, and of course we cannot know who that one is. But the odds are 1,000 to 1 against it being any given one of those left to die. Mourning relatives can therefore believe only that there is one chance in a thousand that the boatman is responsible for their relative's death, and modulate their resentment accordingly. The two sets of parents of the drowning babies, on the other hand, have a much stronger grievance. The chances that the lounger is responsible for the death of their child are fifty-fifty. In either case the law could consistently charge the bad samaritan with something like "homicide by omission" on the grounds that the probability of the defendant's being responsible for the death of *someone or other*, on the facts given, is near a hundred percent, even though the victim, in the formulation of the charge, would have to remain nameless.

The more serious flaw in this third account of the rights of the unrescued is that it appears to imply, in the two-baby case, that only one child (we know not which) has a right to be saved by the lounger, even though there are no morally relevant factual differences between the drowning children or their circumstances. This result would appear to violate the rationality of right-ascriptions, in particular what is sometimes called the condition of "supervenience" that all ethical terms, properly employed, must satisfy. Rights and other ethical predicates are said to be supervenient in the sense that their existence derives from other characteristics: we have the right *in virtue of the fact* that we have the other characteristics. It follows from supervenience that if we lacked the right-generating characteristic we would lack the right, and if we have exactly the same characteristics as some other person then we cannot differ from that person in respect to right-ownership. Without supervenience in this sense the language of rights would be fatally infected with arbitrariness.

My preference then is for some variant of the first kind of account, that which recognizes a claim against the undermanned rescuer in all the imperiled parties. Corresponding to these claims, Murphy's lounger has only an imperfect duty, that is to say that he is morally required only to do his best to save as many as he can. If he saves one and the other drowns despite his best efforts, then he has not violated the other's right, for the drowning baby's only claim against him was that he save as many as he could, and that claim was honored. If he let them both die, then he violated the rights of both babies by giving neither any chance at all.

Which one then was his victim? The answer, I should think, is that both babies had rights against him which he violated by his omission but that his victim was the wronged party who would have survived but for that omission. Again, we cannot know who that party was, but it does not follow that this was a "victimless crime," because we *do* know that the victim was either baby *A* or baby *B*. There was definitely a victim then, even though he can not be more definitely named. The victim, it should be emphasized, had no rights that the other drowning baby lacked. This solution does not violate supervenience. The two babies were equally wronged, but the victim was that one whose death was *the consequence* of the lounger's wrongful omission. The lounger committed homicide against one or the other of the children by equally neglecting their rights against him. But given the unhappy circumstances and the lounger's limited opportunity, only one of the children died as a result of his wrongdoing. That one should be quite sufficient, however, to convict him of homicide.

Whatever difficulties may remain for this account of the rights violated in a total default of a duty of imperfect obligation, they are likely to be slight when compared to the moral paradoxes in the view of Professors Murphy and Stell, that neither drowning baby has any right that is violated by the samaritan who omits to aid either of them when he could have rescued one safely and easily. In summary, then, when a person in a situation of scarce resources discharges his duty of imperfect obligation by saving some rather than others from among those equally eligible for his aid, he violates no one's rights, no matter how arbitrary his selection procedures. But when he violates his duty in that situation by giving aid to no one at all, then he violates the rights of at least some, and—on the preferred theory—all of the eligible recipients who suffer subsequent harm.

Determinate duties without correlative rights. It is not entirely clear which of the two typical characteristics of imperfect duties Mill meant to be the defining one: the lack of a determinate beneficiary or the lack of a correlated right to be assisted in the beneficiary or both. If the defining feature is the lack of a particular assignable person at whom the duty can be said to be directed, then there can be perfect duties (with perfectly determinate recipients) which nevertheless cannot be claimed by the person at whom they are directed as his right. Some (but not all) duties toward the third-party beneficiaries of promises may fall into this category. Johnny may promise his mother to smile when he looks at Mrs. Jones, his schoolteacher. He thus has a duty to one determinate recipient, Mrs. Jones, to behave in the promised way, though the promise he made to his mother gave his teacher no right to his smile. Alternatively, Johnny's mother may exploit the authority of her office as parent and *order* Johnny to smile at Mrs. Jones, thus imposing on Johnny a "duty of obedience" toward a determinate third party, but not one that Mrs. Jones can exact from him as *her* right. To take a less trivial example, consider a saintly or heroic person who thinks of himself as having a special duty derived from his personal ideals, or from his self-assigned vocation in life, or from an intuition of compelling appropriateness, or from God, that requires him "to give benefits to others much in excess of what [he believes] is their right."[13] We may dismiss such a person as a moralistic egotist, but we cannot convict him of a conceptual error. It is no contradiction to speak of a duty to help others that is not logically correlated with any right in the recipients to be assisted. Finally, I might mention the duties of *noblesse oblige* that were thought to be owed by nobles even to their unworthy underlings, simply because the duties attached to the station occupied by the nobles and (as we now say) "came with the territory." Lords had duties to their servants, under the feudal system, that the servants could not rightly claim as their due.

It is possible, I suppose, for a philosopher to claim any or all of these duties as models for understanding the pool lounger's duty to rescue the drowning child, or the samaritan's duty to assist the battered victim of crime. It is possible for philosophers to claim anything at all. There is no conclusive way of refuting the claim that the drowning child and the battered victim have no moral right to be rescued correlative to the moral duty that others have to rescue them. However, there is a simple phenomenological test that all these models fail when applied to the child and the victim. When we agree that the bystanders ought to offer assistance in these cases, indeed that they *must* offer assistance, do we also think that *moral indignation* on behalf of the recipient of the duty would be fitting if the bystander failed to do his duty, or would we just give the bystander low moral grades, adding that his flaws are no business of the person he declined to aid, nothing *he* has a right to complain about? If A is pompous, vain, silly, dull-witted, or unimaginative, what is that to B, who is a mere stranger, a passive observer? B can make these adverse judgments about A and avoid his company, but can he claim as a personal grievance against A that A has these failings? Clearly not; and that is a sign that he has no right that A be a better person in these respects. That is A's business, not his. But the parents of the drowned child will feel understandably and plausibly aggrieved, and we can share their indignation vicariously. We would not acknowledge that their child's right was infringed if we thought of the bad samaritan's neglected duty as something like a duty of *noblesse oblige*. But clearly we cannot think of it that way; the persisting sense of grievance will not permit it.

Acts of supererogation. It would hardly be necessary to deny the still stranger view that the lounger and the samaritan, having no duty whatever to give assistance, perform "acts of supererogation" if they do, were it not for the fact that an esteemed legal writer has recently seemed to make this claim about all rescue attempts, even the "minimally decent" ones that would be required by a bad samaritan statute. In an influential article, Richard Epstein refers to the distinction made by "most systems of conventional morality" between "conduct which is required and that which, so to speak, is beyond the call of duty." Then he goes on to argue that "if that distinction is accepted as part of a common morality, then the argument in favor of the traditional common law good samaritan rule is that it, better than any possible alternatives, serves to mark off the first class of activities from the second."[14] In fairness to Epstein, the general drift of his argument is that there is a slippery slope in the application of a bad samaritan rule, so that it is hard to avoid making into duties actions that are in fact genuinely supererogatory once we start down that path by making mandatory even the clear cases of easy rescue that we have been considering. (We shall turn to that argument in the next section.) Nevertheless, it is important to point out that whether the path of legislation is slippery or not, the cases of minimally decent samaritanism with which it starts are anything but supererogatory.

There are two common ways to interpret the concept of a supererogatory act, one quite specific, the other generic. In the specific sense, supererogatory acts tend to be *harder* than most acts required by duty. They are "above and beyond duty." Like the acts of saints and heroes, they are "meritorious, abnormally risky nonduties."[15] Minimally decent acts of easy rescue, *by definition*, are not supererogatory in this sense. There is nothing risky about calling an ambulance or yanking a small child out of the water. In the generic sense, a supererogatory act is any act "whose performance we praise but whose nonperformance we do not condemn."[16] But in that sense, easy rescues like that open to Murphy's pool lounger fail to be supererogatory since everyone (including Murphy) condemns their nonperformance. Indeed Epstein too, though he steadfastly opposes legal enforcement, admits that "failure to aid those in need can invoke . . . moral censure."[17]

3. Lord Macaulay's line-drawing problem

There is no plausibility then in the view that a positive act of assistance *as such* is a "mere conferral of benefit" (either in the sense of profit or the sense of favor) or an act of generosity, charity, or supererogation. The qualifying phrase "as such" is important. The rejection of the view containing this phrase implies that even though some acts of assistance may be gratuitous, etc., they are not so simply and entirely in virtue of their status as positive acts of assistance. If all such acts, "as such," are mere beneficial gifts or favors and the like, then even the minimally decent ones would be too, and that, as we have seen, is not credible. The argument against bad samaritan laws that rests on a purely conceptual analysis of "acts of assistance"—any and all acts of assistance—into gratuitous conferrals fails utterly.

A more plausible argument concedes that the minimally decent samaritan acts required by the European statutes are moral duties correlated with the moral rights of endangered persons to be assisted, but insists that it is impossible in principle for the law to be formulated in such a way that these duties are enforced, without at the same time requiring persons in other contexts to perform acts that are above and beyond their actual moral duties. There is, according to this argument, no nonarbitrary way of drawing and *holding* the line. Any statute designed to enforce minimally decent samaritan rescues in some cases will inevitably enforce "very good" and "splendid samaritanism" in other cases, and that would indeed be to force people by law to live up to the highest moral ideals of saintliness and heroism, instead of merely performing the duties to prevent harm that are incumbent on all minimally decent people. And that would degrade the ideals by depriving genuine heroes of their proper credit, and weaken the law by saddling it with unenforcible duties. In short, this slippery slope leads to a form of legal moralism.

This argument does not rely on the empirical version of the famous slippery slope argument. (See Chap. 27, §1.) Its point is not that if laws are passed requiring minimally decent samaritanism then power-greedy, legal-moralist legislatures will have their foot in the door, and will in time be foisting their more demanding statutes on us too. Rather the argument employs something like the logical version of the slippery slope. The difficulty it points to is not in the political situation but in our concepts themselves. It claims that there is no way of formulating even the minimal statute which can clearly mark off the class of properly enforcible moral duties from the class of improperly enforcible gratuities—no way short of arbitrary stipulation. Epstein makes the claim somewhat more modestly. He does not characterize the difficulty as "logical," and he does not allege that its solution is impossible in principle, but he does regard the difficulty as one for draftsmanship, and given our slippery concepts, he suggests, that difficulty is formidable: "Once one decides that as a matter of statutory or common law duty, an individual is required under some circumstances to act at his own cost for the exclusive benefit of another, then it is very hard to set out in a principled manner the limits of social interference with individual liberty."[18]

The classic statement of the line-drawing objection to bad samaritan statutes is that of Lord Macaulay, who discussed the question in the introductory notes he wrote in 1837 for the commission to revise the Indian penal code, of which he was a member.[19] Macaulay begins by asking to what extent omissions should be punishable when they "correspond to," that is produce the same consequences as, those positive acts that are punishable because of their harmfulness. Very wisely, he decides to steer a middle course right from the start, rejecting both the view that all such omissions should be punishable and the view that none should. His problem then is to draw the line that separates the harmful omissions that are punishable from those that are not. He concludes by drawing the line where the Anglo-American law has always drawn it, in effect to immunize "samaritans," those persons in a position to help others in distress to whom they stand in no "special relations."

Macaulay's method is to list clear cases of punishable and nonpunishable failures to prevent harm and then attempt to extract the implicit principle of distinction from the examples themselves. Clear cases of punishable omissions include that of the jailor who declines to feed his prisoner, leading to the latter's death in his jail cell, and the nurse who intentionally allows the death of a baby entrusted to her professional care by omitting to remove it from a tub of water into which it has fallen. It is equally clear, on the other side, that a person should not be convicted of murder because he omitted to relieve a beggar, and (in Macaulay's most famous example) that a surgeon ought not to be "treated as a murderer for refusing to go from Calcutta to Meerut to perform an operation, although it should be absolutely certain that this surgeon was the only person in India who could perform it, and that if it were not performed, the person who required it would die."[20]

In what way do the prisoner-starving and baby-neglecting cases differ from the beggar-rebuffing and surgical nonrescue cases that makes the former punishable and the latter legally innocent? Jailors are assigned a legal duty, one that helps define their job, to feed their prisoners, and professional nurses contract to exercise protective care over their wards, whereas no compartment of the law imposes a duty on private individuals to feed starving beggars or to travel by primitive railroad across an entire subcontinent to operate on an unknown patient. Hence Macaulay concludes that harmful omissions should be punished in the same manner as the harmful actions to which they correspond, "provided that such omissions were on other grounds illegal."[21] This formula at first appears to be circular, decreeing that omissions should be made contrary to law only in those cases where they are already contrary to law, but that is not quite Macaulay's meaning. He means that harmful omissions should be made *criminal* only when they breach some legal duty or other, including those enforced by noncriminal rules like duties to honor agreements or duties to exercise due care, violations of which are grounds for *civil* actions, or injunctions, forfeitures, or other legal remedies. The common ground of these heterogeneous duties is some prior special relationship between the omitter and his victim. They must be related as master-servant, actor-agent, promisor-promisee, employer-employee, vendor-purchaser, salesman-customer, nurse-patient, lifeguard-swimmer, carrier-passenger, innkeeper-guest, nursemaid–entrusted child, jailor-prisoner, owner of dangerous pet or instrument–party endangered by the pet or instrument, etc. There is no civil liability and neither, Macaulay concludes, should there be criminal liability, for an omitter who is a mere stranger ("samaritan") to the injured party with no duty to him derived from prior agreements, special status, or job. For example:

> A omits to tell Z that a river is swollen so high that Z cannot safely attempt to ford it, and by this omission voluntarily causes Z's death. This is murder if A is a person stationed by authority to warn travellers from attempting to ford the river. It is murder if A is a guide who had contracted to conduct Z. It is not murder if A is a person on whom Z *has no other claim than that of humanity.*[22]

Macaulay does not explain why a claim based simply on "common humanity" cannot, or should not, be the ground of some kind of affirmative duty to give assistance *somewhere* or other in the law, and his peremptory exclusion of the possibility must strike the modern reader as question-begging after all. The unrelated bystander, *A*, goes scot-free despite allowing *Z* to go to his death. Why? Because he had no duty to rescue that the law elsewhere recognizes. But whether the law *should* recognize duties based on the relationship of common humanity is precisely the point at issue.

Macaulay is not entirely satisfied with his way of drawing the line, but he thinks that further efforts to extend criminal liability for omitters would yield even more counterintuitive results. "Wherever the line of demarcation is drawn, it will, we fear, include some cases which we might wish to exempt, and will exempt some which we might wish to include."[23] Still Macaulay is certain that his line is more plausible than that suggested by the nineteenth-century American Edward Livingston in his proposed code for the territory of Louisiana.[24] Livingston's formula is strongly suggestive of the twentieth-century bad samaritan statutes enacted in Europe. He would impose liability for homicide on any person, specially related or not, who omits to save an endangered person when he could have done so "without personal danger or pecuniary loss." Macaulay objects on two grounds. Livingston's formula would extend liability unjustly to those, like the Calcutta surgeon, who would suffer immense inconvenience and loss of time even though he is offered "such a fee that he would be a gainer by going." Perhaps then Livingston's formula should include "great inconvenience" along with personal danger and pecuniary loss as grounds of exemption. But that would still leave vulnerable the person of ample wealth who "refuses to disburse an anna to save the life" of a solitary and unthreatening beggar. So Livingston's criterion is too severe. But Macaulay's second objection is that for a certain range of cases it is also too lenient. Some persons should be convicted of murder for omitting to attempt rescues even when doing so *would* involve personal danger, pecuniary loss, or great inconvenience. These culpable nonrescuers are precisely those who have special legal duties based on contract or status relationships with the endangered party. Even if it costs parents their last penny, they must provide food for their infant, and, in a second example, "a nurse hired to attend a person suffering from an infectious disease cannot perform her duty without running some risk of infection. Yet if she deserts the sick person, and thus voluntarily causes his death, we should be disposed to treat her as a murderer."[25]

I suspect that some improvement can be achieved over both Livingston and Macaulay by combining the better features of their two approaches. This can be done if (1) we abandon the attempt to list precise exempting conditions and speak instead of the absence to the rescuer of *unreasonable* danger, loss, or inconvenience, and (2) we give some added importance to special relationships, especially when they are the basis of special reliance by the threatened party on the party obligated to him, by ascribing perhaps a duty of greater incumbency, and liability to greater punishment. Thus the passerby who declines to warn the traveler, Z, who has been deserted by his guide and also by the sentry posted at the river, that the river is too swollen to cross might be punished for his omission even though he is a stranger to Z, but the derelict guide and sentry would be punished more severely still, perhaps even for murder, because of their specially incumbent duties and Z's special reliance on them. They have not only violated a general duty of humanity held in common with all other members of the community; they have also violated duties assigned uniquely to them, duties which made them objects of a singular trust and dependency. By voluntarily accepting those duties in the first place, they created the very trust they later violated.

Macaulay would explicitly reject my first suggestion, that vague standard-bearing terms like "unreasonable," "excessive," and the like be used in the law of criminal omissions instead of precise or metrical criteria of cost, danger, and inconvenience. And this brings us to the crux of Macaulay's argument, which has the form of a dilemma. The first and more damaging horn of the dilemma is the impossibility in principle of precise criteria. However they are formulated they will fail to match our intuitions of appropriate severity or lenience in all cases. But the only alternative to them—the other horn of the dilemma—is vague terms like "unreasonable" which (I think Macaulay and surely Epstein would say) permit prosecutors and juries unbridled, and indeed unprincipled, discretion in deciding whether or not a given omission is criminal. Admittedly inadequate as Macaulay's own line of demarcation is as a reflection of our judgments of fairness, we had better hold the line there, he insists, exempting from the duty to rescue all persons who lack special relationships to the victim. Once we open the door to samaritan liabilities, the line-drawing problem becomes more than difficult; it becomes impossible, and there will be no nonarbitrary way of stopping short of liability for *all* harmful omitters, including rebuffers of beggars and inconvenienced traveling surgeons.

Macaulay returns to the example of the river fording to illustrate his central contention that precise line-drawing, once we allowed criminal liability for samaritan omissions, would be impossible:

> It is true that none but a very depraved man would suffer another to be drowned when he might prevent it by a word. But if we punish such a man where are we to stop? How much exertion are we to require? Is a person to be a murderer if he does not go fifty yards through the sun of Bengal at noon in

May in order to caution a traveller against a swollen river? Is he to be a murderer if he does not go a hundred yards?—if he does not go a mile?—if he does not go ten? What is the precise amount of trouble and inconvenience which he is to endure? The distinction between the guide who is bound to conduct the traveller as safely as he can, and a mere stranger, is a clear distinction. But the distinction between a stranger who will not give a halloo to save a man's life, and a stranger who will not run a mile to save a man's life, is very far from being equally clear.[26]

This first horn of Macaulay's dilemma does indeed threaten to gore the advocate of bad samaritan statutes who is put by it in a familiar kind of quandary. If it is reasonable to impose a duty to walk one step to warn the traveler, then surely it is reasonable to require two steps. The difference between two steps and one is so insignificant morally that it would be inconsistent to charge a bad samaritan with murder for failing to take one step, while letting another off for failing to take two. But the difference between two steps and three is equally insignificant, so it would be unreasonable to draw the line of duty at two steps. Similarly insignificant is the difference between three steps and four, or between twenty-nine and thirty, or between 999 and 1,000. So there will be no place to draw the line, the argument goes, that will not mark an arbitrary difference between those made liable and those exempted.

Clearly something has again gone wrong with the argument. There may be no morally relevant difference between any two adjacent places on the spectrum, but there is a very clear difference between widely separated ones. It would be inconsistent to exempt one bad samaritan for failing to take two steps while convicting another for failure to take one, but there would be no inconsistency in convicting one for failure to take half a dozen steps while exempting another for failure to run two miles. So the distinction between clearly good and clearly bad samaritans is not undermined.

One way of coping with Macaulay's quandary is to extend liability very cautiously only to those samaritans who could warn, assist, report, or rescue without *any* peril, and without *any* cost (the apparent approach of the Vermont statute) and even, what is more, without *any* inconvenience. (See Diagram 5.) That way we could convict Murphy's pool lounger and similar crystal clear cases, while exempting everyone else. We would punish the very worst of the bad samaritans without requiring others even to measure up to a plausibly minimal standard of reasonable conduct. Something would be lost, but at least we would obviate Macaulay's line-drawing problem, without adopting his stricter test.

A better tack still would be that illustrated by Diagram 6, to divide up the spectrum of hypothetical cases into three segments: (1) clear cases of

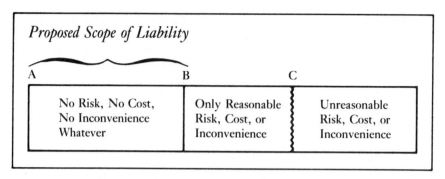

Diagram 5. Samaritan liability for harmful omissions: first proposal.

opportunity to rescue with no unreasonable risk, cost, or inconvenience whatever; (2) cases of opportunity to rescue but only at clearly unreasonable risk, cost, or inconvenience to the rescuer or others; and (3) everything in the vast no-man's-land of uncertain cases in between the extremes. To err on the side of caution, we would hold no one in the middle (uncertain) category liable, and thus draw the line of demarcation at point B. That would be to hold everyone liable who *clearly* deserves to be liable, while exempting all those who do not clearly deserve to be liable—both those who clearly deserve *not* to be liable, and those whose deserts are uncertain. In the river-fording case, perhaps that point would be at the limits of shouting range from the endangered traveler. Of course it might be hard to determine exactly where point B is in a given case, and the line between point B and a place on the line just short of point B may seem as arbitrary a place as any other to draw a line. But careful draftsmanship of statutes could leave it up to juries to decide where reasonable doubts begin. After all, our tradition restricts jury findings of guilt to the stage before *any* reasonable doubts appear anyway, so there is no lack of precedent for using juries to determine such points. This solution to Macaulay's quandary has two very attractive merits. First, it allows for the ascription of criminal responsibility to some very bad samaritans who would escape altogether if Macaulay's test or even the Vermont test were used; and second, it avoids the absurdity of holding that there is no moral difference between widely separated points on the scale just because there is none between any two nearly adjacent ones. Murphy's lounger and others only slightly further from the swimming pool deserve to be punished for not rescuing the child, whereas observers 100 and 200 yards away do not.

My proposed solution to Macaulay's problem then is to grasp (but gingerly) the second horn of his dilemma and formulate bad samaritan statutes

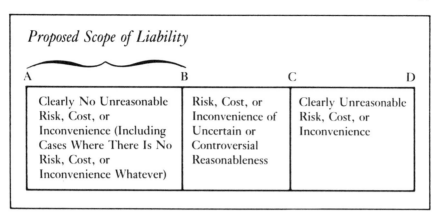

Diagram 6. Samaritan liability for harmful omissions: preferred proposal.

in relatively vague terms that allow juries the discretion to apply standards of reasonable danger, cost, and inconvenience. Juries in civil cases have long been entrusted with such judgments, deciding case by case, for example, whether defendants in negligence suits have exercised "reasonable care." Even in the criminal law, as Thomas Grey points out,[27] juries have traditionally been assigned such responsibilities, for example when they are charged with deciding whether the accused suffered provocation that even a "reasonable man" might not bear, or whether an admitted killer pleading self-defense retreated as far as he reasonably could (ten steps? fifty yards? two miles?), and used deadly force only because it was reasonable in the circumstances to believe that lesser force would not protect him. Are not these judgments of reasonableness as much a matter of degree, asks Grey, as judgments of "how far one should have to walk in the midday heat to save the life of another?"[28] As for the danger of uncontrolled prosecutorial discretion and its malicious use against decent but unheroic samaritans, I think the interpretation I have suggested of the unreasonable-risk standard should be an adequate guard against the danger. Prosecutors have no motive for bringing charges against nonrescuers whom they know juries will not convict, and juries in nonrescue cases would be instructed to acquit defendants if they judge that the personal risks of rescue had reached the threshhold not of actual unreasonableness but of the first germs of doubt about unreasonableness. Prosecutors could hope for convictions only in those cases where the reasonableness of the required effort's costs was uninfected by the slightest trace of uncertainty.[29]

Before leaving Macaulay, we should consider one of his favorite types of examples of nonpunishable omissions: failure to give money to starving

beggars.[30] He was writing, of course, about India in 1837, and these examples were by no means as quaint as they may seem to some of us in a
twentieth-century welfare state. In the India of Macaulay's time, a resident
Englishman would encounter hordes of beggars on every street corner, and
thousands of these would die every year of malnutrition or starvation. It
was manifestly absurd to hold that each time a wealthy man encountered a
beggar, he had a duty to rescue him by making a small contribution. Such
rescues were not at all analogous to pulling drowning children out of the
water and thus eliminating their peril once and for all; rather the inevitable
harm could only be forestalled. One way of looking at the contributions
when they did occur was as beneficent gifts or favors beyond the call both
of the donor's duty and the recipient's right. Perhaps a more plausible
interpretation of them was as acts of charity discharging an imperfect obligation to give help to some, when help to all was impossible. In theory it
might be possible to require everyone, to a degree proportionate to his
ability to pay, to contribute a fixed percentage of his income to some
beggars or other, or to some charitable agencies or other, on pain of punishment, but the complexities of administration would be staggering. The
problems would be too many even to mention here, but the most striking of
them would be the coordination problem. Many beggars would still starve,
since no one of them would have an enforceable right against any particular
benefactor, and many might simply be overlooked in the confusion. Other
recipients might collect from numerous sources, if only by lucky accident,
while the most guileful of the mendicants might acquire fortunes.

Any practical, fair-minded person would be opposed to such a system of
enforced "imperfect duties," but if such a person were also humane, he
would desire instead some sort of scheme of coordination that would allow
the starving as a class to be rescued by the wealthy as a class without unjust
enrichments of the unworthy or unfair disproportions in the contributions
exacted from the donors. A modern state's welfare system, with its maintenance of an income floor for indigents paid out of taxes from those able to
pay, is just such a system. Now no one can plausibly be charged with
failure to prevent a beggar's death by not making him a direct contribution,
since agencies of the state will not permit the beggar to die in any case, and
one can always plead in one's own defense that the state's money for this
purpose comes from tax funds to which one has already contributed one's
fair share. It may have seemed obvious to Macaulay that no unrelated
samaritan has a duty to save a starving person's life by giving him money,
but now we all have a general duty, enforced in a coordinated way, to
support welfare with taxes, and the reasonableness of that duty is no longer
seriously questioned.[31]

On the other hand, the random and unpredictable emergencies of life that require time and effort, rather than money, from chance passersby are not obviated by state welfare systems. As Ernest Weinrib writes, "Often an imminent peril cannot wait assistance from the appropriate social institutions. . . . Moreover, there are no unfairness problems in singling out a particular person to receive the aid [thus the rescuer's duty is "perfect" and determinate] and *easy* rescues do not unfairly burden the chance rescuer."[32] It is consistent, therefore, to defend a bad samaritan statute for the latter cases, while preferring a state system of income maintenance to handle the hungry mendicant cases.

4. Omissions and other inactions

Macaulay poses his problem as a question about the punishability of harmful omissions. This formulation presupposes (1) that omissions can be harmful or have harmful consequences, and (2) that Macaulay is talking not about all inactions, but only that relatively narrow class of nondoings that are properly called "omissions." The latter point might seem to suggest another way round to Macaulay's thesis. One might be tempted to argue that bad samaritans are not omitters at all, but only nondoers, and thus are not punishable for the "harmful omissions" wrongly ascribed to them. On this account, an omission is the nondoing of an act one had a duty to do, and duties come only from special relations to the endangered party. The bad samaritan, having no such special relationship to the endangered party, had no duty to assist him. Therefore, although he did not assist him, it is false that he *omitted* to do so. To punish him, therefore, for failing to do what he had no duty to do would be as unfair as to punish any of the millions of other people who also did not assist the imperiled party. The key question about this argument concerns the truth of the premise that an omission presupposes a duty derived from special relationships. The claim that omissions presuppose nonperformance of duties is, as we shall see, very close to, but not quite the truth. But the claim that there are no duties but those derived from prior agreements and status relationships is the critical controversial step, and simply to assume it without argument is to beg the question.

What does it mean to say that A omitted to do X (i.e. assist B)? The first condition of a full answer, of course, is—

1. A did not in fact do X.

But that hardly distinguishes A from the rest of the human race. When Baker drowns off the beach at Atlantic City because no one has responded to his cries for help, it is as true of Charles, who was asleep at the time in a San Francisco hotel, as it is of Donald, the lifeguard on duty, and Abel, a swimming champion only twenty feet away, that he did not in fact rescue Baker. But surely it would be false to say that Charles omitted to save Baker, or that he neglected, failed, declined, or refused to do so, or even that he refrained or abstained from doing so. Hence we must add another condition to our analysis—

2. *A had a reasonable opportunity to do X.*

This new condition narrows the class of nondoers very substantially. It gets Charles, asleep in San Francisco, and almost all the rest of the human race, off the hook. The word "reasonable" in the statement of this condition can be taken to imply that effective help could have been given by *A* without unreasonable risk or cost to himself or to others, or unreasonably inconvenient trouble (time and effort) to himself. Suppose, however, that George, only twenty feet from Baker in the Atlantic City drowning example, and therefore, unlike Charles, possessed of ample opportunity to swim out and help Baker, does not do so because he does not know how to swim. To exclude him from the class of omitters we need another condition—

3. *A had the ability to do X.*

Even conditions (1) through (3), however, will not exclude poor Herbert who does not realize that he is standing right next to a life preserver with an attached rope. He has the opportunity to help Baker by throwing the inflated tube to him, and he surely has the ability to do so, but alas, he does not see that the implements are near at hand. Since we cannot fairly say that Herbert omitted to save Baker, we must add—

4. *A believed that there is at least good chance that there is a person in peril and that he has sufficient ability and a reasonable opportunity to rescue that person.*

To show that even conditions (1)–(4) together are not sufficient, let us turn to a less dramatic example of the garden variety. Suppose that *B* owns a house with a flower garden. He leaves for a month's vacation, having rented the house to *A* for that interval. *A* agrees to care for it, and explicitly to water the flowers. Hence *A*, in virtue of his special role (tenant) and relationship (promisor) to *B*, has a duty to water the flowers. Of course, he also has the ability and opportunity to do so, and knows that he does, and he can do so without unreasonable risk or cost to himself. Still, he does not do so, and the flowers all wilt and die. We can conclude that *A* omitted (also refrained and failed) to water the flowers, and that in so refraining, he allowed the flowers to die.

So much is clear. But now consider C, a neighbor who lives down the block. He sees that the flowers are not being watered. He too has the ability and the opportunity to water them, and knows that he does, and he can do so without unreasonable risk or cost to himself (only some very minor inconvenience). But he has no special relationship of a strong and relevant kind to B (only "down-the-block-neighbor"), and has made B no promises. Hence he has no duty to water the flowers. We would surely wish to say that although it is true that C did not water the flowers, it does not follow that C omitted to water them (though perhaps he did *refrain* from doing so, having briefly considered the matter and then decided against it). There is some plausibility then in adding a fifth condition requiring that A had a prior duty to do X, derived either from his special status, job, or relationship to B, or from some prior agreement with B. But this would be too hasty, since such duties are not always *necessary* conditions, even though they are often contributing members of a set of conditions that are jointly sufficient to render nondoings into omissions. I should like to suggest that the full statement of a fifth condition that is always necessary should be formulated disjunctively as follows—

5. It was in some way reasonable to expect A to do X in the circumstances, either because
   a. A or people in A's position ordinarily do X,[33] or because
   b. A had a special duty to do X in virtue of his job, his socially assigned role, or his special relationship to B, or because
   c. A had a moral obligation to B to do X in virtue of a prior agreement between them, or a promisory commitment, or because
   d. for some other reason there is a moral requirement that people in the position A found himself in, do X.[34]

If each morning, regularly, A brings his newspaper in from the driveway where the delivery boy has thrown it, but then late one morning a neighbor sees the paper still in the driveway, the neighbor may wonder whether A had no opportunity to bring it in (is he away on a trip?), or no ability (is he ill?), or no knowledge (can't he see it there by the side of the grass?), or whether A simply refrained from bringing the paper in for his own reasons. If A decided that the newspaper is boring, or that it is time someone else shared the burden of bringing it in, or that he wanted to prove to his neighbors that he is not a predictable automaton, then we should say that he intentionally *omitted* to bring the paper in, even though there was never any duty or obligation to do so. We could say this simply in virtue of the reasonableness of the expectation or prediction that he would. He also did not bring in the paper of his neighbor, Mrs. B, but since it was not his regular habit to do so, *and* he had no duty to do so, it would not have been reasonable to expect him to do so. Therefore, it is false that on this morning he omitted to do so. If, on the other hand, he had always been in the habit of bringing Mrs. *B*'s paper to her front door, and he did not on this singular occasion, we could say that he *omitted* to give her this customary assistance. Hence, condition (5a) in our definition.

Nonperformance of duties and obligations derived from special roles and relationships are of course other ways in which nondoings, given known ability and opportunity (hence "refrainings"), become omissions. These are well known and need not be discussed further. But might there not be valid moral rules, or properly applicable moral principles, that impose genuine moral duties on *A* to help *B*, even when *A* stands in no special relationship whatever to *B?* Can a mere bystander, a total stranger, have a moral *duty* to assist another? Well, surely there are many situations in which the bystander has no duty to help even though some other assignable person, standing in a special relationship to the party in need, does have a duty to help. These in fact may be the more typical situations. The lifeguard has a duty to rescue the drowning swimmer and unless he is perceived to be absent or remiss, no mere bystander has that duty. Similarly, the tenant has the duty to water *B*'s flowers, and no mere neighbor does. If there is a "samaritan's" moral duty to give assistance, I should think it would be only in situations in which the endangered party stands in dire peril—immediate danger to life or limb—as opposed to lesser kinds of harm or inconvenience, and secondly where no person with a relationship-based duty is likely to undertake the assistance himself. Where there is a relationship-derived duty or obligation, and a person prepared to discharge it, then that duty takes precedence, and there may be nothing required of the samaritan.

Some might argue as a matter of linguistic usage that there can be no *duties* (properly speaking) without special roles, stations, offices, and relationships, and no *obligations* without prior voluntary agreements or promises. There is indeed support for this view in ordinary usage.[35] But we can avoid that difficulty by speaking of "moral requirements" that are not "duties" or "obligations" in the strict or narrow sense, but that can be every bit as incumbent upon us.[36] (Alternatively, as suggested above, we can think of the requirements as *duties* derived from the not-so-special relationship of "common humanity.")

The rest of the argument for the "moral requirements" of samaritans must rest with intuition. It seems beyond question to me, as a matter of both critical morality and the morality that governs us here and now for better or worse, that a mere samaritan *is* morally required to come to the aid of another party who is in dire peril of losing his life or suffering severe physical injury, if there is no person willing and able to effect the rescue who has a prior duty or obligation to the endangered party and can do so without help, and if the samaritan has, and knows that he has, the ability and the reasonable opportunity to do so without unreasonable risk, etc., to himself or to others. Moreover, corresponding to this "requirement" is a perfectly determinate *right* in the imperiled party to the samaritan's aid, implied in his understandable sense of grievance if the samaritan should withhold his assistance. Therefore, if all of these conditions are present, and the samaritan does nothing, he has *omitted* to save the other party, and his omission falls within the scope of Macaulay's question, being both harmful and, unlike the surprising omission of the habitual newspaper retriever, wrongful as well. When we consider that the harm principle legitimizes criminalization of wrongful conduct that leads to harm, then it would seem, in the absence of further objections, that bad samaritan statutes can be morally legitimate.

5. Are legal duties to rescue undue interferences with liberty?

But there are other objections. One way of arguing against bad samaritan statutes is to concede at the start that the prevention of harm to others is a good reason for that kind of state interference with liberty that consists in a *prohibition against harmful actions* but insist that statutes imposing affirmative duties to act are much greater interferences with liberty than mere prohibitions. At the very least, the argument continues, the reasons for *requirements to act* must be proportionately weightier than reasons for *prohibitions against acting* if they are to be legitimate. On the strongest version of the argument, the reasons for a general duty to rescue others even in the absence of special relationships are *never* weighty enough to counterbalance the severe interference with liberty they would require.

Are affirmative duties—like the duties to inform the police, to call an ambulance, to protect others by installing safety devices, to warn another of pitfalls, or to effect easy rescue of another in peril—are these in their very nature more restrictive of personal liberty than prohibitions? Obviously not. Some affirmative duties can be very intrusive; others hardly intrusive at all. Some prohibitions may be very onerous; others hardly at all. What accounts for these differences are factors other than whether the legal requirements are "affirmative" or "prohibitive." If the law required doctors to travel all over the country treating patients, that obligation would be very intrusive, but a law requiring a closely situated bystander to warn a blind person that he is about to step into an open manhole requires only a spoken word, which hardly limits his other options at all. Similarly, a legal prohibition against driving more than ten miles per hour in a school zone limits one's liberty more narrowly (and a good thing too) than would an enforced limit of fifty miles per hour. Therefore, when one compares the degree of intrusiveness of a requirement to act (like paying one's taxes or aiding a crime victim) against that of a prohibitive restriction (like not leaving one's home or not exceeding some speed limit) one is as likely to find the one as the other more restrictive of liberty, depending not on whether it is affirmative or prohibitive, but rather on its impact on one's options (See Chap. 5, §7). Often the degrees of liberty restriction will seem roughly equal, as Thomas Grey suggests when he asks rhetorically: "Is it more of a deprivation of liberty to be told that you have to call the police if you see a person in danger than to be told you cannot turn right against a red stop light?"[37]

Nevertheless, there is a point in the complaint that bad samaritan statutes are more invasive than ordinary criminal prohibitions, for they limit our ability to anticipate occasions on which legal duties may drop on us out of the blue, and consequently they weaken our control over our own affairs. Think of how easy it would be, in the absence of unpredictable duties to aid strangers, for us to pursue single-mindedly some purely personal objectives in life while keeping our moral slates clean. Once we renounce the right, and thoroughly repress the intention, ever to assault, beat, rob, steal, defraud, rape, or kill other human beings, then the rest would be rather easy. There would be some relatively predictable affirmative duties like tax and rent payments, but once these had been allowed for, one could then live one's whole life "minding one's own business" exclusively, without fear of ever committing a legal wrong, without ever being answerable to others, without ever stumbling into distracting duties or punitive liabilities. One could pay the claims of citizenship and community membership their due, avoid the entanglements of "special relationships," honor the requirements of minimally decent morality, and then go one's own way, painting pictures, writing poems, collecting string, or doing one's thing, whatever that should be. With bad samaritan statutes, however, one would never know when some new and unanticipated obligation might devolve on one. Legal duties would be matters beyond one's control, and bad luck might intervene to spoil everything.[38]

There is little doubt, therefore, that in weakening the degree of anticipation and control people have over their lives, bad samaritan statutes are greater interferences with liberty, other things being equal, than most prohibitive criminal statutes. For that reason they require a weightier case on the other side of the scales in order to be fully justified. The harm whose prevention renders the invasion of liberty legitimate must be a proportionately greater harm, as indeed it is in most of the European-style statutes. The Vermont law, for example, restricts liability to the case where the needy party is "exposed to grave physical harm." By that means, the law shows its concern for the unlucky samaritan who stumbles into a legal obligation that is in no way the product of his own making and who then protests with some bitterness, "Why me?" It is impossible, however, for the element of luck to be removed altogether from the operation of a system of criminal laws, even from those that are backup sanctions for various uncontroversial civic duties. "It is bad luck," Woozley admits, "that through no fault of your own, you find yourself in a situation where you have no choice but to act in a certain way if you are not to find yourself facing a charge. But it is no worse luck than that of a person served with a subpoena summons to give testimony on a crime which he happened to witness, or than that of the young man who, if he is not to face a charge, has to fight in a war which he stumbled into by becoming eighteen years old at the wrong time."[39] The "unfairness" of unpredictable *moral* obligations is a much more familiar part of our experience. We expect to stumble into such duties, and take our vulnerability to be simply another of the inevitable "facts of life." "It would be an unduly narrow view of the moral life," adds Landesman, "to hold that we can have no moral requirements except those voluntarily undertaken or agreed to."[40] The legal duties we have to rescue strangers from perils to which *we* did not contribute are themselves enforcements of moral duties that we have not voluntarily undertaken, and they need not surprise us any more than the other moral duties (e.g. the duty to support one's aged parents even though one did not "ask to be born" of them) in that category. Bad samaritan statutes, however, are not thereby *mere* "enforcements of morality" of the sort repugnant to liberals, for the moral requirements they enforce are logically correlative to moral rights of the imperiled to be saved. They do not, by any means, create "crimes without victims."

6. The moral significance of causation

The final argument against bad samaritan statutes is the most impressive and difficult. It involves two central claims. The first, which we shall not examine critically until §7, is that a failure to prevent harm the risk of which was created either by other parties or "by accident" cannot be the *cause* of the harm that ensues. The party who omits to prevent the harmful upshot of a causal process begun by a natural event or by some third party can be said to have *allowed*[41] the harm to occur, but not himself to have *caused* that harm, and in no circumstances can allowing be itself a kind of causing. We can refer to this contention as the "restricted causation claim."

The second claim, and the one we shall now proceed to examine, is that there is great moral significance in the distinction between causing harm and merely allowing it to happen, and that this significance is important enough to warrant imposing criminal liability for those who intentionally cause certain harms while withholding criminal liability from those who merely fail to prevent those harms when they can. This second claim we can call the "moral significance claim."

If we reject the "moral significance claim," then the restricted causation claim is rendered moot so far as the controversy over bad samaritan laws is concerned. Those laws do not forbid killing; the ordinary homicide statutes do that. They do not prohibit causing grievous physical harm. What they do proscribe is *not-preventing* deaths and other serious harms. Why shouldn't a penal code infused with the spirit of the harm principle punish people for not-preventing harms *as well as* for causing them (even assuming that these are irreducibly different)? The statute would be formulated in terms of giving aid to those in peril, an affirmative duty, but the rationale of the duty would be the prevention of harm, a legislative purpose certified as legitimate by the harm principle, at least in its vague original formulation. (See Introduction, p. 11.) According to that liberty-limiting principle, it is always a relevant reason in support of criminal legislation that it is needed to prevent harm to persons other than the actor, and harm to others can be prevented both by prohibitions against harming *and* requirements to attempt rescue, that is to prevent the continuation of a process already begun that is clearly headed toward harm to another. Whether it is action or inaction that is prohibited, the objective is the prevention of harm. On the other hand, if there is a significant moral difference between causing and not-preventing (allowing), then we may have good reason to reformulate the harm principle to restrict its application to acts that *cause* harm. In that case, it would become crucially important to decide whether not-preventing harm can itself be the cause of a harm, and the restricted causation thesis would by no means be moot.

Assuming then that one causes harm to another by initiating a causal process that leads directly to a harmful result unless it is stopped short, and that one "allows" or fails to prevent harm when one does not intervene to stop a causal process already begun (but not by oneself), what does it matter morally whether A causes harm to B or fails to prevent harm to B when it is easy to do so? Typically one's intentions and motives are malign when one chooses to cause harm, whereas failures to prevent harm are often merely negligent or fearful, and thus less blameworthy, or blameworthy in a different way. But the question becomes more difficult if we compare an action and an omission that have exactly the same intentions and motives, and indeed are the same in all other morally relevant respects, except that one causes, and the other merely allows, the same harmful result. When we focus our attention on a certain class of examples, where the harm done or not prevented is extreme, and the effort required to prevent it is utterly trivial, and other morally relevant factors are identical, it is impossible to avoid the conclusion that there is no morally significant difference between them, or at least no moral difference sufficient to bear any legal weight. Thomas Grey gives one such example.

> B has a heart attack, and reaches for the bottle of medicine that will save him. What difference does it make . . . if (i) A pushes the bottle out of his reach or (ii) it is just out of his reach and A could easily give it to him, but does not? Are not the morally relevant features of the situation A's state of mind and the consequences? Yet in both versions these are the same: A wants B dead, and he dies. The only difference is that in version (i) a slight movement would be required of A to avert B's death while in (ii) A can achieve his desires without moving a muscle. Is this a morally relevant difference?[42]

Even if we must say that in (i) A *caused* B's death while in (ii) he "merely" *allowed* B to die, we cannot see why that difference should be at all relevant to the moral judgments we make about A in this example. An even purer example of this "moral symmetry" is Jeffrie Murphy's story (*supra*, §2) of the pool lounger's omission to pull the drowning child out of the pool when paired with the complementary story of the same person idly pushing the child into the pool, when the lounger's motivation in the two stories is the same.

The "moral symmetry principle"[43] does not fare as well, however, when applied to another class of examples. Heidi Malm describes circumstances in which "the effort or risk required to prevent a harm is great enough to justify the *failure to prevent* that harm yet not great enough to justify *causing* similar harm in similar circumstances:"

> Risk to my own health may justify my not donating the kidney you need to stay alive, but it would not justify my killing you if I needed your kidney in order to prevent the same risk to my own health. Or, as another example, suppose it would cost me one thousand dollars to alter my plans in order to avoid killing someone. This risk to my own interests would not, I think, relieve me of my duty not to cause a death. But if it would cost me the same amount in order to save a life (whose impending death is not my fault) then such risk to my own interests may be sufficient to relieve me of my legal duty to prevent a harm. . . . If it were true that, other things being equal, there were no moral difference between causing a harm and failing to prevent a harm, then we should have to judge the above pairs of acts equally permissible or impermissible.[44]

Malm has pointed to a striking asymmetry between the duty not to cause harm and the duty to stop harmful processes already underway, when the efforts or risks involved in intervention are more than minimal. This asymmetry challenges the moral philosopher to give an explanation. Malm's own view is that this asymmetry in our attitudes and practices is justified by the "value our society places on personal autonomy." That value, she adds, explains "why it simply would not be fair to require persons to risk sacrificing their most important aims or interests in order to prevent a potential harm which they had no responsibility for initiating."[45] The account of autonomy invoked in such an explanation, however, would probably already assume the very asymmetry to be explained. How else could it explain why requiring persons to "risk sacrificing their most important aims or interests" by refraining from imposing harms on others (e.g. killing them) is not equally a violation of their personal autonomy?

In any event, the bad samaritan statutes we are considering apply only to cases where the harm to be prevented is extreme ("grave physical harm") and the effort or risk required to prevent it is trivial ("not unreasonable"). They require no one to risk his "most important aims or interests." With *these* cases, the moral symmetry principle seems to make an almost perfect fit. The duty to attempt an easy rescue, to call the police or summon an ambulance, seems every bit as stringent in these cases, *ceteris paribus*, as the corresponding duty not to cause the harm directly by one's own action. If it does not matter morally in these cases whether the harm was caused or merely not-prevented, then the question whether nonpreventings can themselves be causes of harm is indeed moot in the sense that the case for bad samaritan statutes holds however it is resolved.

It remains however to give an account of Malm's asymmetry as it applies to cases where more than minimal effort or risk is required. There seems no doubt that in some cases, although not the cases bad samaritan statutes would cover, "we are under greater obligation to avoid taking a life than to save a life even though effort and motivation are constants,"[46] and that "we feel obligated to go to almost any length to avoid killing someone, but not under equally great obligation to save someone."[47] If it is the *certainty* of an endangered party's death to be weighed against only a *risk* of harm to ourselves, and his gravely serious harm against our mere effort, or inconvenience or expense, however great, why should we not be obligated to go to "almost any length" to save him? After all, everything else being the same, we are obligated to endure almost any sacrifice in preference to killing him. Even though minimalist bad samaritan statutes can be justified independently of these questions, the questions cry out for our attention. We should attempt to come to terms with them partly for their inherent inter-

est, and partly because of the possibility they raise that juries should employ a much stricter test than I have suggested of the "unreasonableness" of
the risk, cost, or inconvenience required by a rescue effort. (*Supra*, §3.)

The greater stringency of duties not to harm when compared to duties to
rescue in cases where the required effort is more than minimal is morally
mysterious only if the distinction between the "positiveness" and "negativeness" of the compared duties is taken to have moral significance in itself.[48]
That would be to convert an apparently arbitrary difference between certain classes of duties into a kind of moral ultimate, ungrounded in distinctions more basic than itself. That account of the matter would be especially
unsettling given the quite unmysterious importance of the general requirement of avoiding harm, by one means or another, to others.

Tracing the superiority of negative over positive duties to the deeper
distinctions on which it is based is a complex matter, and only a light sketch
is possible here. One underlying reason for the general superiority of the
negative duties is that positive duties, if framed in the same unconditional
terms ("Thou must save all of those in need that thou can") would lead to
unsolvable coordination problems. Moral duties, whether positive or negative, are derived from "moral rules" which, like all regulatory rules, are
inherently social in scope and in function. Rules allocate *shares* of social
responsibility to individuals. Their imposed requirements are the dues we
pay for our membership in the collective community. They also assign
persons to jobs, roles, and offices defined by special duties or delegated
tasks. Public morality is not simply a general name for the sum of all the
autonomous private moralities; rather it is essentially a way of coordinating
private efforts for common goals. In some matters it makes no sense to
determine what an individual's duty is in isolation from the public system
of assigned shares and responsibilities. The very concept of a "share" implies a division among a cooperative group. One does not determine each
person's fair share in independence of similar assignments to all the others,
and then hope that the results balance out. Rather each person's duty is
determined in part by the nature and scope of the duties assigned to the
others. In many cases, the content of one's duty is not determined in an
isolated private vacuum; rather it depends essentially on the conventions of
coordination agreed to by all. "What side of the road is it my duty to drive
on?" can *only* be answered by determining what side the other drivers have
agreed to.

Assigning certain important negative duties can normally be done in a
simple and unqualified way for each citizen without raising difficult coordination and motivational problems. As Trammel points out, a negative
duty (e.g. the duty not to kill others) can be discharged completely, and

the duty rarely costs us great effort or sacrifice. "It is a rare case when we must really exert ourselves to keep from killing a person."[49] Thus each of us is capable of assigning to himself the unqualified moral duty—"Thou shalt not kill." On the other hand, we must in principle consult with our fellow citizens to determine a suitable rule, even a *moral* rule, governing our positive duty to rescue, because an individual duty to aid everyone who needs aid cannot be discharged completely. It would be unfair to those who attempt to do so on their own if others do not make similar efforts, and utterly chaotic if everyone tried, on his own, to discharge such a duty, independently of any known assignments of "shares" and special responsibilities.

It is true, therefore, that each has a duty to go to almost any length to avoid killing another, but not a parallel duty to go to almost any length to save others. But this moral truism can be very misleading. Part of the reason why I don't have a duty to maximize the harm-preventing I can achieve on my own is that society collectively has preempted that duty and reassigned it in fair shares to private individuals. *Collectively* there *is* hardly any limit to how far we are prepared to go to prevent serious harms to individuals. Suppose a small child falls in a well. I am a mere bystander unrelated to the child's family, merely one of a crowd of frightened and concerned citizens drawn to the scene. There is very little that can be required of me, beyond passive cooperation and noninterference. But that is partly because I pay my share of the costs for rescue efforts. The actual rescue attempt will be made by individuals who have been assigned that responsibility by political authorities or specially related parties. They are the instruments of our combined social effort, and we all contribute (in theory) our own fair share of the costs. Collectively we regard one child's life as a precious thing, almost beyond price, and no effort is spared to save it. But if each of us were charged simply and vaguely with the duty of doing the maximal amount of harm-preventing we possibly can, then there would be an uncoordinated mess. A system of such duties would be socially self-defeating, and full of inequities in the sharing of burdens as well as the receiving of needed assistance. Moreover, it would encourage officious intermeddling by the overzealous, among other forms of harmful blundering.

Each of us has a duty to call the fire department whenever we discover a fire. Beyond that we have no positive duty to fight the flames. That is the special responsibility of the skilled professionals we support with our funds. The reason why we have the duty to report the fire but not the duty to fight it is not just that there is minimal effort required in the one case and not in the other. It is rather that the very strict social duty of putting out fires is most effectively and equitably discharged if it is split up in advance through the sharing of burdens and the assigning of special tasks. Positive duties to rescue *are* every bit as serious and weighty as negative duties not to harm. Unlike the latter, however, they must be divided into parts, allocated in shares, and (often) executed by appropriate specialists. That way their full crushing weight does not fall equally on all shoulders in all cases, but is more efficiently and equitably borne by the community as a whole.

When all is said and done, however, there remains one class of positive duties to give assistance that cannot be discharged by institutional mechanisms and special assignments, namely those cases of sudden and unanticipated peril to others that require immediate attention, and are such that a bystander can either make an "easy rescue" himself or else sound the alarm to notify those whose job it is to make difficult rescues. These positive duties, like corresponding negative ones, can be discharged completely and without exertion or risk. A sound system of social coordination would assign them to everyone. A citizen's duty to call the fire department, after all, is a vital part of our coordinated system of fire-fighting. Even samaritans can be required to do these social duties, for their cost is not burdensome, and the consequences of their omission can be disastrous.

7. The consequences of omissions

I am therefore unimpressed with the "moral significance claim." Where minimal effort is required of a samaritan there seems to be no morally significant difference between his allowing an imperiled person to suffer severe harm and his causing that harm by direct action, other things (intention, motive) being the same. Even in some cases where more than minimal effort is required, this moral symmetry seems to hold. I have in mind emergencies in which institutional procedures cannot be put immediately into operation and even sounding an alarm takes considerable trouble. When a samaritan stumbles into such a situation, his duty to give the appropriate aid is virtually as stringent as his duty not to produce a corresponding harm—whatever we would say, in the wake of his subsequent omission, about "the cause" of the resultant harm. If he encounters a seriously injured hiker alone on a remote mountain trail, for example, he would have a duty at least to inform the proper authorities, even if it cost him many hours retracing his steps to do so. That is the kind of duty whose burden would rarely fall on one, and whose assignment leads to no coordination problems. It is by no means as unrestricted as a duty to go looking, as a full-time job, for persons in peril whom one can help. That "duty" (unless it were one's professional job) could have very little stringency, but that is not because of its "positiveness" *per se*, but, as we have seen, because social coordination problems would make its universal assignment irrational.[50]

If I am right in rejecting the moral significance claim, then the restricted causation claim that often complements it is indeed moot, and we could leave it unevaluated. A person can behave wrongly, and properly incur criminal liability in some cases, for allowing harm to occur to another party, even if we would not say afterward that he harmed him or caused harm to him by his omission. Simply not-preventing, in these cases, is enough, and its difference from causing (if any) is morally insignificant. Yet I propose to examine the restricted causation claim anyway, for two reasons. First, I might not be right in rejecting the moral significance claim, in which case the legitimacy of bad samaritan statutes might well rest on the restricted causation claim. Second, the negative causal claim is independently important anyway.

Can A's nonprevention of a harm to B ever be called, after the fact, the cause of that harm to B? To begin with, if any nonpreventings can be causes, they must be those that are *omissions* to act. (See *supra*, §4). It would be absurd to attribute B's harm to A's not-preventing it, if A lacked either the opportunity, the ability, or the knowledge to prevent it, or if it was not reasonable to expect or require him to do so. We can reformulate our question then as follows: Can an *omission* to act be the cause of a harm, and if so, under what conditions? We should also note at the start that often the question of whether a given inaction is an omission rides on the question of whether the omitter was under a moral requirement to act. If there was no moral requirement that he act, then his inaction was not an omission to act, and, by the principle we have just adopted, it cannot have been the cause of the subsequent harm he could have prevented had he acted. Often then we must know whether the nonrescuer had a duty (or other "moral requirement") to act before we can know whether he caused harm by not acting (assuming that is possible), rather than the other way round.[51]

The continuum of causal idioms. The causal status of omissions is obscured by the great variety of idioms we have for linking conduct to subsequent harms, and by the puzzling variations in appropriateness among these idioms, even though they are all in some sense *causal* idioms. Let us apply each in turn to a standard case where a causal process has already been initiated, either by accident or by the intentional action of a third party, and it seems headed toward a result harmful to B unless someone intervenes to prevent it, and only A, an unrelated "samaritan" bystander, is in a position to prevent it. Suppose B, a nonswimmer, falls off a bridge into the river. (In a variation on this tale, a villainous third party C pushes him off and then flees.) *A* is standing on the bridge one step away from a life preserver which he can easily drop by an attached rope to *B*. No one else is within miles of the scene. *A* is a misanthrope generally, who is happy to see anyone die, but he especially loathes *B* and hopes that he drowns. He casually saunters away leaving *B* to his fate. If we can assume that *A* violated a moral duty (or other "requirement") to save *B*, we can characterize his failure to do so in the circumstances as an omission, and we can ask whether *B*'s death can be causally attributed to that omission. This question can be posed in any of the following idioms: (1) Was *B*'s death a *consequence* or *result* of *A*'s omission? (2) Was *A*'s omission *a cause* of, or "causal factor" in, *B*'s death? (3) Was it *the cause* of *B*'s death? (4) Did *A cause B*'s death (by omitting to prevent it)? (5) Did *A* drown *B*?

Cause and consequence. That omissions have consequences sounds much more natural to the ear than that they have effects. At a given moment, just after *B* falls into the river, it is true that if *A* throws him the life preserver he will not drown then and there, and that if *A* omits to throw him the life preserver he will drown then and there. It is entirely up to *A*; he is in control of *B*'s destiny. Whatever he chooses to do will have important consequences for *B*. If he acts, *B* will survive *as a consequence*; if he omits to act, *B* will drown *as a consequence*. *B*'s life hinges on the decision, since *ex hypothesi* there is no other way in which he can be saved. *A* then decides to refrain and *B* dies *as a result*. *A*'s intervention was necessary to *B*'s survival and, in the given circumstances, it would have been sufficient to tip the balance from death to life. *A*'s omission to act, on the other hand, was a factor but for which *B* would have survived; hence it was a necessary condition of his drowning. Indeed to say that *A* was "in control" at this point, that it was "in his power" to determine whether *B* lived or died, logically *entails* that one of these outcomes can happen only if *A* lets it happen. And *A*'s omission to act, conjoined with the other circumstances, was sufficient for *B*'s drowning. It completed the sufficiency of a set of conditions which without it (given its necessity) would have been insufficient to produce that result.

The claim of sufficiency, however, is the controversial step. The other circumstances themselves, it might be said, were sufficient for the drowning, and an omission to act literally adds nothing to them. If *A* stays out of the picture, they will be quite able on their own to produce that result. Thus nothing pertaining to *A*'s conduct is included in the set of conditions jointly sufficient for *B*'s death, and nothing pertaining to *A*'s conduct was necessary to the sufficiency of that set since the other conditions could have produced *B*'s death quite on their own even if *A* had not been on the scene. So the argument goes.

It must be admitted in reply that the other conditions would have been sufficient to produce *B*'s death had *A* not been on the scene. But *A was on the scene* with the power to block that result, and the other circumstances would not have been sufficient to produce *B*'s drowning anyway, whatever *A* chose to do. *A*'s decision to refrain then *was* necessary to the sufficiency of the other conditions. In the circumstances, if he had decided otherwise the result they produced would not have happened. And if his decision to omit rescue was necessary for the drowning to occur, the other circumstances could not have been sufficient without it. They formed a collectively sufficient set only when *A*'s negative decision was added to it. All of that seems implied, at any rate, by the statement that the death was a consequence of *A*'s decision to omit rescue, a judgment to which common sense is thoroughly committed. The principle involved is this: when one has the *power* to affect events one way or another depending on one's choice, then the way events are subsequently affected is a consequence of the way that power was exercised.

Causal factors. A full explanation of how something came about will usually mention a large number of contributing factors that came together to produce the result to be explained. Some of these "causally relevant factors" will be preexisting normal conditions (e.g. oxygen in the air); some will be preexisting abnormal conditions (e.g. the presence of a flammable gas in the laboratory); some may be omissions (the failure of a guard to lock the laboratory door); some will be precipitating events (the trespasser lights a match). The result in the example is an explosion. The result of what? Each of the factors mentioned was a contributing condition. Sometimes we say that each was "*a* cause," and that "*the* cause" was their all coming together in the way they did. On the other hand, we sometimes think that "a cause" is by itself sufficiently important to be cited as "the cause." Most causal factors are necessary conditions of the caused result. Some are obvious and unenlightening when later cited (the presence of oxygen); some are critical (the lighted match, the unlocked door, the escape into the room of the volatile gas). But some causal factors are not necessary conditions. (See Chap. 3, §7.) Simultaneous events, either of which would have been sufficient for a given result, are neither of them necessary, but both are "causally relevant" to the occurrence of that result. Similarly, "additional causes" are causally relevant but not necessary: "*A* gives *B* a fatal dose of poison but before it takes effect *C* shoots and kills him; *A* starts a fire which is about to burn down *B*'s house when a flood, bursting through a dam broken by *C*, extinguishes the fire and sweeps away the house."[52] On the other hand, many necessary conditions are not causally relevant factors.

Hart and Honoré mention those merely "analytic connections" that are logically but not causally necessary—"If she had never married she would not have been a widow"[53]—and "incidental connections" (but for a motorist's exceeding the speed limit he would not have arrived at a point on the road at just the moment when a huge tree there fell over, crushing his car. His speeding was not a causally relevant factor though it was a necessary condition for the accident). For the most part, however, the class of causally relevant factors explaining an occurrence will overlap substantially with the class of prior causally necessary conditions. Even ancient history can contribute causally necessary conditions that are causal factors in the explanation of much later events. Julius Caesar's failure to conquer the German tribes, for example, has been said to be "a cause" of the Protestant Reformation. But when the separation in time is great, the "relevance" is rarely even that evident, and will often depend on alleged step-by-step sequences of events and generalizations connecting them that are easily subjected to doubt.

Insofar as A on the bridge had exclusive control of the course of events regarding B in the water, his deliberate choice to refrain from intervening is surely an important element in the narrative account of B's death in the circumstances. Given his power to prevent that result, his failure to exercise it for B's sake had an important role in the sequence of events leading to B's death. We might hesitate to call it a *causal* role, insofar as causation suggests to us an active as opposed to a passive participation, but it seems a modest enough claim to say that A's omission was among the causal factors, along with the falling in, the depth of the water at that point, the direction and velocity of the current, and B's inability to swim, that led to B's death. It was, in short, *a* cause, even if not *the* cause of the harm. (After all, B died "as a result.")

A's inaction, given his exclusive control, was a causally necessary condition of B's drowning. In this respect, it is like millions of other nondoings by millions of other persons at the time and in past history, without which the harm would not have occurred. But in the example, A's was the only nondoing that could be correctly described as an *omission* to save B from drowning. Thus there is nothing arbitrary in elevating it, and only it, among all nondoings, to causal status. Suppose, to vary the example, that A was not alone, but was one of a random group totaling a dozen, all of whom were on the bridge in a position to throw the life preserver, and that all of them intentionally omitted to do so. In that case, I submit, we would take all twelve omissions to be causally relevant factors in the tragedy, although no one of them alone was "the cause." We might say, for abbreviative convenience, that the collective omission of the group, or of anyone in the group, to aid the swimmer, was "a cause" of his death. Indeed, it was a critically relevant factor in the production of the harm. It would still be true that A's omission was a necessary condition of the harm. But for it, the harm would not have happened. And the same can be said, of course, of each individual omission, as well as the collective omission of the group. And given the fall, the condition of the river, and the omissions of the other eleven people—given all that—A's omission was sufficient in those circumstances to cause B's death.

Causal citations. Often we are not content with complicated causal explanations that mention a large number of "causally relevant factors." Rather, for some practical purpose, for moral judgment, or to allay a very particular cognitive puzzlement, we ask that one causal factor (or a small number of causal factors) be separated out from the others and cited as *the* cause of the event in question. In an earlier work, I described in more detail how causal citations are determined:

> The point of a causal citation is to single out one of the certified causal candidates that is especially *interesting* to us, given our various practical purposes and cognitive concerns. These purposes and concerns provide a convenient way of classifying the "contexts of inquiry" in which causal citations are made. The primary division is between explanatory and nonexplanatory contexts. The occasion for an explanatory citation is one in which there is intellectual puzzlement of a quite specific kind. A surprising or unusual event has occurred which is a deviation from what is understood to be the normal course of things. A teetotaler is drunk, or an alcoholic sober; a punctual man is tardy, or a dilatory man early; it rains in the dry season, or it fails to rain in the wet season. Sometimes the breach of routine is disappointing, and we wish to know what went wrong this time. But sometimes the surprise is pleasant or, more commonly, simply stimulating to one's curiosity. We ask what caused the surprising event and expect an explanation that will cite a factor normally present but absent this time, or normally absent but present this time, that made the difference. The occasion for explanation is a breach of routine; the explanatory judgment cites another deviation from routine to correlate with it.
>
> Very often one of the causal conditions for a given upshot is a faulty human action. Human failings tend to be more "interesting" factors than events of other kinds, even for purely explanatory purposes; but it is important to notice that this need not always be the case. Faulty human actions usually do *not* fall within the normal course of events, so that a dereliction of duty, for example, when it is a causally necessary condition for some puzzling breach of routine, being itself a departure from the normal course of things, is a prime candidate for causal citation. But when the faulty conduct of Flavius is constant and unrelieved and known to be such to Titus, it will not relieve Titus's perplexity over how a given unhappy event came about simply to cite Flavius's habitual negligence or customary dereliction of duty as "the cause": What Titus wishes to know is what new intrusive event made the difference *this* time; and it won't

help *him* to mention a causal factor that has always been present even on those occasions when no unhappy result ensued.

Not all causal explanations by any means employ causal citations. Especially when we are puzzled about the "normal course of events" itself and wish explanations for standardly recurring regularities (Why do the tides come in? Why do released objects fall? Why do flowers bloom in the spring?), mere brief citations will not do. In such cases we require long stories involving the descriptions of diverse states of affairs and the invocation of various laws of nature. Similarly, not all causal citations are explanatory. Sometimes there is no gap in a person's understanding of how a given interesting event came about, and yet he may seek nevertheless to learn its "real" or "most important" cause. Nonexplanatory citations are those made for some purpose other than the desire simply to put one's curiosity to rest. Most frequently they cite the causal factor that is of a kind that is easiest to manipulate or control. Engineers and other practical persons may be concerned to eliminate events of the kind that occasioned the inquiry if they are harmful or to produce more of them if they are beneficial. In either case, when they seek "the cause," they seek the causal factor that has a handle on it (in Collingwood's phrase)[54] that they can get hold of and manipulate. Another of our practical purposes in making causal citations is to *fix the blame*, a purpose which introduces considerations not present when all the leading causal factors are things other than human actions (as they often are in agricultural, medical, or engineering inquiries). Insects, viruses, and mechanical stresses and strains are often "blamed" for harms, but the word "blame" in these uses, of course, has a metaphorical sense.

In summary, causal citations can be divided into those made from explanatory and those made from nonexplanatory standpoints, and the latter group into those made from the "engineering" and those made from the "blaming" standpoints. Explanatory citations single out abnormal interferences with the normal course of events or hitherto unknown missing links in a person's understanding. They are designed simply to remove puzzlement by citing the causal factor that can shed the most light. Hence we can refer to the criterion of selection in explanatory contexts (for short) as *the lantern criterion*. Causal citations made from the "engineering standpoint" are made with a view to facilitating control over future events by citing the most efficiently and economically manipulable causal factor. The criterion for selection in engineering contexts can thus be called (for short) *the handle criterion*. The point of causal citations in purely blaming contexts is simply to pin the label of blame on the appropriate causal factor for further notice and practical use. These judgments cite a causal factor that is a human act or omission "stained" (as an ancient figure of speech would have it) with fault. The criterion in blaming contexts can be called (for short) *the stain criterion*. When we look for "the cause," then, we may be looking for the causal factor that has either a lantern, a handle, or a stain on it.[55]

I see no reason to change this account of causal citations except to add that it applies not only to citations of "the cause," but to some degree to certification of the "causal candidates" themselves. What is "the cause" of an outcome is subject to a certain amount of relativity. What throws light on one person's understanding may not be the same factor that illuminates another's, or what has a handle for one practical purpose may lack one for another. Many mere causal factors will have no helpful lantern, handle, or stain for any actual person's perplexity or purposes. These will nonetheless remain qualified though unlikely candidates for causal citation—genuine and relevant causal factors—provided only that there is some conceivable if not actual gap in understanding they might fill or practical purpose they might serve. A prior necessary condition that could do no such work for any remotely likely person, much less any actual one, would not even be "a cause" and thus not an eligible candidate for citation as "the cause." Thus the absence of a dinosaur on the track, though a necessary condition for the successful first run of the Paris-Lyons express train, was not a cause of that momentous event, not only because it is too obvious or trivial to help any actual inquiries, but because we cannot conceive how anyone who *could* come to understand how this event came to pass could at the same time have the expectation that there might be dinosaurs roaming the countryside of modern France. Moreover, since dinosaurs no longer exist, and cannot be *made* to reexist, their absence is not a factor with a handle on it that could in theory be used to cause, prevent, or control future railroad accidents.

Let us return then to the tragedy of the drowning B. Suppose that someone asks what "the cause" of B's death was. If we assume that the questioner is at least partially ignorant of what happened, we will look for a causal factor that will shed light on his areas of ignorance. "The cause of death was drowning," we might say. "Oh, I know *that*," he might reply; "I just don't understand how that could have happened, since B doesn't know how to swim, and he would not have risked going into the water." "He slipped and *fell* in the water," we might add. "*That* was the cause of his death." Another person may know that virtually everybody in that area swims. When he asks for the cause of B's death, we may allay his puzzlement by citing B's unusual inability. A legislator and a safety inspector may be looking for the causal factor with a handle on it. They want to prevent such accidents in the future. They might conclude their investigation with the judgment that the cause of the dreadful accident was the slippery condition of the bridge or perhaps the lack of a wall or side railings. Another person who knows about the conspicuously marked life preserver and rope might exclaim: "With all those people on the bridge how could B have failed to be rescued?" We will tell him that only A was on the bridge and he didn't want B to be rescued. Our inquirer will then cite A's omission as "the cause." That citation will also satisfy an inquirer who is concerned with blame, for of all the causal factors, A's omission is the one that most evidently satisfies the stain criterion. There is then no one correct causal citation for all inquiries. The one accepted by a given inquirer will be that which settles his puzzlement or answers to his practical purposes (legislating, making safety devices, assigning blame). In hardly any actual case will a satisfactory citation mention the depth of the water, the strength of the current, etc. All of that is assumed to be already understood, hence unenlightening, or else beyond economical manipulation.

Another example of a causal citation that selects a human omission may be more persuasive. Suppose *B* dies in his hospital bed several days after being sent to the hospital for a routine bacterial respiratory infection. What was the cause of his death? The verdict of the medical inquest is that the cause of death was pneumonia. That judgment is true, and it will satisfy the type of curiosity at which it is directed. But many observers will remain puzzled. Patients commonly enter the hospital with bacterial respiratory infections, and they hardly ever die of pneumonia. What was different this time? What unusual cause accounts for this unusual result? The pathological diagnosis is unhelpfully silent about that. The inquest verdict may leave practical purposes unsatisfied too. If human fault is involved, who is to blame? (Whose negligence or wrongdoing was "the cause"?) What causal factor can be eliminated so that such freak accidents can be prevented in the future? Further investigation discloses that upon his entrance into the hospital *B* was assigned to Dr. *A*, who recognized him as an old enemy and rival. Dr. *A* then withheld the usual treatment with antibiotics, and *B*'s condition began to worsen. Even then Dr. *A* deliberately omitted to prescribe the usual medication, and *B* died *as a result.* (Dr. *A* was delighted.) *A*, of course, is no samaritan. As *B*'s physician he stands in a special moral relationship to him, and has a duty to try to cure him. So perhaps *A* could be held criminally liable even without a bad samaritan statute. But our question here is not about that; it is the purely conceptual question whether *A*'s omission can properly be called "the cause." Should we insist for all purposes that the disease caused *B*'s death and *A* merely allowed it to happen, or can we say for some purposes that *A*'s "allowing" was itself the cause? Dr. *A*'s "allowing" was the only *omission* among the causal factors, since only he could have been expected to provide the appropriate medication, being the one physician whose duty it was to do so. The unusual feature of the story that explains why *B* died whereas thousands of others just like him survived was precisely Dr. *A*'s omission. It was the element that explains how this case differed from all the others, and thus provides the missing link for the puzzled understanding. It is the only causal factor with a stain on it, and the one with the most economically manipulable handle on it. It is therefore multiply qualified to be cited as "the cause."

Causing as making to happen. Common usage supports the application in special circumstances of the first three types of causal idioms to omissions, though perhaps not without some strain. When we come to the active transitive verb "to cause," however, the strain becomes too great. How can a person cause another to die by doing nothing at all? How can a physician cause pneumonia by simply ignoring his patient? How can he make a patient die by passively standing aside? These skeptical questions have force because of the well-established association of the active verb "causing" with active doing, and especially with the manipulation of objects. The putting of "matter in motion" by pushing, pulling, twisting, tearing, pounding, and the like remains a persistent model of causation in the minds of us all. This physical impact model, however, no longer can do justice to our more sophisticated (admittedly causal) techniques for making things happen, for example closing electrical circuits, initiating chemical transformations, or providing psychological motivations, where no obvious pushing or shoving of material objects is involved. But even in respect to these more sophisticated techniques, as Max Black points out, "we continue to model descriptions of cases remote from the prototypes on the simpler primitive cases, often by using metaphors literally applicable only to those clear cases."[56]

There is no longer any linguistic strain in describing people as making things happen by dropping chemicals into boiling water (as opposed to pushing, pulling, etc.) or by pressing buttons (ever so lightly) to connect electrical circuits, or even by merely speaking certain words conveying threats, incentives, reminders, or commands to other persons. But usage still draws the line short of causing things to happen by doing nothing except letting events take their course without intervention. The action required by the active verb may be minimal and even involve no impact of matter in motion, but it must involve some kind of bodily doing, if only speaking a word. We do *get* things to happen without *making* them happen, sometimes simply by overseeing their happening, or "seeing to it that they happen," but when the "getting to happen" consists merely in omitting to prevent, then the contrast with simpler models of making and forcing things to happen is too stark, and most people balk at speaking of causing at all. When the villainous A "gets B to die" of diabetes by not giving him the insulin B had every right to expect, then even though A has carefully and deliberately "seen to it" that B dies, we are not likely to say he *caused B's* death. Instead we will have to settle for other causal idioms: A's wrongful omission was "the cause" of the death, or he omitted to give B his insulin, and B died "as a result."

Causing as a determinate mode of making to happen. We come now to the very opposite end of the spectrum of causal idioms from the ones with which we began. Here there is no doubt that the causal idiom is inappropriately applied to omissions. *A* omitted to throw *B* the life preserver, and *B* died, we can say, as a consequence. Very likely we can also say that *A*'s omission was a causal factor in *B*'s death, and even, in some contexts of inquiry, that it was *the* cause of the death. That *A* caused *B*'s death, however, we are probably barred from saying. (The river currents, a much more active force, did that.) If we say that *A* *killed B* (caused him to die) this will probably be taken as passionate hyperbole, the equivalent of claiming that he is "no better than a murderer," which is surely true, even if he did not literally kill (cause, make, or force to die), but only "saw to it that the death occurred." One thing that *A* *certainly* did not do, however, was *to drown B* himself. Similarly, *A*'s namesake in the hospital saw to it that his patient died of infection, but *he* did not infect the patient; the bacteria did that. The more specific action verbs imply not only that a person actively caused (made, forced, manipulated, etc.) something to happen, but that he did so in a direct and determinate manner—forcing him down beneath the surface of the water, in the one case, destroying the tissues of his lungs in the other. *A* did not even get into the water in the one case, nor come into contact with the lungs in the other. His omissions may have been a contributing cause of death, and even the critically important cause. He may even be no better than a direct active killer. But he is no drowner, and no infectious germ. Those judgments would stretch the causal idiom too far.

8. The exclusion of causally irrelevant necessary conditions

In a recent article, Professor Eric Mack has argued vigorously, and in a large number of ways, against the view that nonpreventings can ever be causes. The main difficulty he poses for a theory like the one sketched here, I think, is that it "cannot avoid commitment to the . . . claim that *any* absence of an action (or event) is a cause of outcome *Y* if that action (or event) would have prevented *Y*."[57] My restriction of the class of inactions that are causally relevant factors to omissions, he apparently regards as merely *ad hoc* and arbitrary. Moreover, he rightly points out that "the negative causation theorist" (like me) is committed to including among the causally relevant factors in the occurrence of some outcomes the nonoccurrence of impersonal events preventing that outcome. "The absence of rainfall was a cause of the crop failure" is one such example. Mack then challenges us to find a principled

way of excluding from the class of causally relevant factors explaining a given
occurrence the infinitude of other nonevents which if they had happened
would have prevented the occurrence in question. Surely we wish to avoid
saying that the causes of President Carter's election included "for example,
Brown's failure to assassinate Carter, Carter's not killing himself, Carter's
failure to beat his wife in public, the public's not believing that Carter beats
his wife, the non-explosion of the solar system in 1937, the non-collapse of
the galaxy in 1936, and so on."[58] We have already noted that not every earlier
causally necessary condition of an outcome is a causal factor in the genesis of
that outcome, but now to meet Mack's challenge we shall have to provide
more explicit principles of exclusion.

Let us consider four categories of causally necessary conditions that contain both causally relevant and causally irrelevant members, and then try to
draw a clearer line, in each category, between genuine and spurious causal
factors. We can consider, in turn, actions, inactions, events, and nonevents.
Whichever category we are concerned with, we shall notice certain recurrent
patterns: prior necessary conditions are not causes when (1) their connection
with the outcome exemplifies no generalizations or natural laws connecting
conditions of their type with outcomes of that type (this applies mainly to
actions and events) or when (2) the connection is so trivial, obvious, or remote
that it can cast light on no conceivable perplexity, or provide a handle for no
conceivable practical purpose, or reveal a stain for no conceivable moral
inquiry (this applies mainly to inactions and nonevents).

Actions. A pushed B, who was standing on an icy surface at the time, and B
fell down. But for the push, but for the ice, but for B's being off balance, B
would not have fallen. A's act of pushing then was one of the necessary
conditions for the outcome. It was also a causally relevant factor, because
we know of reliable generalizations connecting events (acts) of its type with
outcomes of the kind in question. Pushes tend to produce falls; but for this
push this fall would not have occurred; therefore this push was a cause of
this fall.

I borrow the contrasting example once more from Hart and Honoré.
Motorist A, "having speeded earlier, either was not speeding at the time of
the accident or his speeding at the time of the accident was admittedly
irrelevant."[59] When he arrives (now driving carefully) at a certain point in
the road, a large tree falls over and lands on top of his car, leading to an
accident that injures his passenger B. The earlier speeding was a prior
necessary condition of the accident since "had he not speeded he would not
have arrived at the scene of the accident at the time he did, and so there
would have been no accident."[60] But clearly the earlier speeding was not a

causal factor in this accident, since there is no causal generalization connecting driving at any given speed with the falling of aged trees, though "there are, of course, many types of cases where driving at an excessive speed may quite properly be said to be the cause or a cause of an accident; it may, for example, lead through easily traceable stages to the driver losing control and thus in turn to a collision. . . . In such cases not only is it true that if the driver had not speeded the accident would not have happened, but the sequence of events, traceable stage by stage, exemplifies general connections between kinds of events, statable in broad generalizations, holding good for other instances at other times and places, even though we cannot specify all the limits within which they do so."[61]

John and Mary Doe move from Denver to Los Angeles when their daughter Gwendolyn is three years old. Fifteen years later she meets George, a boy in her high school class; they fall in love, marry, and produce their own offspring, Elbert and Erica. But for her parents' move years earlier, Gwendolyn would never have married George (since she would never have met him). Moreover, Elbert and Erica would never have come into existence, and therefore would not have stolen candy a few years later from Mr. Economides' grocery store. The original move to Los Angeles, while a necessary condition for these later events, is connected to them only incidentally. But let us suppose that a necessary condition of Elbert and Erica's shoplifting was a given character flaw, and that but for the way Gwendolyn and George toilet-trained them, they would not have acquired that flaw. If, as some psychologists have claimed, there are reliable causal generalizations connecting events of these types, then in virtue of those generalizations, the manner of toilet-training was not merely a necessary condition; it was a causal factor, even though separated by years from the outcome. Moreover, it is not difficult to conceive of types of intellectual perplexity for which this factor would shed light, types of practical purpose for which it would provide a handle, and types of blaming inquiries for which it would reveal a stain.

Inactions. Mack's examples of the negative factors behind President Carter's election are indeed examples of necessary conditions that were not causes. These necessary conditions fail to attain causal status, however, despite the fact that there are reliable generalizations connecting such things as nonassassinations and non–wife-beatings with victories in elections. People don't usually vote for dead candidates or for candidates who publicly beat their wives, so these are not mere incidental connections. The explanation of their failure to be genuine causes then must rest on the contextual factors I characterized in connection with causal citations. In fact, none of us have any perplexities about Carter's election that these nonactions cast any light on. If there were numerous assassination attempts during our election campaigns, or if Carter's chief rival had been himself assassinated, then, given that there would be some reason to expect that Carter too would be a target, one might well think of the nonassassination as a cause of his election (though probably not so fundamentally illuminating as to be *the* cause). Similarly, if there is no reason whatever to suspect that Carter has ever beaten his wife, it doesn't explain anything to cite his nonbeatings as a cause even though but for them he would not have been elected. Only if Carter's nonbeatings of his wife were also *omissions* to beat his wife could they have any causal status.

Events. A windstorm causes *B*'s barn to collapse. But for the wind the barn would not have collapsed; so the wind was a *conditio sine qua non.* Moreover, the sequence of events exemplified well-confirmed generalizations connecting winds of certain velocities with the collapse of structures of certain kinds, so the necessary condition is also a causal factor, and an illuminating one at that—a cause with a lantern, if not a handle and a stain.

In contrast, consider a scenario in which the same windstorm plays a necessary part. The damage is too expensive for the owners to repair. They sell their farm and move from Iowa to Los Angeles, where their daughter fifteen years later meets a neighbor boy, falls in love with him, marries him, and raises a family of Californians. None of these things would have happened but for that earlier freak wind, but the wind in Iowa was not a cause of that great variety of subsequent events into the endless future for which it was a necessary condition. It will not explain why the farmer's grandchildren get good or bad grades in school; nor does it exemplify a generalization connecting windstorms with love affairs.

Nonevents. For an example of a nonevent which is both a necessary condition for, and a cause of, a subsequent occurrence, we can mention once more an unexpected decline in the usual amount of rainfall but for which a subsequent famine would not have happened. Given the usual and expected amount of rain the crops would have been plentiful and there would have been no widespread shortage of food, so the failure to rain was a necessary condition of the famine. Moreover, the connection between the drought and the famine exemplified familiar generalizations connecting nonevents of just these types, "holding good for other instances at other times and places." Moreover, citing the lack of rain has explanatory force in this example precisely because of the "reasonable expectation" that a larger amount of rain would fall. Failure of an event to occur when it could reasonably have been expected explains why an unexpected and unusual outcome resulted.

In this respect the nonoccurrence of the rain is analogous to those inactions which are omissions.

In contrast, there was no reason to expect the explosion of the solar system in 1937, so it is an event utterly disanalogous to an omission. Not only does it lack any explanatory force in an account of Carter's election, it is not possible to conceive of how it could shed any light on that particular event for any conceivable form of puzzlement about it. As a necessary condition of *any* human event whatever after 1937, it sheds no light on any event in particular. Even someone who expected the world to end in 1937 would not find that its failure to do so added any to his understanding of why Carter and not Ford was elected. There are no familiar generalizations connecting vast astronomical nonevents with the relative popularity of various types of political candidates and platforms.

Mack's argument against negative causation in the case of human omissions depends on his claim that if "my failing to rescue Smith" can be a cause of his drowning, then "every absence of an action (or event) that would have prevented Smith's subsequent death counts just as much as a cause of that death as any other."[62] Even this very brief sketch of a theory of causal relevance shows that the concept of negative causation need be nowhere near as promiscuous as that.

9. Summary

Among other questions raised in this chapter, two are primary: (1) Are bad samaritan statutes morally legitimate? and (2) To show their legitimacy must we resort to the principle of legal moralism or can the harm to others principle certify them? I have answered the first question affirmatively and argued, in response to the second question, that bad samaritan statutes and the harm principle can be reconciled.

The presumptive case for bad samaritan statutes rests on the social importance of avoiding, at reasonable cost, serious harms to personal interests, and the plausibility of the moral claim that imperiled individuals have a right to be saved by those who can do so without unreasonable risk, cost, or inconvenience. The leading arguments on the other side have been examined and found wanting. Bad samaritan statutes do not require unlucky persons to confer windfall profits ("mere benefits") on others; they do not make gifts and favors mandatory; they do not force people to contribute to charity (i.e. to discharge even their imperfect obligations); they do not enforce duties which, like those of *noblesse oblige*, are uncorrelated with the rights of their beneficiaries; they do not force people to perform heroic or self-sacrificing acts of supererogation. It is not impossible, furthermore, to draw a serviceable and principled distinction between legal duties of aid

that require only minimal ("reasonable") trouble and those that would require acts that are morally gratuitous, imperfectly obligatory, supererogatory, and the like. Finally, even though we must concede that criminal
statutes requiring persons to give assistance do weaken the control people
have over their own affairs more than the typical criminal prohibitions do,
that slight surcharge on liberty is easily balanced on the weighing scales by
the requirement that the harm we are obligated to prevent be restricted to
grave physical injury or death.

Bad samaritan statutes can be reconciled with the harm principle in either
of two ways. If we take the harm principle in its original, somewhat vague,
interpretation (p. 26), its endorsement of bad samaritan statutes is quite
obvious. Both statutes prohibiting persons from causing harm and statutes
requiring persons to prevent harm have as their rationales the need to
prevent harm, precisely the rationale whose legitimacy is endorsed by the
harm principle as initially formulated. On the other hand, in explicating the
concept of harm in Chapters 2 and 3, we have taken harm to be a state of
set-back interests which is the *product* of the wrongful (right-violating) conduct of another party. If nonpreventings cannot be causes, then the set-back
interests of unrescued persons are not the "product" of those nondoings.
The harm principle as newly formulated cannot endorse the prohibition of
omissions, if omissions don't cause harm. Thus to reconcile the harm principle in its more precise formulation with bad samaritan statutes we must
show that omissions, under certain conditions, do cause harm, and this I
have attempted to do in sections 7 and 8. From the moral point of view,
however, this undertaking is not important, because the distinction between
causing harm and not-preventing it, even if indissoluble, is not in itself of
great moral significance. It would be a morally acceptable consequence of
the failure of my argument in sections 7 and 8 that we formulate an expanded liberty-limiting principle: It is always a good reason in support of
criminal legislation that it is necessary *either* to prevent people from harming
(causing harm to) others *or* to get them to make reasonable efforts to prevent
others from being harmed. It is especially clear that the distinction between
harming and not-preventing is morally insignificant in precisely those cases
that would be covered by bad samaritan statutes, where the effort required
is minimal and intention, motivation, and degree of harm are the same as in
the corresponding case of active causation. Where the amounts of effort and
risk are greater, then the affirmative duties of prevention admittedly become much less strict than the corresponding negative duties, but that, I
have argued, is because of the increasing complexity of social coordination
problems, not because of some inherent moral significance in the distinction
between activity and passivity.

5

Assessing and Comparing Harms

1. Mediating maxims for the application of the harm principle

As it has been formulated here, the harm-to-others principle is virtually beyond controversy. Few would deny that it is always a morally relevant reason in support of a proposed criminal prohibition that its enactment would prevent harm to parties other than the persons whose conduct is to be constrained. Since the principle purports to state neither a necessary nor a sufficient condition for justified state coercion (see Introduction, §3), it is not vulnerable to obvious and embarrassing counterexamples. Whatever this innocuous statement of the harm principle gains in plausibility, however, it loses in practical utility as a guide to legislative decisions. Legislators must decide not only *whether* to use the harm principle in this somewhat dilute formulation, but also *how* to use it in cases of merely minor harms, moderately probable harms, reasonable and unreasonable risks of harm, aggregative harms, harms to some interests preventable only at the cost of harms to other interests irreconcilable with them, structured competitive harms, accumulative harms, imitative harms, and so on. Solutions to these problems cannot be provided by the harm principle in its simply stated form, but absolutely require the help of supplementary principles, some of which represent controversial moral decisions and maxims of justice.

I shall use the term "mediating maxim" as an umbrella term for further specifications of meaning (in this case of the term "harm"), for guides to the application of a liberty-limiting principle in practical contexts of various special kinds and in conditions of uncertainty, and for maxims of fairness to serve as guideposts to mark moral boundaries. Some of the maxims in this miscellany look to the parties likely to be restrained by proposed legislation in order to assess the fairness of imputing harm or danger to their conduct, or the fairness of coercing them without that imputation. Others look to the endangered interests whose protection is under consideration, in order to direct assessments of their relevant dimensions and degree of importance, and to compare them with one another and with the interests of the parties to be constrained. Both this and the following chapter consider maxims in both of these categories. These chapters are designed to suggest strategies for coping with gaping uncertainties about how to apply the harm principle in tricky circumstances. They are meant to help the hypothetical legislator by providing his nearly vacuous guiding principle with a little more content, a little clearer direction.

2. The magnitude of the harm

Interests vary from person to person, and so do personal defenses and vulnerabilities. Some interests are so singular and eccentric that only a handful of persons possess them. Other interests are so widespread as to be almost universal, yet none of these, not even the welfare interest in continued life, is possessed by everyone without exception. The criminal law, however, must employ general rules that are applicable to everyone, and are reasonably simple. Multiform interests must be protected by uniform rules. The problem is solved by the positing of a "standard person" who can be protected from standard forms of harm to "standard interests." The law gains greatly in convenience and clarity and loses little or nothing in justice by "presuming" that certain interests are possessed in common by everyone and then imposing uniform duties of noninterference with them. The standard person has certain standard welfare interests including, for example, interests in continued life, health, economic sufficiency, and political liberty. Laws, therefore, can be put generally: harm to *these* interests, at least, must be prevented.

But how great must the harm be in order for the harm principle to warrant legal coercion to prevent it? It goes without saying, of course, that the proscribed actions must tend to cause genuine harm and not mere annoyance, inconvenience, hurt, or offense. But bare minimal invasions of interest just above the threshold of harm are not the appropriate objects of legal coercion either, and a plausible version of the harm principle must be qualified to exclude them. No one would seriously suggest, for example, that repeated rude and disrespectful remarks to parents, spouses, teachers, and others who have a right to better treatment should be forbidden by criminal statutes, even though such discourtesies not only "wound feelings," but indirectly harm the interest in personal efficiency by causing depression and anger sufficiently great to distract and debilitate. Similarly, few would advocate the jailing of mischievous party hosts for putting too much gin in their unsuspecting (and nondriving) guests' drinks, even though the hangovers thereby produced may be sufficiently unsettling to cost their victims an efficient day's work. As the venerable legal maxim has it, *De minimis non curat lex* ("The law does not concern itself with trifles").

Why must minor harms be excluded from the class of evils from which we are given legal protection? One rationale for the *De minimis* maxim is suggested by the harm principle itself: interference with trivia will cause more harm than it prevents. This at least is a rationale that accords with the spirit of the harm principle, and insofar as the harm principle derives from a more general utilitarian moral philosophy enjoining everyone, citizens and legislators alike, to maximize benefits and minimize harms, the *De minimis* maxim finds clear support in it. The utilitarian moral philosophy, however, pays no attention to how harms and benefits are distributed, and therein lies its chief apparent weakness. On the purely utilitarian interpretation of the *De minimis* maxim, the harm that A threatens to B must be greater than the harm that would be caused to A by government interference, else coercion will do more harm than good on balance. But this way of qualifying the harm principle is not likely to satisfy us in every case. If B is entirely innocent and A is about to inflict a wrongful injury on him of a relatively minor kind, it will not be reasonable to refuse to prevent A from doing so by the threat of punishment, simply on the ground that such coercion would in the circumstances be more "harmful"[1] to A's interests than A's action would be to B's interests. Suppose, for example, that A can legally acquire $10,000 but only by a course of action that incidentally includes kicking B hard in the calf. If he does so, B will suffer a minor leg injury forcing him to limp painfully for a week. If the law prevents A from kicking B, A will suffer a greater loss in the circumstances than B would incur from the kick (the loss of $10,000). But to use B as a mere means, as A would do, is to treat him unfairly, and to act in a manner that is morally indefensible. (See Chap. 3, §3.) Other things being equal, wrongdoers are less deserving of protection from harm (or the loss of benefit) than the innocent are—a consideration of justice that utilitarianism does not take into account.

There is a more general reason, however, why legal coercion should not be used to prevent minor harms, even though in theory it would be morally legitimate to do so: namely that chances are always good that such a use of power would cause harm to wrongdoers out of all proportion both to their guilt *and* to the harm they would otherwise cause, even when the priority of innocent interests is taken into account. Moreover, such an interference with liberty would frequently do more indirect harm to the innocent parties themselves than the conduct it constrains might have done. The threat to punish rudeness, for example, could not be made credible without a kind of secret "moral police" and a readiness to inform that would itself poison human relations. The use of force, whether by direct compulsion or by threat of punishment, is not a precise instrument of "social engineering" subject to firm control and precise gradation. Using it to prevent such harms as those sometimes induced by wounded feelings would be like smashing mosquitos with a club.

3. The probability of the harm

The legislative application of the harm principle must also be based upon empirical generalizations about the likely effects on protected standard interests of various standard kinds of threatening actions. Harm to standard interests must be prevented by prohibiting actions that are likely to invade them, but how probable must the harm be if it is to justify criminal prohibition? The question hardly applies to most of the standard actions forbidden by criminal codes, for their harmful consequences are immediate and certain. Aiming a loaded gun at a nearby human being and pulling the trigger, for example, is virtually certain to cause him harm, especially if we presume that he has the standard welfare interests. At the other extreme, we can never be equally certain that a given pattern of behavior will cause *no* harm, but in the case of some forms of conduct, for example walking to a corner shop to purchase groceries, our confidence has as high a warrant as any optimistic expectation in a dangerous world. The problem for legislators concerns the spectrum of cases between these extremes.

It will not do to say simply that only harm whose occurrence as a consequence of a given activity is *more probable than not* will justify preventive coercion. If the harm in question is very great, then a very small likelihood of its occurrence will do. For that reason the state is justified in forbidding citizens from firing guns randomly in the air. The chances are small that the spent bullets will land on vulnerable targets with sufficient velocity to cause them harm, but there is a chance that that could happen, and the consequences in that unlikely case would be so grave that we cannot take *any chance* of their occurring. Similarly, the state is justified in prohibiting cars (even powerful, well tuned, and thoroughly inspected ones) from exceeding fifty-five miles per hour on multilane interstate freeways, even though the chance of harm to others in any given case is slight. Conversely, if the harm in question is relatively small (though above a threshold fixed by the *De minimis* maxim) it may be worth running a substantial risk of its occurrence in order to avoid using coercion, though we should rarely, if ever, tolerate a probability of more than half. The inverse variation between magnitude and probability of harm can be expressed in concise formulas: the greater the probability of harm, the less grave the harm need be to justify coercion; the greater the gravity of the envisioned harm, the less probable it need be.

The important concept for the legislator, then, is neither magnitude of harm nor probability of harm alone, but rather the compound of the two, which is called *risk*. The degree of risk, which varies directly with both its magnitude and its probability, must be of vital concern to the legislator guided by the harm principle. Still another factor must be considered, however, by the legislator who is concerned to assess the reasonableness of permitting actions that create a given degree of risk. That crucial third factor is the independent value of the risk-creating conduct both to the actor himself, to others directly affected by it, and to society in general. There is very little "value" in shooting a rifle randomly in the air: perhaps some small diversionary pleasure to the actor if he is odd enough to have a taste for that sort of thing, and some tiny profit to ammunition merchants. Against that negligible value, the legislator must balance a substantial risk, itself compounded of low probability but high magnitude of harm. The scales will surely tilt sharply away from liberty. On the other hand, the social value of expeditious delivery of the seriously ill to hospitals is so great that ambulances should be permitted to run greater risks (but not of course unlimited risks) than ordinary motorists. In general, the greater the social utility of the act or activity in question, the greater must be the risk of harm (itself compounded of gravity and probability) for its prohibition to be justified.

Every form of voluntary activity, of course, can be presumed to have some value for those who choose to engage in it. In every case of legal prohibition, therefore, some probability of harm in excess of a mere "remote and speculative tendency" is required. But where the private interests served by the activity are powerfully reenforced by public interests, the risk that coercion will produce more harm than it prevents to innocent interests can be avoided only by the use of a very stringent standard of probability. Where the "dangerous" activity in question is deemed of vital public importance, as is for example the expression of opinion in speech or in writing, legislators might well incorporate into the laws some analogue of the "clear and present danger test" often used by the courts to protect first amendment rights. The need to minimize social harm provides a ready rationale for the clear and present danger test applied to the criminalization of expressions of opinion, which could well be extended to other types of activity deemed of comparable social value. That rationale is roughly as follows. There is a public interest, reenforcing substantial private ones, in the discovery and dissemination of all information that can have any bearing on public policy, and of all opinions about what public policy should be. The dangers to the country at large (and thus to most of its individual citizens) that come from neglecting *that* interest are enormous at all times. Some have argued that only the interest in national safety can outweigh the public interest in open discussion,[2] but *that* interest sits in the scale only to the degree that it is actually imperiled. From the point of view of the public interest alone, with no consideration whatever of individual rights, it would be folly to sacrifice the benefits of free speech for the bare possibility that the public safety may be somewhat affected. The greater the certainty and imminence of danger, however, the more the interest in public safety moves on to the scale, until at the point of clear and present danger it is heavy enough to tip the scales its way.[3]

Another consequence of the necessity that statutes be formulated in general and simple terms is that the persons affected by various kinds of standard activities must themselves be presumed to have standard vulnerabilities to harm from them. Persons with abnormally low susceptibilities to injury must usually be given the same protection by general rules as persons of normal vulnerability. Thus, it will be punishable assault and battery for a ninety-pound weakling ineffectually to pummel a powerful giant. The statute forbidding such conduct will be perfectly general, and no more qualified (and complicated) by references to size and strength of attacker and attacked than by references to the presence or absence of standard interests.

Abnormally high susceptibilities to harm create more difficult problems. Persons with rare vulnerabilities should be protected by criminal statutes against deliberate and malicious attempts to exploit their special weaknesses, but they cannot always demand that other people's vigorous but normally harmless activities be suspended by government power for their protection. Thus, a person with a rare and extreme allergy to common table salt must be protected from persons who would secretly put salt into his food with the intention of harming him, just as the rest of us deserve protection from enemies who would poison our food with arsenic or strychnine. Perhaps he could wear or carry some easily recognizable symbol of his fatal vulnerability, like the white cane of blind persons, and the law could prohibit others from knowingly serving salted food to him and to others similarly identified. In that way, perhaps, special consideration for abnormally vulnerable persons could be made mandatory at little or no cost to the interests of others. But such a person could hardly claim, invoking the harm principle, that legislation should be passed making it a crime generally for any one in a public place to serve food seasoned with salt. He can demand protection from the criminal law only from conduct that would harm the normal person in his position. The further protection that he needs he must provide for himself—and of course he must be permitted to provide for himself—by noncoercive methods.

The same point applies to the protection provided by the civil law of nuisance. (See Chap. 7, §2.) There too, abnormal susceptibilities are protected only from deliberately malicious actions. A plaintiff can neither recover damages nor be awarded injunctive relief from a defendant who causes him harm through the normal and faultless performance of his everyday job when that job has social value (or at least no disvalue) and is harmless to persons of normal susceptibility. In an 1888 Massachusetts case (*Rogers v. Elliot*),[4] the court, in a typical ruling, decided against the epileptic plaintiff, holding that "it is not a nuisance to ring a church bell merely because it throws a hypersensitive individual into convulsions." (Operation of industrial machinery that threw most of the town into convulsions, on the other hand, would be instantly silenced by any court.) The abnormally vulnerable person should be protected by the criminal and/or civil law, however, from deliberate and malicious attempts to seek him out, pursue and harass him, and exploit his vulnerability for no respectable purpose. The properly mediated harm principle would surely warrant legal interference with Mr. Elliot if he pursued Mr. Rogers all over New England ringing bells at him.

4. Aggregative harms

The most difficult problem raised by hypothetical estimates of probable harm is of a still different kind. Specific instances of generally harmful activities are sometimes themselves quite harmless. In these cases a blanket prohibition will (probably) diminish or eliminate the general harm but only at the cost of preventing the harmless or beneficial instances too. There might thus be a net gain, from the point of view of harm prevention, in the blanket prohibition, but there would be a greater gain still in a system of selective permissions and prohibitions that reduced the general harm at a lower cost to innocent activity. Probably more harm is done generally by the practice of imbibing alcoholic beverages than would occur if no one ever drank. More than half of all fatal automobile accidents, for example, involve at least one drunken driver. But if the use of liquor is simply banned across the board, millions of citizens will be deprived of their wholly innocent and harmless pleasures. Many or even most users of alcohol drink moderately to promote pleasant relaxation in company or to cope with stress, and do not thereby make themselves the slightest bit dangerous to others. Similarly, if handguns were effectively banned throughout the country, thousands of accidental and deliberate maimings and killings would be prevented. Yet some persons living in unusually dangerous circumstances can plausibly claim to need the protection afforded by a private weapon, and some of these, no doubt, can be trusted not to endanger others by their possession. If the state prohibits these persons from possessing handguns, it must tell them, in effect, that *they* cannot do something which is harmless, because *others* cannot be trusted to do the same thing without causing grievous harm.

It is not always possible to find a satisfactory solution to problems of this general kind, but it is at least clear in what direction a legislator employing a sensibly mediated harm principle must look. There is often an alternative to the Scylla of blanket permission and the Charybdis of blanket prohibition, namely a system of state-enforced licensure. All and only those who are qualified to drive automobiles are permitted to do so, and qualification is determined by an objective, state-administered examination, and rewarded by a license which is itself a revocable privilege. Qualification for gun ownership would be determined not by a similar test of skill but by objective standards of need and trustworthiness. Similarly, "qualification" for the use or possession of spiritous liquors would be established not by a test of ability, but by standards of age and general competence, and would be revocable for misuse.

Unfortunately, all schemes of licensure bear social costs; many are subject to serious abuses; some cannot avoid arbitrariness in the determination of "qualification." Still, they are always worth considering when a legislature faces the problem of generally-but-not-necessarily-harmful activities ("aggregative harms"); for the two alternatives—tolerance of serious preventable harms and blunt coercion exercised against the harmless—are usually even less acceptable.

Two kinds of licensing schemes can be distinguished, although the differences between them are largely a matter of degree. The first is closer to blanket prohibition than to blanket permission. It regulates an inherently dangerous activity, like practicing surgery or carrying loaded firearms, by restricting licenses to a specially qualified minority. The second, which is closer to blanket permission, grants revocable licenses to a majority of persons, based on some minimal qualification like age or citizenship, and basic operational competence, and controls abuses by revoking licenses of those who misbehave. The most familiar example is the licensing of automobile drivers. (Our society, since its disastrous experience with Prohibition, has declined to place the use of alcoholic beverages even in so unrestrictive a category as this.)

Licensure is likely to be more efficiently administered in those situations in which a generally dangerous practice (like handgun possession) is prohibited for all except an exceptional few who can shoulder the burden of proving their own special need and competence. Rules for the police would be clear-cut. Anyone observed to be carrying a weapon of the regulated type would be presumed to be in violation of the law unless he could show a license. It would be easier in principle, given effective enforcement, to restrict the dangerous weapons to those people licensed to have them than it would be in the less restrictive kind of system where the excluded minority could often benefit from a spillover of the restricted objects from their widespread use by the majority. Where all but a few have license to possess and use alcoholic beverages, for example, it is much more difficult to keep the restricted items out of the hands of the unlicensed. Under our present system, older teenagers often acquire liquor or beer from the recently licensed young adults who still have frequent contacts with them.

Under the more restrictive kind of licensing scheme, moreover, much harm could be anticipated and prevented because the state would not have to give each person one opportunity to abuse a license before withdrawing it from him. When the more restrictive scheme is used to regulate activities that are *truly* inherently dangerous, it would not have to honor the adage that "every dog is entitled to his first bite." There is a sense, I think, in which firearms are inherently dangerous and alcoholic beverages, which God knows are dangerous enough, are not dangerous "inherently." A loaded weapon is always in a position to go off, and when it does, somebody is likely to be severely injured or killed by it. Liquor bottles do not in an analogous way "go off" all at once, and even their particular uses (e.g. a given healthy swig) are not so explosive as to carry an immediate threat of total extinction to anyone who gets in their path. Harming others, after all, is primarily what handguns are *for*.

Moreover, speaking generally, it would make the work of the police in many localities (though perhaps not in others) more difficult if householders were permitted their own "do-it-yourself" crime-prevention instruments. The point of having police is to provide a more effective mode of protection than private initiative. Furthermore, the bare existence of millions of unregistered handguns, even though the large majority are owned by noncriminals, is a threat of the most serious harm to all of us, and not only to those who would commit muggings and burglaries if they could. For every criminal who is deterred or apprehended because of private gun use, there are probably many innocent persons shot accidentally, children killed playing with their parents' weapons, hot-headed bar patrons with sensitive egos killed in escalating quarrels, spouses killed in angry domestic disagreements, and so on. For all these reasons, the harm principle endorses a presumption against legalized handgun ownership. But police detectives off duty, householders in remote and vulnerable locations, bank messengers and money truck employees who carry large sums of cash and have been trained in the controlled use of firearms, and others in exposed circumstances, might qualify for special privileges (licenses) of gun possession without weakening the general protection accorded by prohibitive statutes.

We could, of course, license all persons above a minimal age and above a minimal competence to own firearms, and revoke the licenses only of those who prove their unworthiness by committing felonies and other abuses, just as we license nearly everyone to drive automobiles. This would be only slightly more restrictive than the policy of blanket permission without licensing that has prevailed throughout much of the United States. The costs of this more permissive licensing scheme (compared to those of the plan described in the previous paragraph) would be a greater number of deliberate, impulsive, and negligent killings by the noncriminal classes, and an inducement to the shrunken number of muggers and burglars themselves to carry arms and to "shoot first and ask questions later." Shootouts would be more frequent; more innocent bystanders would be hurt; killings would more frequently avenge insults and settle trivial quarrels. The advantages would be a marginal increase in the sense of security (often illusory) of innocent householders who fear burglaries, and law-abiding pedestrians who fear muggings or rapes.[5] The opposite policy of declining to give licenses to all but a special minority might in fact increase to some small degree the dangers that many people would have to endure, and many of these people would feel wrongly deprived of protection they could provide for themselves without risk to others. Responsible persons would have to tolerate an increased level of danger because less responsible persons—other persons—could not be trusted to use *their* defensive weapons safely. There is some unfairness in that restriction, but there is also unfairness in the alternative arrangement in which larger numbers of preventable deaths occur. It is "unfair" to a person (to put it mildly) to be shot in an argument over a minor traffic accident, or shot by a mentally ill assassin using legally possessed, even legally licensed, weapons. Ideal justice could be achieved only by a system which both minimized net deaths and injuries and allowed responsible self-protection, but this would require a degree of foreknowledge in the issuing of licenses that is practically impossible.

The prohibition, with licensed exceptions, of handgun possession is only the most dramatic and controversial example of legal policies that involve a conflict between net harm reduction and fairness to responsible parties who are unavoidably burdened. There are many examples of restrictions "on the just and unjust alike" that cannot be obviated by *any* kind of licensing scheme, either because of the inherent fallibility of all methods for distinguishing reliable from unreliable users, or because of the vast administrative complications in doing so. To cite only one example, and that from the category of blanket prohibitions rather than limited licensing, there is the federal law requiring pharmaceutical companies to market medicines in containers whose tops are designed to be too difficult for small children to open. That means that some responsible childless adults who want aspirins in the middle of the night must first grope for their eyeglasses, and then struggle in their drowsy condition with a diabolically recalcitrant container, to their great irritation. It is estimated, however, that the lives of 200 children a year were saved by this law in the period from 1976, when it was enacted, to 1981, and most adults will think their inconvenience a reasonable price to pay for that net reduction of harm, given that the licensing alternative is impracticable.

It is often more difficult, though rarely impossible, to devise a workable system of licensure for activities that are meant to be permitted to most, and prohibited only for a minority. Such activities are not dangerous to others in themselves (as carrying loaded weapons is, for example), but are harmful in the aggregate only because a significant minority of those who engage in them abuse their liberty to do so. This is somewhat contrary to the firearms situation, as I have interpreted it, for there the presumption is that gun possession is inherently dangerous for everyone and therefore impermissible except for those who can show both trustworthiness and special need. Drinking liquor is a good example of the kind of activity that lends itself to relatively unrestricted licensing, although its difference from gun possession is only a matter of degree. Under most state laws at present, the only "license" required for this activity, which is socially harmful in the aggregate, is a birth certificate showing that one is of age. Consequently, large numbers of irresponsible adult drinkers (though themselves only a small minority of *all* drinkers) continue to cause harmful accidents and commit harmful crimes attributable in part to their drinking. But suppose that the state issued every competent person a drinking license at the time he or she reached the legal age, and then reserved to itself under law the power to withdraw the licenses from those who abuse them. It is hard to imagine state boards using such a power in a sensitive, flexible way, free of arbitrariness and other abuses. People have even been

denied driver's licenses and occupational licenses for reasons having nothing to do with public danger (e.g. Communist Party membership and
refusal to take loyalty oaths). The temptation to strike out at generally
disapproved persons by withholding drinking licenses might be greater
still.

One way to prevent the arbitrary use of discretion, of course, is to do
away with discretion altogether, and substitute clearly specified, objectively
determinable conditions in the statutes themselves. The danger of this
method, however, is even greater, for it removes sensitive flexibility (the
original point of a licensure scheme) from the system altogether. There is
nothing more "objective" than the fact of prior conviction for a felony, for
example, but to throw in loss of license for *that* (as lawmakers are often
tempted to do) would be to add to an already discharged punishment a
further penalty having no clear relation either to the ex-convict's guilt or to
his dangerousness. The most likely group to be singled out by statute for
automatic cancellation of drinking privileges would be those who, through
powerful psychological habit or physical addiction, have been unable in the
past to drink with moderation and responsibility. But this is precisely the
group that is least deterrable by threat. Many of these would be certain to
resort to illegal means to secure drink, and the legislation in question would
simply solve their problem by dumping them on our prisons, a most uneconomical solution indeed.

Still, there are licensing techniques that contribute toward the solution of
the problem, are workable within their narrow scopes, and at least have the
merit of avoiding both Scylla and Charybdis, whatever other rocks they
must scrape by. Experience has shown, for example, that it is easier to
license automobile driving than drinking, under a system that requires
revocation of license for drunk driving, and easier to license the sale of
liquor than its use, under a system that requires revocation of license for
continued sales to a person who is already obviously drunk, to minors, or
after hours. Finding an alternative to blanket permission and blanket prohibition is a technical problem requiring imagination and patience. Only
when that problem is for all practical purposes unsolvable is the legislator
employing the harm principle justified in voting for blanket prohibition.
What cases of the general kind under consideration show is that the task of
the legislator who is committed to the harm principle is not always simply
to compare the relative probabilities of harm under blanket permission and
blanket prohibition and then let probability be his guide to decision. That
kind of rigid mechanical approach is neither required nor permitted by any
version of the harm principle that makes a claim to plausibility.

5. Statistical discrimination and the net reduction of harm

One kind of ground that is often proposed for automatic disqualification for a license raises special problems: being a member of a clearly defined class of persons that has a statistical property of a relevant sort, whether or not the individual in question has that property himself. Statistical criteria are commonly employed by insurance companies and other firms whose expertise consists in knowing how to let probability be a guide to profits. Whenever the state makes some kind of insurance a prerequisite for a license it implicates itself in the discriminatory premium schedule. Most automobile accident insurance companies, for example, have charged higher premiums to young men than to young women, and higher premiums to persons under twenty-five than to persons above that age, entirely on the basis of statistics that show greater frequency of accidents in the one group than in the other. Annuity companies similarly have paid higher benefits to retired men than to retired women, entirely because of the actuarial expectation that women live longer than men, even though there is no necessity that every retired woman will live longer than every retired man. Insofar as the state makes automobile insurance mandatory, it becomes a party to the statistically based discrimination against young adults, particularly young men, and insofar as its agencies contract exclusively with discriminating annuity companies for its employee retirement plans, it becomes a party to the prejudicial treatment of older women.

Prejudice is a kind of unfairness that is literally "pre-judging," that is attributing a property to an individual person, and acting accordingly, in the absence of any direct evidence that he or she has that property, but only the very indirect evidence that other persons who share some resemblance to that person have it. Sometimes prejudging cannot be avoided, as in the life-insurance business, for example. Even then it can seem quite unfair in its particular application, particularly to the person who must be treated as if he has a property that he knows, in fact, he lacks. But where prejudice *is* avoidable, it no longer can be justified as a "necessary evil," and thus cannot be justified at all.

Even if arbitrary discrimination cannot be avoided in such areas of life as the insurance business (where it is used not to annul liberty but to make one's living costs marginally higher), it can be avoided by legislators when they formulate the qualification conditions for licensing systems enforced by criminal sanctions. Arguments of the purely statistical kind could be used (as they were in the United States in the 1920s) to support the banning of *all* use of alcoholic beverages, on the ground that drinkers as a class are more likely than nondrinkers as a class to cause harmful accidents. Assuming adequate enforceability (the assumption that failed in the 1920s), there could be a very significant reduction in the number of serious injuries and deaths if total prohibition were enacted. The legitimacy of such extreme legislation is moot now in the United States, because of the general belief that enforcement would be impossible except at unacceptable social costs.

We now hear similar arguments, however, for withholding legal drinking privileges from people in the eighteen to twenty-one age group, even though the members of this group have full rights and responsibilities of citizenship in various other respects. There are several very forceful arguments against taking this step, which almost any nineteen-year-old will recite with conviction. Charges of unfairness and inconsistency, in particular, are easily made. People in the eighteen to twenty-one-year group are old enough to be conscripted into the military services in time of war as well as peace, yet legally deprived of so common and elementary a pleasure as a bottle of beer. They are mature enough to vote, to pay taxes, to get married, and to have babies, yet in respect to having a cocktail before dinner, they are treated by the rest of adult society as children. On the other side of the argument, the whole case for the exclusion of this entire group from legal drinking privileges rests on incontrovertible evidence that we can thereby reduce substantially the number of deaths and serious injuries from automobile accidents.[6]

The direct appeal to statistical harm is indeed a forceful one. State legislators are understandably reluctant to forego the opportunity to save several hundred lives each year. But obviously it cannot always carry the day when legislatures deliberate over such matters, even when their devotion to the harm principle is unanimous and unreserved. Suppose that the drinking age is raised from eighteen or nineteen to twenty-one, thus saving a certain impressive number of lives. Further research, let us imagine, then shows that the next worst drunken-accident record is that of the twenty-one to twenty-four age group, closely followed by the fifty-five to fifty-eight age group. More lives could be saved—let us suppose a number equal to that already saved by withholding licenses from the eighteen to twenty-one group—by excluding those age groups too from the drinking privilege. (Similar arguments might support withdrawal of the *driving* privilege from those over, say, seventy-five.) Alternatively, suppose a statistical survey discloses a significantly higher percentage of alcohol abuse among American Indians, Irish, and Russians than in other ethnic groups. Imagine that statistical projections show that a likely saving of one hundred lives a year could be achieved by withdrawing legal permission to drink from those persons. The indignation that would greet such discriminatory legislation would be boundless, and resistance to its enforcement would reach violent levels.

The statistical discrimination in these hypothetical examples, despite its effectiveness in reducing harm, is obviously illegitimate, and the reason is clear. The correlation between statistical class membership and a specified type of behavior in these examples does not connect that behavior to any causally relevant factor operating in each member of the class. That a given person is a member of the statistically dangerous class is a ground for suspecting that he might have a property that is causally connected with danger, but the class membership itself is not that property. There is nothing in the property of being a septuagenarian, as such, that is linked necessarily and in every individual case (or even in most individual cases) to being a dangerous driver. Those individuals who are exceptionally danger-ous are so not in virtue of being a certain age, but in virtue of being in a certain physical condition frequently but not universally produced by being so aged. Similarly, we would not be justified in inferring a causal connec-tion between being an American Indian or being Irish, Russian, etc., and being prone to drunkenness, even if it were discovered that there is a genetic basis for alcoholism and that the responsible genes are found more commonly in these groups than in others. If a laboratory test could be devised for determining the presence of these genes, then there would be no obvious unfairness in excluding from the drinking privilege all who have the genetic propensity to harmful drunkenness (harmful, that is, to *others*), re-gardless of what ethnic group they happen to belong to.

Similarly, there is no injustice in barring epileptics, or at least those epileptics who are prone to unforeseeable seizures, from the privilege of driving automobiles or operating heavy machinery. But if it should turn out that only 1 percent of Americans are epileptics, but that 8 percent of all Ruritanian-Americans are epileptics, it would be unfair to enact a statute disqualifying all Ruritanian-Americans from having driver's licenses. In this example, of course, it would not only be unfair; it would be, from the perspective of the harm principle, *unnecessary*. The same reduction of harm could be achieved by a statute disqualifying epileptics directly without mention of ethnic groups at all. As a rule of thumb, whenever a legislature is tempted to withhold licenses on the basis of statistical correlations be-tween group membership and danger-proneness, it should first make every reasonable effort to establish a genuine causal connection between the danger-proneness and some trait that is relatively common in that group, and then legislate directly against that trait, no matter which group it is found in. Only when such efforts at separation fail should statistical discrimination even be thought to be an option, and even when it is a possible option, its attractions as a harm-reducer, in all but extreme cases, will be outweighed by its glaring unfairness.

I *would* conclude, therefore, that proposals currently under consideration in many state legislatures to withdraw drinking privileges from the eighteen to twenty-one age group should be rejected, were it not for one consideration hitherto unmentioned. Age discrimination tends to be much less invidious than discrimination based on other arbitrary factors like race, sex, ethnic group, religious belief, and so on. Indeed, there is a sense in which age discrimination is not even very *discriminatory*. Except for those who die prematurely, everyone is equally at every age at some time or other in his life. To discriminate, as a matter of permanent policy, against *all* eighteen-year-olds is to discriminate against everyone, since everyone, *ex hypothesi*, will be eighteen at some time in his life. But to discriminate equally against everyone, of course, is not to discriminate at all. (Only eighteen-year-olds destined never to become twenty-one-year-olds could complain that their exclusion from drinking privileges is in the present sense discriminatory, and they are a tiny and usually not identifiable group.) It is not true, on the other hand, that everyone equally is at one time in life black, female, Irish, atheist, etc., so racial, ethnic, sexual, and religious discrimination is genuine discrimination, whereas age discrimination is not. For this reason it is at least arguable that exclusion of a whole adult age group from a licensed privilege could be legitimate, even without the direct causal linkage I have claimed necessary in the other cases of statistical discrimination. But even in age discrimination cases, legislatures should not act until they have exhausted other alternatives, in particular the alternative of finding a workable test for the presence of a property that is causally linked to dangerousness, irrespective of age.

6. The relative importance of the harm

The harm principle as so far clarified is a clear and univocal guide to the legislator only for that range of cases where he has no need of a guide at all. He knows that he wants the law to prohibit killings, beatings, burglaries, and frauds, and to permit walking, reading, conversing, and eating, and the harm principle provides him with a ready and obvious rationale for these preferences. Killing, beating, and the like cause harm to their victims, and that fact (the harm principle tells him) is a good and relevant reason for prohibiting them. Since no equally cogent reason can be offered for permitting these patently harmful activities, the case for forbidding them is conclusive. Walking, reading, and the like (considered simply as such), on the other hand, do not normally cause harm, and thus the harm principle provides no reasons for forbidding them. Since no clear reason for prohibition appears from any other quarter, the case for permitting them is conclusive.

Where the legislator urgently needs guidance, however, the harm principle as so far clarified, being largely an empty formula, lets him down. Genuinely problematic cases for the legislator have a common form: a certain kind of activity has a tendency to cause harm to people who are affected by it, but effective prohibition of that activity would tend to cause harm to those who have an interest in engaging in it, and not merely in the often trivial respect in which *all* restrictions of liberty (even the liberty to murder) are *pro tanto* harmful to the persons whose alternatives are narrowed, but rather because other substantial interests of these persons are totally thwarted. In all such cases, to prevent A from harming B's interest in Y would be to harm A's interest in X (as well as his general interest in liberty, for whatever that is worth). So the legislator must decide whether B's interest in Y is more or less important—more or less worth protecting— in itself (questions of degree of risk aside) than A's interest in X. And the legislator must think not merely of some specific persons A and B, but of *all* persons of types A and B, that is, of standard A's and B's. The harm principle, as so far clarified, tells him that protecting B's interest from harm is a good and relevant reason for restraining A, but that is all it tells him. It doesn't tell him *how* good a reason it is compared with the obvious reason, itself derived from the need to minimize harms, for permitting A to pursue *his* interest untrammeled. In order for a legislator, using the harm principle only, to find a sufficient reason for or against legislating constraints in these hard cases, he must have some method for comparing the relative importance of conflicting interests.[7]

It is impossible to prepare a detailed manual with the exact "weights" of all human interests, the degree to which they are advanced or thwarted by all possible actions and activities, duly discounted by objective improbabilities mathematically designated. Drafting legislation can never be made as rote as cooking a casserole by the provision of some analogue of a cookbook of recipes. In the end, it is the legislator himself, using his own fallible judgment rather than spurious formulas and "measurements," who must compare conflicting interests and judge which are the more important. Here we can only discuss in a general way how legislators can and do go about it, which "dimensions" of interest are relevant, and what "interest-balancing" must involve.

Typical hard cases for the legislator involve conflicts between the *active interests* (as we can call them) of some persons to come and go as they please, say what they wish, employ instruments of various kinds toward their ends, and the like, and the *passive interests* of other persons in being unassailed, enjoying their property in peace and quiet, keeping their affairs secret, and so on. In general, we have a variety of active interests in engaging in vigorous activities and doing as we please, and a variety of passive interests in being let alone, or not being "done to" in certain ways by others.

The conflict between a newspaper's interest in publishing news and a private person's interest in not being known about, or in general between the public curiosity and the personal interest in privacy, is a model for the cases in which the harm principle needs supplementation by procedures for interest-balancing, but it is hardly unique. In defamation cases in the civil law there is often a conflict between the public interest in truth and the plaintiff's interest in his own good name. In nuisance law, there is a conflict between the plaintiff's interest in the peaceful enjoyment of his land and the defendant's interest in keeping a hogpen, or a howling dog, or a small boiler factory. In suburban neighborhoods, the residents' interests in quiet conflict with motorcyclists' interests in cheap and speedy transportation. In buses and trains, one passenger's interest in privacy and the absence of painfully distracting boredom can conflict with another's "interest" (if it amounts to such) in listening to a portable radio or the interests of two nearby passengers in making unavoidably audible, but avoidably inane, conversation. The principle directing us to minimize harm all around doesn't tell us, by itself, whether or how the law should intervene in such conflicts.

To be sure, we should protect an interest that is certain to be harmed in preference to one whose liability to harm is only conjectural, other things being equal, and we should deem it more important to prevent the total thwarting of one interest than the mere invasion to some small degree of another interest, other things being equal. Harm is the setback of an interest, and setbacks do differ in degree, but when interests of quite different kinds are invaded to the same degree, where is the greater harm? That depends, of course, on which of the two kinds of interest is the more *important*. To measure importance, legislators must consider at least three ways in which interests can differ: (1) in their "vitality," (2) in the degree to which they are reenforced by other interests, private and public, and (3) in their inherent moral quality. These relevant dimensions of interests can now be explained briefly. (A fourth criterion is added in Volume IV, Chap. 29, §4.)

Some interests are more important than others in the sense that harm to them is likely to lead to greater damage to the whole economy of personal (or as the case may be, community) interests than harm to the lesser interest will do, just as harm to one's heart or brain will do more damage to one's bodily health than an "equal degree" of harm to less vital organs. Thus, the interest of a standard person in X may be more important than his interest in Y in that it is, in an analogous sense, more "vital" in his whole interest network than is his interest in Y. A person's welfare interests tend to be his most vital ones, and also to be equally vital. Where a standard person's interest of high vitality in his system conflicts with another standard person's interest of relatively low vitality in *his* system, then, other things being equal, the former interest can be deemed more important than the latter. Thus courts have ruled (to take one of many possible examples) that a rape victim's interest in not being publicly identified as such is more important to her than a newspaper reader's interest in knowing the minute details of the day's news is to him.

Determining which interests are the more vital is no easy task, especially when we are restricted to a consideration of the interest systems of various types of "standard persons," but even if we could settle this matter, there would remain difficult complexities. Interests tend to pile up and reinforce one another. My interest as a professional scholar residing in the suburbs in peace and quiet may be more vital in my system than the motorcyclist's interests in speed, excitement, and economy are in his, but there is also the interest of the cyclist's employer in having workers efficiently transported to his factory, and the economic interest of the community in general (including me) in the flourishing of the factory owner's business; the interest of the motorcycle manufacturers in their own profits; the interest of the police and others (perhaps including me) in providing a relatively harmless outlet for adolescent exuberance, and in not having a difficult rule to enforce. There may be nowhere near so great a buildup of reinforcing interests, personal and public, in the quietude of my neighborhood. For that reason, the motorcyclist's interest may be a more vital component of the system of *community interests* than mine, though when we also consider the effects of his noise on property values and on the attractiveness of the community to peace-loving outsiders who would otherwise be tempted to move into it and contribute their talents, the question can be seen in its full complexity as a close and difficult one.

There is still another kind of consideration that complicates the delicate task of interest-balancing. Interests differ not only in the extent to which they are thwarted, in their importance or "vitality," and in the degree to which they are backed up by other interests, but also in their inherent moral quality. (See Chap. 3, §4.) This factor will not always come into play, for there is no very plausible way of ranking all normal and innocent interests on an objective moral scale, but in certain extreme cases, all reasonable persons can be expected to agree that certain interests, simply by reason of their own natures, quite apart from their relations to other interests, are less worth protecting than others. The "stake" in knowing, as an end in itself, the intimate details of Brigitte Bardot's married sex life (once the subject of a sensational lawsuit in France) was a morally repugnant peeping tom's interest. The sadist's interest in having others suffer pain is a morbid interest. The interest in divulging a celebrity's private conversations is a busybody's interest. It is probably not conducive to the public good to encourage development of the character flaws from which these interests[8] spring, but even if there were social advantage in the individual vices, there would be a case against protecting their spawned interests, based upon their inherent unworthiness. The interests in understanding, diagnosing, and simply being apprised of newsworthy events might well outbalance a given individual's reluctance to be known about, but photographs and descriptions with no plausible appeal except to the morbid and sensational can have very little moral "weight."

7. The interest in liberty on the scales

Two intertwined questions can arise when interest-balancers turn their attention to the interest in liberty. Whenever a person's interest in X is thwarted, say by a legal prohibition against anyone's doing, pursuing, or possessing X's, an interest in liberty is also impeded, namely, the interest in having a choice whether to do, possess, or pursue X or not. We can ask, then, how important generally speaking is the interest in being free to choose, and also in a given case of legal coercion, how great an invasion has been made of that general interest. The latter question presupposes that we can make sense of quantitative expressions about "greater" and "lesser" depletions of liberty.

If our personal liberties were totally destroyed by some ruthlessly efficient totalitarian state, most of us would be no more able to pursue the ultimate interests that constitute our good than if the sources of our economic income were destroyed or our health ruined. For that reason our interest in liberty is best understood as a basic welfare interest. When some specific kind of conduct is made illegal, every citizen's liberty is diminished in at least one respect: no one is at liberty to engage in the newly prohibited conduct. But it does not follow, by any means, that everyone's welfare interest in liberty has been thwarted by new legal prohibitions any more than a new tax, as such, is an invasion of the welfare interest in economic sufficiency. These welfare interests, as we have seen, are not violated until they are brought below a tolerable minimum level. There may also be a nonwelfare, transminimal interest in liberty analogous to the interest some people have in possessing as much money as possible, though the image of the "liberty-miser" is sufficiently blurred to weaken the analogy somewhat. Invasions of the interest in having as much money (or liberty) as possible, of course, are much less harmful than invasions of the interest in having enough money (or liberty) for a decent life, and possess correspondingly less weight on the interest-balancing scales.

Everyone has a derivative interest, however, in possessing more money or liberty than he actually needs, as a "cushion" against possible future invasions of his welfare interest in having enough to get along. Consequently, the closer are one's assets (in money, liberty, or health) to the minimum line, the more harmful are depletions of them above the minimum line. For all welfare interests there is some analogue of the principle of the diminishing marginal utility of money. The legislative interest-balancer then will ascribe some weight to all legitimate interests including all interests in liberty, but he will ascribe greater weight to the welfare interest in liberty than to the security interest in cushioning that welfare interest, and greater weight to the interest in securing minimal liberty than to the interest in accumulating extensive transminimal liberty or "as much liberty as possible."

There is a standing presumption against all proposals to criminalize conduct that is derived simply from the interest "standard persons" are presumed to have in political liberty, but the strength of this presumption varies not only with the type of interest in liberty (welfare, security, or accumulative) but also with the degree to which that interest is actually invaded by the proposed legislation. Invasions of the interest in liberty are as much matter of degree as invasions of the interest in money, though we lack clear-cut conventional units for measuring them corresponding to dollars, pounds, and francs. The interest in liberty *as such*—as opposed to the various interests we have in doing the things we may be free or unfree to do—is an interest in having as many *open options* as possible with respect to various kinds of action, omission, and possession. I have an open option with respect to a given act X when I am permitted to do X and I am also permitted to do *not-X* (that is to omit doing X), so that it is up to me entirely whether I do X or not. If I am permitted to do X but not permitted to do *not-X*, I am not in any usual sense at liberty to do X, for if X is the only thing I am permitted to do, it follows that I am compelled to do X, and compulsion, of course, is the plain opposite of liberty. The possession of a liberty is simply the possession of alternative possibilities of action, and the more alternatives, the more liberty. Some criminal statutes reduce our alternatives more than others, though as Isaiah Berlin reminds us, "possibilities of action are not discrete entites like apples which can be exhaustively enumerated,"[9] nor like shillings and pence (we might add) which can be accurately counted. Counting and evaluating options, therefore, "can never be more than impressionistic,"[10] but there are better and worse ways of gathering one's impressions, and some persons' impressions may be more accurate than others', for all that.

We can think of life as a kind of maze of railroad tracks connected and disjoined, here and there, by switches. Wherever there is an unlocked switch which can be pulled one way or the other, there is an "open option"; wherever the switch is locked in one position the option is "closed." As we chug along our various tracks in the maze, other persons are busily locking and unlocking, opening and closing switches, thereby enlarging and restricting our various possibilities of movement. Some of these switchmen are part of a team of legislators, policemen, and judges; they claim authority for their switch positionings. Other switchmen operate illicitly at night, often undoing what was authoritatively arranged in the daylight. This model, of course, is simpler than the real world where the "tracks" and "switches" are not so clearly marked; but it does give us a sense of how some closed options can be more restrictive of liberty than others. When a switchman closes and locks a switch, he forces us to continue straight on, or stop, or back up. What we cannot do is move on to a different track heading off in a different direction from the one we are on. Before the switch was locked we had the option of continuing on or else moving to the new track, but now that particular option is closed to us. If the track from which we are barred is only a short line leading to a siding, and coming to a dead end in a country village, then our liberty has not been *much* diminished. We are not at liberty to go to one precise destination, but the whole network of tracks with all its diverse possibilities may yet be open before us. If, on the other hand, the closed switch prevents us from turning onto a trunk line, which itself is connected at a large number of switching points with branch lines heading off in many directions, then our liberty has been severely diminished, since we are debarred not only from turning at this one point, but also from enjoying a vast number of (otherwise) open options at points along the trunk line and its branches. In this case, one locked switch effectively closes dozens of options further up the line. Options that lead to many further options can be called "fecund"; those that are relatively unfecund can be called "limited." The closing of fecund options, then, is more restrictive of liberty, other things being equal, than the closing of limited options, and the more fecund the option closed, the more harm is done to the general interest in liberty.

The railroad model is inadequate in a number of respects. It is an approximate rendering of our idea of liberty of movement, but it is difficult to apply to liberty of expression and opinion, or to "passive liberties" like the freedom to be let alone, and the like. Moreover, it needs many complications before it can adequately render the full complexity of choices designated by the single word "options." Free people are often faced with choices of the form "to X or not to X": to vote or not to vote, to buy a car or not to buy a car, to travel or to stay at home. Even our more complicated decisions can be crammed into this logical form, but the form in which they present themselves to our minds is often many-sided: to vote for candidate A or B or C or D? to buy a Ford or a Chevrolet or a Datsun or a Volkswagen or a Renault? to travel to England or France or Holland or Sweden or Spain or Italy? to marry Tom or Dick or Harry or . . . ? Our options in these cases are shaped more like tuning forks than wedges, and a barrier at the base of the fork restricts our liberty more than one at the base of a single prong. Other options disjoin conjunctions of alternatives rather than single possibilities. When the highwayman sticks his gun in one's ribs and says "Your money or your life," he allows one the option of giving or not giving one's money, and the option of staying or not staying alive, but he closes the option of keeping *both* one's money *and* one's life—a most fecund option indeed.

The "open option" theory of liberty is to be preferred, I think, to its main rival, the theory of liberty as the absence of barriers to one's actual desires, whatever they should happen to be. Suppose that Martin Chuzzlewit finds himself on a trunk line with all of its switches closed and locked, and with other trains moving in the same direction on the same track at his rear, so that he has no choice at all but to continue moving straight ahead to destination D. On the "open option" theory of liberty, this is the clearest example of a total lack of liberty: all of his options are closed, there are no alternative possibilities, he is forced to move to D. But now let us suppose that getting to D is Chuzzlewit's highest ambition in life and his most intensely felt desire. In that case, he is sure to get the thing in life he wants most. Does that affect the way the situation should be described in respect to liberty? According to the theory that one is at liberty to the extent that one can do what one wants, a theory held by the ancient Stoics and Epicureans and many modern writers too, Chuzzlewit enjoys perfect liberty in this situation because he can do what he wants, even though he can do nothing else. But since this theory blurs the distinction between liberty and compulsion, and in this one extreme hypothetical case actually identifies the two, it does not recommend itself to common sense.

Common sense may seem to pose difficulties for the "open option" theory too. The problem for that analysis of liberty is to explain why we attach so great a value to liberty if it is understood to have no necessary connection to our actual desires. Suppose Tom Pinch's highest ambition in life (again speaking in the terms of the railroad metaphor) is to go to destination E, a small siding at a warehouse on a dead-end line of a minor branch. Suppose further that the switch enabling trains to move on to that track is unalterably locked in the position barring entry, and is, furthermore, the only locked switch in the entire network of tracks. It may be a small consolation indeed to our frustrated traveler that he is perfectly free to go everywhere except to the one place he wants most to go. The problem for the open-options account is to explain why Chuzzlewit, who *can* do what he wants most to do, but nothing else, *lacks* something of value, and also why Pinch, who *cannot* do what he wants most to do but can do everything else, *possesses* something of value (his liberty).

There are two moves open to a theorist who accepts this challenge. The first is to compromise his open-option theory (as Berlin apparently does) by admitting other elements. Berlin, in a qualifying footnote, suggests that the total amount of liberty enjoyed by a given person at a given time is a function not only of the number and fecundity of his open options, but also of "the value [that] not merely the agent, but the general sentiment of the society in which he lives, puts on the various possibilities."[11] If we accept Berlin's suggestion some strange consequences follow. Chuzzlewit, who in our example is compelled to go to D whatever he might wish, is not really unfree after all, provided D is considered a desirable destination both by Chuzzlewit and "the society in which he lives." I fail to see how the desirability of D affects one way or the other the question whether Chuzzlewit has any choice about going there. If Chuzzlewit is allowed no alternative to D, it follows that he is forced willy-nilly to go to D. His situation pleases him, no doubt, but that simply shows that persons can do quite willingly what they are compelled to do, that they can be contented in their unfreedom, a fact of experience that has been much observed and long known. As for our poor frustrated traveler Pinch, Berlin's suggestion can take away his last consolation. If his preferred destination is deemed a desirable place to be both by himself and by the "general sentiment" of his society, then he is not very free after all, even though his options to move through the system of tracks are almost completely open. He may in fact be no freer, or even less free, than Chuzzlewit, although this is hard to determine since Berlin, who accepts both the number and the value of open possibilities as liberty-determining factors, gives us no clue as to their relative importance. If society at large does not agree with Pinch's eccentric estimate of the desirability of his destination (a fact that Pinch might be expected to find irrelevant to the question of how free he is) and thus finds the barriers to his desire not only singular and limited, but also of no great disvalue, it will tell him that he is "truly free" no matter how frustrated he feels.

A more plausible way of accounting for the value of liberty will make firm but more modest claims on its behalf. As Berlin himself says many times in his main text, liberty is a thing of solid value, but not the only thing that is valuable. In particular, it is implausible to identify liberty with happiness or contentment, other states to which most persons attach high value. Chuzzlewit may be contented with his heart's desire in the absence of alternative possibilities; indeed he may even be better off, on balance, contented and unfree, than he would be free and uncontented. And Pinch might understandably be willing to trade a great amount of unneeded liberty for the one thing that is necessary to his contentment. But what these examples show is not that "true freedom is contentment" or that compulsion and freedom are compatible (when one is contented with the compulsion), but rather that freedom is one thing and contentment another, that they are both valuable, but sometimes in conflict with one another so that one cannot have both.[12]

What then is the basis of our interest in liberty? Why should it matter that we have few "open-options" if we have everything else we want and our other interests are flourishing? Our welfare interest in having a tolerable bare minimum of liberty is perhaps the easiest to account for of the various kinds of interests persons have in liberty. If human beings had no alternative possibilities at all, if all their actions at all times were the *only* actions permitted them, they might yet be contented provided their desires for alternative possibilities were all thoroughly repressed or extinguished, and they might even achieve things of value, provided that they were wisely programmed to do so. But they could take no credit or blame for any of their achievements, and they could no more be responsible for their lives, in prospect or retrospect, than are robots, or the trains in our fertile metaphor that must run in "predestined grooves." They could not develop and pursue new interests, nor guide the pursuit of old interests into new and congenial channels, for their lack of keys to life's important switches would make it impossible for them to maneuver out of their narrow grooves. Only a small number of kinds of ultimate interests would be consistent with what was permitted, and there would be no point in wanting to develop new ones more harmonious with one's temperament or natural propensities. There would be no point, in fact, in thinking of changing in any important way, in changing one's mind, one's purpose, one's ambitions, or one's desires, for without the flexibility that freedom confers, movements in new directions would be defeated by old barriers. The self-monitoring and self-critical capacities, so essential to human nature, might as well dry up and wither; they would no longer have any function. The contentment with which all of this might still be consistent would not be a recognizably human happiness.

Most of us have fallen into fairly settled grooves by middle life, so the enjoyment of a vast number of open options beyond the requirements of the welfare interest in liberty may not seem very urgent to us. There is no particular comfort in the thought that if I should happen to change my desires or ambitions there will be no externally imposed barrier to my pursuit of the new ones, when the probability of such change seems virtually nil. Still there is something very appealing in the realization that just in case there should be changes in me or my circumstances (contrary to my present expectation), the world will not frustrate and defeat me. The "breathing space" conferred by alternative possibilities then is an important kind of security.

Another source of the interest in liberty is quite independent of security. Enjoyment of open options is valued by many persons for its own sake, in quite the same way as the enjoyment of a pleasing natural and social environment. There is a kind of symbolic value in possessing a library with more books than one will ever read, or having access to a museum with more exhibits than one can ever see, or eating in a restaurant which offers more dishes than that which one wants most to choose. It is good to have a choice to exercise even when one would be content anyway without it. Alternative options not only secure a person against the possibility of changes of preference, they also permit an appreciation of the richness and diversity of the world's possibilities, and form themselves an environment in which it is pleasant to live.

For young persons whose characters are not fully formed, however, and even for older persons who have not become fixed in their ways, the primary base of the interest in liberty is the necessity to experiment with modes and styles of life, and to search among as large as possible a stock of possible careers for the one that best fits the shape of one's ideals, aptitudes, and preferences. For such persons, open options may be more a vital need than a luxury. But for others, the accumulation of open-options well beyond necessity or security may be itself a kind of ulterior interest, one of those focal aims whose joint advancement constitutes a person's well-being. For some persons an accumulative interest in liberty may have the same status and footing as the interests others may have in the beauty of their surroundings, or in blooming health beyond mere instrumental utility, or in vast wealth or power.

Two points about the interest in liberty should be reemphasized before we conclude. The first is that the interest in liberty is not derived simply from the prior interests we have in things we may or may not be at liberty to do. The motorcyclist's interest in getting to his job quickly and inexpensively is not the same as his interest in having a choice among alternative ways to get to his job, and the suburban scholar's interest in the peace and quiet of his neighborhood is not the same as his interest in having various alternative places where he might study. When we come to "weigh" and "balance" the conflicting interests of the motorcyclist and the scholar, their interests in speed, economy, and quiet will go directly and entirely on the scales, but their respective interests in liberty are only fractionally involved. The person against whose interests the legislature or court decides will still have left a great deal of liberty in other respects even though one of his options, in the case at hand, will be authoritatively closed. The weight to be ascribed to the respective interests in liberty, then, will be only part of the total weight of interests each party puts on the scale, and whether it is greater or lesser than the rival's interest in liberty will depend on their respective degrees of fecundity.[13] Criminal proscriptions sometimes infringe our interest in doing the thing prohibited, though this is not frequently the case, since most of us have no interest in the prohibited conduct to begin with, but the interest in open options is something of quite independent value, and is *always* invaded to some degree by criminalization even when no other actual interest is. That fact has little moral bearing, however, except when the options closed by criminal statutes are relatively fecund, in which case it is a fact of high moral importance.

The second point about the interest in liberty derives from the fact that options can effectively be closed by illicit actions of private individuals as well as by the authoritative decrees of legislators as enforced by the police, the courts, and the prisons. Criminal laws are designed to protect interests, including the interest in having open options, from such private incursions. Contemplating criminal legislation, therefore, always involves appraisals of the "trade-off" between diminished political liberty for *A* and enlarged *de facto* freedom for *B*. When the statute is clearly justified by the harm principle, most of us *usually* make a gain in *de facto* freedom that more than compensates us for any loss of liberty to engage in the proscribed conduct.

Since legislators normally have in mind interests other than the interest in liberty when they prohibit or discourage certain kinds of conduct, it is difficult to think of clear examples of criminal statutes that enlarge freedom on balance. The clearest cases, of course, are laws prohibiting false imprisonment, kidnapping, hijacking, forcible detention, and other direct incursions of the liberty of victims to come and go as they wish. When a person is wrongfully locked in a room, for example, it is as if he were an engine on a siding when the only switch connecting to the main track network is locked against his entry. The option thus closed is therefore an extremely fecund one. On the other side, no matter how circumstances may have brought the "false imprisoner's" interest in his own liberty into the situation, that interest will surely not sit on the legislative scales with anywhere near so great a weight, since the option closed by the prohibition against false imprisonment, in all but the most exceptional cases,[14] will not be as fecund as the options protected.

Most criminal prohibitions, however, are designed primarily to protect interests in life and limb, health, property, privacy, and the like, and protect liberty only incidentally. Even these statutes often find some justification in their net enlargement of liberty, though they would be fully justified by the harm principle in any case because of their protection of other interests. The law forbidding rape, for example, while designed to prevent women from psychological trauma and physical harm, and fully justified on those grounds, also protects the interest in liberty to whatever minor extent that interest sits on the scales. That law closes one relatively unfecund option of most adult males while depriving females of no liberty whatever.[15] At the same time it not only protects the interest that all females have in the absence of harmful and traumatically offensive bodily contacts (an independent merit that looms much larger than liberty in the law's rationale), it protects various of their relatively fecund open options from forcible closure by private individuals. All females, therefore, gain protection of fecund open options with no sacrifice of any other liberty, while most males suffer the closure of one small limited option—a clear net gain for liberty. Criminal legislation, however, is not always and necessarily so good a trade from the point of view of liberty.[16] And in any case, it is the weights of affected interests other than liberty that are likely to be decisive when interests conflict.

8. Summary of restrictions on the harm principle

At first sight, the harm principle seems a straightforward and unproblematic guide to legislative decision-making. Indeed, insofar as our models for understanding harm are broken bones and stolen purses, we can preserve that illusion and think of harm as a simple, determinate, even purely empirical notion. The analysis proposed in this and the preceding chapters, however, reveals that harm is a very complex concept with hidden normative dimensions, and that partly because of this, the harm principle cannot be applied in a plausible way in large ranges of circumstance without supplementary criteria (or "mediating maxims"), some of which are provided by independent moral principles. The following is a summary of proposals

I have made in this and earlier chapters of restrictions on the sense of "harm" and supplementary maxims to guide the application of a properly mediated harm principle in special circumstances. The list will be continued in Chapter 6.

1. The term "harm" as it is used in the harm principle refers to those states of set-back interest that are the consequence of wrongful acts or omissions by others. This interpretation thus excludes set-back interests produced by justified or excused conduct ("harms" that are not wrongs), and violations of rights that do not set back interests (wrongs that are not "harms"). A harm in the appropriate sense then will be produced by morally indefensible conduct that not only sets back the victim's interest, but also violates his right. A right, in turn, was analyzed as a valid claim against another's conduct, and what gives cogency to a claim is the set of reasons that can be proffered in its support. There is room for normative controversy over which kinds of consideration constitute good reasons for a claim, but I have concluded (subject to the exceptions mentioned in [2] below) that any interest simply *qua* interest constitutes a proper kind of reason (among others) in support of claims against other people. A claim becomes valid, and thus a right, when its rational support is not merely relevant and cogent, but decisive.

2. If there are such things as malicious interests, or patently wicked or morbid interests (and their existence may well be doubted), then these are exceptions to the generalization that all interests simply as such provide good reasons in support of claims to noninterference by, or assistance from, others. Consequently, the thwarting of a sadistic or morbid interest would not count as "harm" in the sense that term bears in the harm principle, and the technical sense of "harm" is further narrowed.

3. When B voluntarily consents to an action of A's that sets back one of his own interests, or voluntarily assumes the risk, in advance, that A's action will adversely affect one of his interests, then A's action is not "indefensible," since B's consent has given him a justification. B's consent is a waiver of his right, hence even if A's action causes B harm (in the sense of set-back interest) it does him no wrong, and does not therefore count as "harm" in the special sense required by the harm principle. *Volenti non fit injuria* is a mediating maxim for the application of the harm principle.

4. The analysis of "harm" even in the broad untechnical sense rules out mere transitory disappointments, minor physical and mental "hurts,"

and a miscellany of disliked states of mind, including various forms of offendedness, anxiety, and boredom as harms, since harm in the broad sense is any setback of an interest, and there is (typically) no interest in the avoidance of such states. (Although they are not harms, however, nothing need prevent us from judging them evils of another kind than harm.)

5. Minor or trivial harms *are* harms despite their minor magnitude and triviality, but below a certain threshold they are not to count as harms for the purposes of the harm principle, for legal interference with trivia is likely to cause more harm than it prevents, not only to the person directly interfered with, but even to his innocent victim (whose interests must be given priority in our legislative calculations) and to various third parties. *De minimis non curat lex*, interpreted in a way that is consistent with the priority of innocent over mischievous interests, is a mediating maxim for the application of the harm principle.

6. For cases where harm or the lack thereof is a less then certain consequence of a given kind of conduct, that is, where the kind of conduct in question is neither perfectly harmless nor directly and necessarily harmful, so far as we can tell, but does create a danger to some degree, legislators employing the harm principle must use various rules of thumb as best they can:

    a. the greater the *gravity* of a possible harm, the less probable its occurrence need be to justify prohibition of the conduct that threatens to produce it;

    b. the greater the *probability* of harm, the less grave the harm need be to justify coercion;

    c. the greater the *magnitude of the risk* of harm, itself compounded out of gravity and probability, the less reasonable it is to accept the risk;

    d. the more *valuable* (useful) the dangerous conduct, both to the actor and to others, the more reasonable it is to take the risk of harmful consequences, and for extremely valuable conduct it is reasonable to run risks up to the point of clear and present danger;

    e. the more *reasonable* the risk of harm (the danger), the weaker is the case for prohibiting the conduct that creates it.

7. For unavoidable practical reasons, persons with abnormally low susceptibilities to injury are to be given the same protection by general rules as persons of normal vulnerability.

8. Persons with rare vulnerabilities to harm, however, cannot properly claim against the state that it protect them by using the criminal law to suspend the vigorous and normally harmless activities of other people. In those respects in which others can modulate their conduct without

serious inconvenience to avoid harming vulnerable people when those people are easily identifiable (like the blind), then the law can legitimately require them to do so. And in any case, the abnormally vulnerable person should be protected by the law from unnecessary, deliberate, and malicious efforts to exploit his vulnerability.

9. Where *aggregative harms* are unevenly produced by persons engaging in a common form of dangerous activity, so that blanket permission would not prevent the harms, whereas blanket prohibition would interfere with harmless and beneficial as well as harmful instances of the activity, the legislature should attempt to regulate the activity through a system of selective licensure, and resort to blanket prohibition only when licensing schemes are unworkable. That morally significant differences among the persons who engage in an activity should be treated differently by the law when it is practicable to do so, is a mediating maxim for the application of the harm principle.

10. When opposed interests of different kinds are related in such a way that if the law is silent then the one will be set back to a certain degree, whereas if the law protects that one then the other will be thwarted to the same degree, the legislature should protect that interest which is the more *important*. Relative importance is a function of three different respects in which opposed interests can be compared:
    a. how "vital" they are in the interest networks of their possessors;
    b. the degree to which they are reenforced by other interests, private and public;
    c. their inherent moral quality.

11. Since an invasion of the *interest in liberty* is a harm, it follows that all legal prohibitions, insofar as they narrow options, cause some harm which must be taken into account in the calculations of the legislator. The legislative invasion of citizens' interests in liberty can be justified by the harm principle only if necessary to prevent the greater harm still that would be caused to victims of the proscribed conduct. But the interest in liberty plays a relevant role in these calculations only to the extent that it would actually be invaded by the contemplated legislation. The more *fecund* the option closed, the greater the invasion of liberty, so legislation that closes many key options indirectly by closing a given option directly is more difficult to justify, other things being equal, than legislation that closes only a limited option. Invasions of interests of the latter kind are "trivial harms" merely. In most cases, the interests that are seriously invaded by coercive legislation are interests other than the generalized interest in liberty.

6

Fairly Imputing Harms

1. Competitive interests

The world is full of situations which are such that the interests of one party can be advanced only at the expense of the interests of others, and vice versa, or—even more unhappily—such that the interests of one party can avoid being defeated or thwarted only if that party acts in a way that will set back the interests of another party and vice versa. In the absence of an "invisible hand" reconciling conflicting interests, what is good for producers may in some circumstances be bad for consumers, and what is good for farmers may be bad for ranchers. In many of our procedures for resolving conflicts, a vote, judgment, or verdict that helps one contending party must inevitably harm the opposing party. Where there are shortages of needed goods and instrumentalities, often one party cannot claim his share without depriving another party of what he needs, thereby causing "harm" to his interests. Some of these conflicts are eliminable by the redesign of defective institutions or the elimination of shortages; others, like the competition between suitors for a lady's hand, seem for all practical purposes to be inherent in the human condition.

Interests of different persons that are related to one another in such a way that one can avoid being harmed only if another is harmed instead, can be called "competitive interests." Some competitive interests are aimed at particular objectives that could *in principle* be achieved without harming others. These are only contingently competitive. One can always conceive of the elimination of a particular shortage, or the disappearance of a particular rival, or a compromise that would cost the contending parties very little. The conflict between the interests of the motorcyclist and the suburban scholar, in our previous example (Chap. 5, §6), is only contingently competitive in this sense. The parties might both accept a rule allowing motorcycle traffic in the area only at certain hours, or only if motors are properly muffled, or the like. Other interests, however, are "competitive" in a much stronger sense. These are aimed at achieving, partly for its own sake, a certain position relative to others. Priority, victory, ascendance over others, are essential to their very conception, rather than incidental and unwanted byproducts of the context in which they are nourished. There are many highly competitive persons who possess as stable ulterior goals or focal aims an interest in being superior to others in some respect. There are various ways, for example, of having an interest in playing tennis. One can seek tennis-playing opportunities as a means of promoting one's welfare interest in health, or as a way of cultivating a special form of excellence valued (as one's own ballet dancing or painting may be valued) as an end in itself. But if one's interest in tennis is primarily an interest in winning cups, trophies, and high rankings relative to others, then that interest is an intrinsically (not merely contingently) competitive one. The significant characteristic of intrinsically competitive interests taken as a group is that some must necessarily be set back (thus "harmed") in the very nature of the case. So long as there are tennis matches there will be losers, and as long as players have an interest in winning (as such), some interests will inevitably be thwarted.

In the special sense we have ascribed to the word "harm," however, it is not always true that a person has been harmed when his interests have been thwarted. An interest is harmed in the special sense required by a plausible harm principle only when its possessor is wronged by the action or omission that does the thwarting, and one is wronged only when the interest-invading act has neither justification nor excuse. No one would claim that victors in voluntarily undertaken tennis matches wrong the losers in beating them, or that lovers wrong disappointed suitors in the very act of marrying. As Mill put it:

> Whoever succeeds in an overcrowded profession, or in a competitive examination; whoever is preferred to another in any contest for an object which both desire, reaps benefit from the loss of others, from their wasted exertion and their disappointment. But it is, by common admission, better for the general interest of mankind, that persons should pursue their objects, undeterred by this sort of consequence. In other words, society admits no right, either legal or moral, in the disappointed competitors to immunity from this kind of suffering. . . .[1]

Not all competitive setbacks then are harmful in the requisite sense.

In fact, defeat in a competition is a harm only when the form of competition itself is somehow morally illegitimate or else the defeat was inflicted in an unfair way—by fraud, treachery, or force. The business of the state then, as determined by the harm principle, is restricted to the prohibition of illegitimate forms of competition and the enforcement of procedural rules governing competitions, at the very most. When is a form of competition "legitimate"? Various clear cases come to mind quickly. Competitive relationships that are natural and inevitable can be mentioned first. These are, in Mill's words, not merely "oppositions of interest" that arise from "bad social institutions [and] are unavoidable while those institutions last," but those which would be "unavoidable under any institutions." Then there are instances of competition of a more artificial kind, made possible by social conventions and structures of rules within institutions that may or may not themselves be defective, but which are entered into in a fully voluntary way by the competitors, each of whom is fully and accurately apprised of the risk, and free of coercive pressure or manipulation. As we have seen, a person cannot be wronged by that to which he voluntarily consents. A person may suffer defeat in the competition, and that may seriously set back his interests, but if he has freely consented to the risk in advance, his loss does not count as a harm for the purposes of a plausible harm principle as mediated by the *Volenti* maxim. A professional boxer, in suffering a crucial defeat, may suffer irreparable harm to his intrinsically competitive interest and also harm to his interests in health and wealth, but these effects would count as wrongs only if boxing matches in general are illegitimate in some way, or if this particular match was unfairly arranged or involuntarily entered, or if the opposing boxer cheated (e.g. by concealing a brick in his glove).

A form of competition is illegitimate if it is "avoidable" in Mill's sense, and also if either (1) it is so structured that genuinely voluntary consent to serious risks is practically impossible to secure or confirm, or else (2) it is necessarily harmful to the interests of third parties or to the interest of the public at large.

An instructive example of a form of competition that is illegitimate in both these ways, but which might at first glance seem not properly prohibitable according to our qualified harm principle, is that of the duel. Under the old *code duello* that governed the conduct of the noble-born for many centuries, one party's affront to the "honor" of another could be answered by a challenge to a test of arms. The recipient of the challenge then had the "option" of accepting or declining it. If he accepted, he was placed in the dreadful position of either killing or endangering another human being or being himself killed (or endangered). If he rejected the challenge, he would become thoroughly disgraced in his own social circle. A single voluntary act of one person (the challenger) imposes an inescapable dilemma on the other: either kill-or-be-killed or be disgraced. The acceptance of the challenge under such circumstances could hardly be described as a fully voluntary assumption of risk, free of coercive pressures. The very social practice of the duel is illegitimate precisely because it forces persons into dreadful risks in circumstances that make genuine consent usually impossible, and at best, always suspect.

But even on the assumption that genuinely mutual consent to a duel would sometimes be possible, there is a strong moral case against the practice of dueling based on other grounds. Homicide is a morally serious matter to which no society that values its own interests can be altogether indifferent. Historically, of course, dueling was confined to a relatively small part of the population, but if it were allowed to take root in a democracy and become a legally recognized method available to *everybody* for gaining "satisfaction" for insults, one might reasonably expect the toll in dead bodies to be so high that the general social well-being would be affected. Every time a duelist was killed or maimed, his widow and children would need support; those who loved him would be directly harmed in their other-regarding interest; those colleagues, contractors, and subordinates who depend on him would be indirectly harmed in their economic or vocational interests; the smooth flow of public business would be disrupted. Moreover, if dueling were the general practice, malicious plots on life would be encouraged; respect for life would diminish; socially useful forms of competition would be avoided for fear of fatal complications; arrogant bullies would terrorize all social intercourse; general insecurity would increase. These results would harm the interests of everyone (with the possible exception of fencing coaches, mobsters, and romantic paranoiacs). In short, even a truly voluntary agreement between two hate-filled enemies would be a "contract" of the kind that is very much against the public interest, and there would be no practical way of privileging exceptional cases by a system of licensure that would not be arbitrary and potentially corrupt.[2]

2. Harm to Public Interests

Much the same kinds of questions can be raised about a working-class analogue of the duel: settling a quarrel by a test of fisticuffs. The rules for this dubious practice are not codified in the precise and complete manner of the *code duello*, but in their general outlines they are well understood. Many a barroom quarrel has culminated in an unfriendly invitation to "step out-side and settle this matter." If the two adversaries then settle their griev-ances in a quiet unobserved place, they cannot be charged with an affray or public disturbance. Each of them can be understood, at least in some clear cases, voluntarily to assume the risk of personal injury to himself, and also to promise tacitly not to inflict a beating on the other beyond what is required to establish a clear victory. Declining an invitation to fight may be a way to lose face with one's acquaintances, but it is hardly as humiliating as the total disgrace that could ruin the life of a nobleman who declined a challenge to duel. Physical injuries would surely result from the fight—lacerations, bruises, broken bones—but these would hardly ever lead to permanent disablement or death. To make such conduct criminal would be to tell grown men that they are not permitted to engage privately in prima-rily self-regarding conduct to which they have both consented. If criminal prohibition of their conduct is to be justified by the harm principle, it must be on the ground that it is necessary to prevent harm to public interests.

The problem is that "the public interest" is so very vague a conception that there is no clear way of applying it to nonobvious cases like the "volun-tary fisticuffs" example. Advocates of legal coercion are always tempted to use the elasticity of the "public interest" to stretch the harm principle so that it will justify criminal prohibition of disapproved conduct that is at first sight harmless to persons other than the actors, so we should proceed very cautiously. The difference between the dueling and fisticuffs ex-amples, of course, is largely one of degree. In both cases social conventions place coercive pressures on the person who must decide whether to accept an offer, but these pressures are more invariant and severe in the dueling example. Likewise, in both cases the activity in question, even when truly voluntary, adversely affects the public interest in the smooth flow of busi-ness, in having a low rate of industrial absenteeism (which would be caused by injuries), in uninhibited social discourse (without fear of arrogant bullies), and in general security. The problem for lawmakers then may be largely empirical: are these interests affected *to a sufficient degree* to outbal-ance the harm involved in the state's invasion of the adversaries' interests in liberty? But the legislator's problem is only partly empirical. He must also understand the elusive concept of a "public interest" that seems to belong to no one in particular, and understand it well enough to identify all the public interests that may be involved, and the source of the weight they have when they *are* involved.

What is a public interest? What kinds of harms are public harms? There are in general two closely connected conceptions. According to one, a "pub-lic interest" is a collection of specific interests of the same kind possessed by a large and indefinite number of private individuals. The interests in the collection do not necessarily belong to everyone, but they could belong to *anyone*, without further specification. These interests are not all based on one and the same goal X, but rather on distinct objectives that are all of the same X-ish kind. Thus Jones may have an interest in his own X, and Smith in *his* own X, and almost anyone picked at random from the general public might have an interest in his own X. Public harms, on this conception, are those produced by generally dangerous activity that threatens no specific persons namable in advance, but almost anyone who happens to be in a position to be affected. These activities produce some common danger to all the members of the community, or in Bentham's words, "to an unassignable indefinite multitude of the whole number of individuals of which the community is composed, although no particular individual should appear more likely to be a sufferer by them than another."[3] Poison dropped in a city's water supply would cause public harm in this sense, not necessarily causing injury to everyone in the city, but causing a "common danger" to all, and actual injury to a large and indefinite number of persons, unidentifiable (or in Bentham's term, "unassignable") in advance, who drink the water before a warning can be disseminated. A large bomb placed in Grand Central Station in Manhattan would also threaten "the public at large" in this fashion and thus constitute a "public harm."

According to the second conception, a public interest is a "common," or widely shared, specific interest. Common interests are interests that all or most persons in a community have in one and precisely the same thing, not an interest that each has in his own X, but an interest that each has in one and the same X. Almost everyone has an interest in the promotion of economic prosperity, that is, in the avoidance of recession and inflation. Almost everyone has an interest in the prevention of other "public disasters": depression, war, plague, famine, drought, contamination of the environment, riots, crime waves, social hatreds, spreading distrust and incivility. Less dramatic but equally real is the interest nearly everyone has in the maintenance of public services: garbage collection (even people who make no garbage of their own have an interest that other people's garbage be collected), street lighting, the provision of electric power, telephone and postal services, police protection, and the like. The collapse of these services too would be a public harm in the second sense: the defeating of a single interest that almost everyone shares.

Not all people, of course, share a given common interest to the same degree. Everyone, perhaps without exception, has an interest in avoiding an economic depression and the widespread suffering, bitterness, and political instability that would inevitably attend it. But depressions are not equally

hard on everyone, and are actually good for some businesses. Bread manufacturers sell more bread when persons cannot afford fancier and more
expensive foods, and thus they profit from depressions much as munitions
makers profit from war. Still, even bread manufacturers, in their capacities
as citizens leery of threatening mobs and totalitarian governments, and as
friends, lovers, or patriots with genuinely other-regarding concerns, share
the common interest in avoiding depressions. In a given case, the economic
interest in profits *may* be a stronger interest on balance—a larger component
of the manufacturer's net interest as a person—than his shared interest in
social contentment and political stability, but to some degree or other,
despite his special circumstances, the latter interests will be his too.

A distinction is thus presupposed between a "component interest" of a
person who plays various social roles, and his "resultant" personal interest
on balance. In respect to common interests, for example interests in avoiding disasters like depressions, epidemics, and wars, the more widely shared
interests will be "component" ones, and it is doubtful whether there is any
"resultant" interest shared perfectly generally by *everybody*. The distinction,
in somewhat different terms, is well explained by Brian Barry:

> . . . a person may be affected in a number of different ways by a certain
> policy as he is impinged upon by it in different roles or capacities. As a
> motorist, tighter enforcement of the speed limit is not in his interest, as a
> pedestrian it is; as an importer of some raw materials it is not in his interests to
> have higher tariffs all around, as a seller who has to compete with foreign rivals
> it is; and so on. I shall therefore distinguish between a man's interests *as a φ*
> (that is, in some particular capacity) and his *net interest* in a policy (that is, how
> he is affected overall, striking a balance between the pluses and minuses in-
> curred in his various capacities).[4]

A public interest in the strongest possible sense would be a resultant interest shared by everybody without exception: a *universal net interest*. There
may actually be universal component interests: virtually everybody (even
here the qualifier is necessary) is a pedestrian and thus has an interest as a
pedestrian. Even some resultant interests may be nearly universal, and
certainly many of them, like the interest in avoiding huge riots and epidemics, approximate that condition closely.

It is sometimes argued against Rousseau's contention that there is a universal net interest in having laws against murder, battery, and theft, that
such laws cannot be in the net interests of the murderers, bullies, and
thieves themselves. But this misses Rousseau's point. It is in the criminal's
interest, not only as a criminal but as a person overall, that there be laws
protecting him as well as everyone else from crimes, and that these laws be
generally observed, but that circumstances be such that *he* can get away

with violating them whenever he chooses to do so. It is in the criminal's net interest as well as nearly everyone else's that there be legal protection of person and property, else life would be a Hobbesian war of all against all, "nasty, brutish, and short." As Barry points out:

> Rousseau does not deny that it may be in your interest to *break* a law which benefits you *qua* member of the community; all he says is that it is certainly in your interests to *vote* for it, and that if you have voted in favor of a certain punishment for a certain crime you have no business to complain if your wish for a certain general policy is applied to you in a particular case.[5]

There are states of affairs, then, that approximately answer to public—that is "common" (universal net)—interests, and among them are the interests in preserving law and order generally and avoiding depressions and epidemics. The next question to answer is why the widely shared interests should be given a great deal of weight, even a priority, over other interests by a legal system designed to minimize harms. Part of the answer, at least, is suggested by the examples to which we are unavoidably driven when we think about common interests. It seems to be a fact that the most widely shared net interests just happen to be those that have the greatest degree of vitality in the interest networks of those who share them, and therefore, the greatest "weight" in our moral deliberations. If nearly everybody just happened to have a net interest, say, in the construction of an enormous pyramid as a tomb for dead presidents, that would be an example of a nearly universally shared net interest of relatively low vitality. But as a matter of fact, there is no such universal interest, and the clearest examples of common interests we can list are of a quite different, and much more "vital," kind. Public interests also derive their considerable weight from social reenforcement. An act that sets back to a small extent a widely shared net interest may do little harm to each person who has the interest, but it does some harm to almost everyone, a consideration that multiplies its significance.

3. Accumulative harms

These are not to be confused with "aggregative harms." (See Chap. 5, §4.) Most of the actions and practices that are thought to be against the public interest are such that their single occurrences cause little or no public harm. If there were only one case each year in the entire country of "voluntary fisticuffs," its actual effect on the public interest would be minuscule at the most. Even if both combatants ended up in the hospital, the effects on the smooth flow of business, the absentee rate, and the general security would be barely measurable. Of course, one might always ask, "What if everybody did it?" If *everybody* took to fisticuffs to "settle" insults and disputes, the effects on the public interest would be conspicuously adverse. But to this observation the natural rejoinder is powerful: not "everybody" would act in the way in question if it were permitted. Indeed, we can ask of the most innocent and harmless actions imaginable, for example walking to the neighborhood grocery to buy some provisions, what would happen if everybody did the same, and the answer would be that chaos would reign supreme. But that is a poor reason against doing the act in question, and still less of a reason for criminally prohibiting that act if it is reasonably believed that not "everybody," or not even very many others, *will* do the same. In applying the harm principle, then, the legislator must acquire the best empirical information he can get about the readiness of persons generally (and also their opportunities and abilities) to act in the way whose prohibition he is considering. If, as a matter of fact, not enough persons will act in the way in question to affect adversely any public interest, then there can be no harm in permitting those actions, even if their general or widespread performance would be disastrous.

The problem, however, is not quite that simple. The legislator must consider not only how many people would refrain from doing certain actions even if those actions were legally permitted, but also *why* they would refrain. Some types of behavior are socially harmful if generally done, socially innocuous if done only by a few, and yet such that not many would want to engage in them, or would find it in their interests to do so, even if they were permitted. The harm principle provides no warrant for the prohibition of such conduct. On the other hand, some types of behavior are harmful if widely done, harmless if done by only a few, and in almost everyone's interest to do; yet even if permitted, these acts would not be done by enough people to cause harm, because many or most people would refrain out of moral scruples or civic spirit from doing what is in their interest. In this example, it is only because many or most people sacrifice their own interests out of higher motives in refraining from doing what is legally permitted, that the conduct in question is "harmless." If the legislature's application of the harm principle is informed by a sense of justice, the conduct in question will not be permitted.

One can imagine a country (otherwise similar to our own) in which tax laws are not enforced by a criminal sanction, so that citizens in effect are left free to pay or not pay a recommended fee as they choose, and yet 99 percent of whom choose voluntarily to pay. In this happy hypothetical land, little harm would be caused by the remaining one percent who choose to be freeloaders. To be sure, if a sufficient number (far fewer than "everyone") chose to evade their taxes, the result would be socially harmful, but in the example, that threshold number is not reached because the vast majority are cooperative and civic-spirited citizens. There would be no public harm in legalizing "tax evasion" in such a community, but only because the evaders, trusting the others to be honorable, could take unfair advantage of their self-denying virtue. A plausible harm principle fairly employed would not permit such a situation.

4. Environmental pollution as a public accumulative harm

Apart from the examples we have already considered, there are two further kinds of problems for legislators who must decide how properly to impute harms before drafting legislation meant to reduce or prevent those harms. Precisely because of imputational obscurities and complexities, these tend (with some exceptions) to be problems for civil law (damage suits) and administrative law (regulative agencies), and not to be the business of the criminal law in the first instance, though criminal enforcement is available as a backup sanction for authoritative orders (see Introduction, §7). We shall consider them here only because they provide challenging hard cases for the concept of *harming*, which of course is centrally important to the theory of criminal legislation. I refer to the setting of standards for the emission of industrial pollutants into the air and water, and to "copycat crimes" whose model for imitation is a widely transmitted work of fiction on television or in motion pictures.

One *could* say simply that air and water pollution, since they threaten a vital public interest, are harmful, and therefore should be prohibited. Henceforth, a hasty legislature might declare, anyone who pollutes the air or water is guilty of a felony and subject to not less than a year in prison and a $10,000 fine. Would this criminal statute be supported by the harm principle? It does satisfy the letter of the harm principle's minimal requirement: it cites the need to prevent harm as a reason for prohibitive legislation. But from the point of view of an actual legislature seriously grappling with a pressing public problem, it is utterly trivial and nearly vacuous to say so little. Since obviously it would also cause serious public dislocations to force the immediate closing of all industrial facilities that emit gases into the atmosphere or chemicals into the groundwater, or to ban all gasoline-powered motor vehicles, it is not in the spirit of the harm principle to fight one set of harms by blunt and sweeping measures that produce many harms of other kinds as side effects. Straightforward first-resort use of criminal sanctions would be much too crude, not to say socially harmful, an approach to a problem of this complexity. Rather, the question a legislature must ask, in the spirit of the harm principle, is this: In the effort to minimize public harms generally, within the limits of efficiency, equity, and fair play, what sort of regulative scheme should be devised?

Moreover, because of imputational obscurities, it would be impossible to know how to recognize a violation of the simpler kind of criminal regulation. Air and water pollution are paradigmatic accumulative harms. If there were only one automobile allowed to operate in the entire state of California, its exhaust fumes would soon be dissipated and no harm to the ambient air would even be worth mentioning. One hundred cars might begin to threaten the air quality but it is unlikely that they would bring it to the threshold of harmfulness. But somewhere between those minor exhaust emissions and those produced by millions of cars without catalytic converters the threshold of harm is reached. Similarly, it will do no harm to the public drinking water to drop a few ounces even of so deadly a poison as potassium cyanide into a reservoir. There is some threshold quantity, however (and a surprisingly large one), at which cyanide concentrations would be lethal. When a person (or company) emits a certain amount of sulfur dioxide into the air, well short of the threshold of harm, he has slightly increased the concentration of dangerous chemicals in the direction of harm, and in that sense his actions are "harmful." (See Chap. 1, §5, and Chap. 4, §2.) But that can hardly be the sense of "harm" in any formulation of the harm principle that can serve as a guide to legislators, since it would provide a "reason" for banning indispensable innocent activities, like car driving and fossil-fuel-fired electricity-generating plants, across the board.

Suppose, however, that some person (or company) emits the same small amount of the same gases, but in circumstances such that concentrations of those gases already present in the air are raised just above the threshold of actual harm. Has that person violated the statute (supposing it to be actually in the penal code) against "polluting the air"? With that question, a host of imputational difficulties are introduced. To be sure, the concentration levels were raised by his act above the permissible threshold, but that is mainly because countless other emitters had already made *their* independent contributions, many of them much larger than those of our hapless defendant, and made them with less care and for socially less valuable purposes. "Why pick on me for contributing so little to the harmful accumulation when so many others, for no better and often worse reasons, contributed so much more?" the indignant scapegoat might ask. "*I* was not the one who harmed the public interest; those others were the true culprits." The others, however, would have similar arguments in their own defense. And no one of the others, we must concede, caused all that harmful concentration. It will not help our confused legislators to say simply that they must make laws to prevent individuals from harming others, when there is no clear way of telling when a particular emission is the one that does the harm. (Of course, above the threshold, all subsequent emissions cause harm, as higher and higher concentrations are ever more injurious, at least up to a further threshold where things are so bad they cannot get worse. From the point of view of the dead, "overkill" is no worse than "kill.")

These legislative problems have a common form. In each case: (1) A threshold of harm is approached, reached, or exceeded through the joint and successive contributions of numerous parties. (2) These contributions are uneven in amount, and unequal in degree of care and in social value. (3) In respect to the harm of pollution, each contribution is "harmless" in itself except that it moves the condition of the environment to a point closer to the threshold of harm. (4) When these accumulations cross the harm-threshold, they constitute *public* harms in that they set back vital net interests shared by almost everyone. (5) Most of the activities that produce these contributions toward pollution are so beneficial in other ways that if they were to be prevented entirely, as a group, the resultant harm to the public would be as great or even greater than the harm they now produce.[6] The legislative problem then is to control emissions so that the chemical accumulations remain below the harm-threshold, while restricting as little as possible the socially valuable activities that produce emissions as regrettable byproducts. A satisfactory solution requires not a simple criminal prohibition, modeled say on the statute against homicide or burglary, but an elaborate scheme of regulation, administered by a state agency empowered to grant, withhold, and suspend licenses, following rules designed to promote fairness and efficiency.[7] The role of the criminal law would be a derivative one: to provide backup sanctions to enforce authoritative orders.

Our concern with such regulative schemes here is only to understand their role in the interpretation of the critical idiom, "*A* harms *B*." Prohibitions are legitimized by the harm principle only when necessary to prevent *A* (the party restrained) from harming *B* (where *B* can be any or all private parties or the widely shared interest of a "public"). When a legislature wishes to prevent a public accumulative harm like pollution, it must know precisely how to describe the prohibitable actions that harm the public interest, so that it can prohibit just those actions. But when the legislature does not know, and has no way of deciding, to just which actions to impute the harm in question, it has no way of formulating the desired statute that avoids vacuousness, arbitrariness, and legislative overkill. If there is no way after the fact to tell to which actions to impute the harm, then there can be no way before the fact for legislatures to decide which actions to prohibit because of their harm production. The harm principle in that case is of no use at all.

My thesis is that it is only against the background of such a regulative system as that suggested above that individual imputations of public accumulative harm make any sense. For A to harm the public interest is for A's wrongful conduct to cause a setback to that interest. In the context of industrial polluting, "wrongful" must mean unlawful as judged by a regulative agency applying rules for allocating permits in accordance with specified requirements of fairness and efficiency. In these contexts, no prior standard of wrongfulness exists. There is nothing inherently wrongful or right-violating in the activity of driving an automobile, generating electricity, or refining copper. These activities can be meaningfully condemned only as violations of an authoritative scheme of allocative priorities. To the more general question—does a legislature have a right to prohibit (say) copper-refining as such?—the only answer yielded by the unsupplemented harm principle is the unhelpful one, "Yes, but only if copper refining causes harm." How do we tell if a given refining operation causes harm? Only by determining whether its contribution to the accumulation of certain gases and materials in the ambient air is more than its permitted share. But we can only know its "permitted share" by reference to an actual allocative scheme, operative and in force.

In 1970, Congress passed the Clean Air Act Amendments which for the first time empowered the Environmental Protection Agency (EPA) to promulgate uniform national ambient air standards for seven pollutants.[8] These standards define for each region regulated the same maximal allowable concentration of each pollutant. In effect then, these standards define the threshold of public harm, as determined by scientists in the employ of the EPA. In the terminology favored by economists and legal commentators, they impose "ceilings" above which the total concentration of a given pollutant is not allowed to rise. In those defined regions in each of the fifty states where the ambient pollution concentration does not now exceed the ceiling, the EPA is to monitor a program of "prevention of significant deterioration" (PSD), assuring that the ceilings are never surpassed.[9] The law now requires each state to develop an implementation plan to protect the PSD ceilings by regulating future economic growth, requiring technical diminution devices, and the like. A key term in the accounting system defined by these requirements is the "PSD increment," which is (speaking very roughly) the allowable total increase, at a given time, in the actual concentration levels. The increment will be roughly the difference between those levels (the "baseline pollution concentration") and the imposed upper ceiling. The baseline, of course, varies (in the preferred terminology, "floats") with changes in the quantity of local emissions. The *available PSD increment* at a given time, therefore, is "the difference between this floating baseline and the local PSD ceiling."[10] Lewis Kontnik explains—

> Increases in local air pollution emissions effectively "consume" PSD increment since the ambient increase resulting from the new emissions will decrease the available increment. Conversely, a reduction in local emissions lowers the floating baseline, which increases the amount of PSD increment available. In other words, reductions in local emissions "liberate" increment. When this occurs, the Act allows the emission reduction and resulting liberation of increment by one source to then be used by another source to "offset" emission increases at a nearby location.[11]

The problem to be solved by each state in its own implementation plan is how to allocate the available increment among prospective new sources of air pollution, and this involves comparing such disparate sources of sulphur dioxide emission (say) as one huge industrial smokestack and 60,000 automobiles.

We can hardly pursue the problem here into its bewildering technicalities, but to appreciate what *kind* of moral problem it is, we should briefly glance at some of the potentially clashing goals of an "increment allocation mechanism." Kontnik classifies them under three headings: efficiency, equity, and feasibility. Even a cursory examination of specific objectives under these headings reveals that conflicts can occur both within and between these categories. Under "efficiency," the regulative agency must consider net productivity ("the total value of goods and services produced by the allocation of increment"), increase in employment, tax revenues generated, new capital investment, and minimal environmental impact apart from pollution. Under "equity," the agency must balance regional and local priorities, including the concerns of neighborhood groups, urban planners, and other "interest groups," and fairness (equal consideration) to competing sources. "Existing sources seeking to continue or increase their present rates of air pollution emissions invite treatment different from that of new sources seeking to locate in an area," but "even though a satisfactory legal basis exists for the classification of sources, mechanisms that treat all sources evenly are preferable to those that do not."[12] Under "feasibility," consideration must be paid to political possibilities and dangers, as well as to legal, administrative, and technical costs of the allocation mechanism itself. Then heed must be paid to the requirements of both certainty (predictability) and flexibility in the allocation decisions.

> Certainty and predictability are necessary in order to permit meaningful business and community planning; uncertainty in environmental regulations has been cited repeatedly as one of the major reasons for the failure of industry to

invest in major new facilities. An inflexible mechanism may render industry unable to meet the future demand for necessities. For example, the abrupt exhaustion of PSD increment raises the possibility of a moratorium in the construction of new power generating facilities. Indeed both environmentalists and advocates of growth have expressed concern that such inflexibility could result in abandonment of the entire PSD program. Thus, any acceptable allocation mechanism must provide a blend of certainty and flexibility.[13]

State implementation plans may incorporate any of various alternative allocation mechanisms, or a blend of them all, in trying to achieve as much as possible of the combined efficiency-equity-feasibility goals. A simple lottery is one such mechanism. Somewhat more complicated "first-come-first-serve" rules are another. "Proprietary-Increment Market Allocation" and "Detailed Land-Use Planning" are still others. In short, responsible legislative consideration of the problem posed by the accumulative public harm of pollution involves the entire range of reasons bearing on policy decisions: the values of environmental protection, economic growth, regional fairness, and equal consideration of competing interests; maxims of justice; costs of administration; predictability without inflexibility, and the like, not to mention the debate between advocates of market mechanisms of various kinds and defenders of long-term governmental planning. We are a long way from the world of simple criminal prohibitions, like that which punishes "littering" by a fine of $100. The harm principle lends legitimacy to legislative efforts to solve the multidimensional problems of air and water pollution, but in its bare formulation without supplement, it offers no guide to policy.

5. Imitative harms

An equally difficult problem for imputation arises when *prima facie* innocent conduct is a "but-for cause" of the commission of a seriously harmful crime by independent parties. (For an earlier necessary condition to be a genuine causal factor, of course, it must neither be a mere analytic connection nor a coincidence. See Chap. 3, §7, and Chap. 4, §8. I shall assume throughout this discussion that "but-for causes" satisfy these requirements.) In particular, the showing of fictitious dramas over television or in motion pictures to audiences of millions sometimes puts the idea of some bizarre crime into the minds of persons who might otherwise never have thought of doing the depicted act. There is always a danger of life imitating art when the fiction depicts some peculiarly ingenious mode of sadistic harm-infliction, but there are also disturbing examples of self-inflicted harms by imitative reckless people or ignorant children. For example, in the two-year period after the release in 1979 of *The Deer Hunter*, a war film in which U.S. soldiers and Vietnamese are shown playing Russian roulette for cash stakes, there were twenty-eight confirmed shootings and twenty-five deaths from private games of Russian roulette played by people who had watched the film on videotapes or television. Dr. Thomas Radecki, president of the National Coalition on Television Violence, pointed out that "automobiles, toys, medications, and other products would have been recalled by the government long before" that many deaths had occurred.[14] (Dr. Radecki had attempted without success to persuade the management of a Chicago television station to delete the Russian roulette scenes seven days before two imitative Chicago-area men lost their lives in a home game.) Provided that the adults in these accidents had assumed the risks knowingly and freely— that is genuinely voluntarily—the harm-to-others principle probably cannot be stretched to cover the persuasive suggestiveness of the film, even on the assumption that the viewing of the film was the cause of the victim's risk-taking. One must resort to legal paternalism (see Chap. 17) to legitimize interventions to prevent *voluntary* self-harm. It is otherwise when the suggested (caused) conduct is that of a person who lacks the full capacity for rational choice because he is inflamed, impaired, or immature. (See Chap. 26.) In Barcelona, an eight-year-old girl was injured in jumping from a second-floor landing "after telling her playmates she was Superman" (having earlier seen the film).[15]

Normal people do not become sadists simply by watching television dramas, but persons who already have sadistic dispositions may discover some especially imaginative cruel acts depicted in an especially vivid manner in a television play, and imitate them in assaults on real-life victims. Similarly, persons don't become neurotic obsessives by watching films, but a film might suggest a particular obsession to an already neurotic person. Examples of both kinds abound in recent newspapers. In 1974 a group of criminals robbed a store in Ogden, Utah, and murdered all the people they encountered. That was hardly an idea that could be attributed to a film-script writer. What was unique in the crime, however, was the manner in which five of the victims were murdered. "Sixteen year old Cortney Naisbitt spewed blood because his executioners—who had never seen him or any of the others in the store they came to rob—tied and gagged him and four other people in the basement and made them drink liquid Drano before shooting them. They got the idea from a Clint Eastwood movie."[16]

The best-known example of an imitative crime by a neurotic obsessive is the attempted assassination of President Reagan by John W. Hinckley. Fifteen times Hinckley had seen *Taxi Driver*, a film which obsessively fascinated him. Increasingly he "identified with the lead character who stalks a presidential candidate, and thought that the movie was speaking to him personally." Hinckley shot the president (he said) in order to win "the respect and love" of Jodie Foster, an actress he had never met.[17] Foster played a supporting role in *Taxi Driver*.

A 1981 film, *Nighthawks*, caused at least one critic to recall *Taxi Driver* with a shudder. This movie was promoted with the slogan, "One man can bring the world to its knees and only one man can stop him." It is a fantasy about a peculiarly unscrupulous and ingenious terrorist. So far as I am aware, no Hinckley has arisen to attempt an imitation of the plot, though it is the sort of fantasy that is "capable of stimulating the most malign of Walter Mitty dreams,"[18] which we can assume are dreamed at least by a few suggestible neurotics in an audience of millions. Robert Hatch accurately characterizes those who could be tempted to be copy-cats, and also the nature of the danger:

> I am not persuaded that ours is a uniquely violent age; seventeenth century London was hardly the Forest of Arden. But the incidence of senseless murders—which however make powerful sense to the murderers—is alarmingly high. It is said that those who commit them tend to be rootless young men who brood on their solitary state. If it should turn out that they are also addicted to movies about murder for self-esteem, I would not be surprised. The danger in *Nighthawks* is not clear and present, so it must be let run its course. But that is not to say that . . . we won't be somewhat safer when it disappears from the screen.[19]

In 1977 a nine-year-old girl was attacked by a gang of teenagers on a beach near San Francisco. She was brutally mistreated in a manner so grotesquely inventive and cruel that it could not have been a coincidence that the assailants had seen precisely that mode of treatment depicted in an NBC television drama shortly before. The girl sued the National Broadcasting Corporation for negligently creating the risk that eventuated in her injury. The trial court refused to impanel a jury and rendered judgment in favor of the defendant corporation. The appellate court overruled that judgment and ordered a new trial, but the suit eventually failed.

The facts of the case, *Olivia N., a minor, v. National Broadcasting Co., Inc.*,[20] appear in the summary of Associate Justice Christian at the appellate hearing:

> Appellant's complaint sought damages from respondents for injuries allegedly inflicted upon her by certain juveniles who were acting upon the stimulus of observing a scene of brutality which had been broadcast in a television drama entitled "Born Innocent." The subject matter of the television film was the harmful effect of a state-run home upon an adolescent girl who had become a ward of the state. In one scene of the film, the young girl enters the community bathroom of the facility to take a shower. She is then shown taking off her

clothes and stepping into the shower, where she bathes for a few moments. Suddenly, the water stops and a look of fear comes across her face. Four adolescent girls are standing across from her in the shower room. One of the girls is carrying a "plumber's helper," waving it suggestively by her side. The four girls violently attack the younger girl, wrestling her to the floor. The young girl is shown naked from the waist up, struggling as the older girls force her legs apart. Then, the television film shows the girl with the plumber's helper making intense thrusting motions with the handle of the plunger until one of the four says, "That's enough." The young girl is left sobbing and naked on the floor.

    . . . It is alleged that appellant, aged nine, was attacked by minors at a beach in San Francisco. It is alleged that the minors attacked appellant and another minor girl, and forcibly and against her will, "artificially raped" appellant with a bottle. The complaint alleges that the assailants had seen the "artificial rape" scene in "Born Innocent," and that the scene "caused them to decide" to do a similar act to a minor girl.[21]

Most of these frightening examples share a common form: A produces and presents to the public a drama; the plot in the drama suggests to B a harm which he might inflict on some victim; in consequence B inflicts that harm on C; and there is strong circumstantial evidence that but for B's watching the drama when he did, he would not have inflicted precisely that harm on precisely that victim at precisely that time. We can now raise four questions about cases of this general kind:

1. Does A harm C on these facts?
2. If so, does this kind of indirect harming constitute a reason, under the harm principle, for criminalizing actions of the sort A undertook?
3. If so, is such a reason likely ever to be a *sufficient* reason for criminalization?
4. Is such a reason (if it is a reason) likely ever to be a sufficient reason for civil liability, prior censorship, or other regulative control (like "recalling" the "defective" tapes and scripts and disallowing reshowing)?

There is a simple way of arguing for a negative answer to the first question which, I think, we should resist. Many will argue that it was not A who harmed C; rather the harm should be imputed to B, who directly inflicted the injury. A did not even know of the victim's existence, and was not himself at the scene of the crime. Moreover, even though it was A who inadvertently "put the idea" into B's head, B acted of his own free will in committing the crime. He did not act under duress or delusion. The idea suggested by A's film appealed to him only because he was already predisposed to act in that kind of way, and A can hardly be held responsible for B's deformed character. The act was entirely B's own, and he must be held responsible for it.

So far, the "simple" argument is entirely convincing. There is no doubt, on our hypothetical facts, that *B* must be held responsible for *C*'s harm. The difficult question is whether *B*'s undoubted responsibility precludes also imputing the harm to *A*. The "simple argument" assumes that the fully voluntary act of a responsible person (*B*) cancels the causal connection between the earlier actions of another party (*A*) and the resultant harm.[22] Getting *B* on the causal hook, according to this argument, is enough to bump *A* off the hook. If the harm to *C* is properly imputable to *B*, it cannot also be imputable to *A*, even though it would not have happened but for *A*'s earlier actions. This account of the matter is highly plausible, as we have already seen, when applied to entirely self-regarding harms like those in the Russian roulette examples. If the losing player voluntarily assumed the risk of shooting himself, then it follows that he alone harmed himself. At most, the film producer can be charged with taking advantage of his reckless disposition (see Chapters 31 and 32), not with harming him. The question is whether this simple account can be extended to the harms suffered by third parties.

There is nothing in the record to suggest that Miss Olivia's assailants acted less than voluntarily. In this respect the facts in *Olivia N. v. NBC* are strikingly different from those alleged by the defendant in *Zamora v. Florida*.[23] In the latter case, Ronny Zamora appealed his conviction for first-degree murder, burglary, and armed robbery, on the ground (among others) that the trial court had refused to permit psychiatric testimony on the effect of television violence upon adolescent viewers, particularly "sociopathic" viewers like Zamora. The defense argument was that Zamora was insane when he committed the acts in question, because of "involuntary subliminal television intoxication." The psychological theory underlying the defense was too speculative to be very convincing to a jury (the judge was so frightened of it that he didn't even allow it to be presented to the jury), but if the facts were as alleged, it would follow that Zamora was not responsible for the harm he admittedly caused. In that case, the harm could still be imputed to the television producers, though they could not be said to have caused it intentionally. On the simple theory, once Zamora is off the imputational hook, there is room once more to put an earlier party whose actions were but-for causes of the eventual harm back on the hook. If the facts were as Zamora (unconvincingly) alleged, then the causation of the crime involved a kind of domino effect; by making *B* television-intoxicated, *A* was unwittingly the cause of the damage his human tool produced, just as if *A* had bumped into *B* and inadvertently pushed him off a balcony to land below on poor *C* causing him harm. Since *B*'s "action" was wholly involuntary, the harm gets traced back to *A*. The same judgments would be made if A dropped a drug into B's drink, and B in a drug-induced fit of violence strangled C. Again, getting B off the imputational hook permits us to put A back on.

The "simple theory" overlooks the possibility that there might be room on the hook for both A and B because there are some cases in which it is true both that A caused B's harmful action, and that B's action was fully voluntary. If there are such cases, then both A and B might be to blame for the harm to C (though not necessarily in the same way or to the same degree), and that harm can be imputed to both of their actions. In such cases it would be a disingenuous trick for either A or B to argue that the other's responsibility is an exculpatory defense for himself. It is impossible to argue here for this more complex view of imputation,[24] except to point out that it is hard to deny some moral and conceptual relevance to the facts that but for what A did, C's injury would not have happened, and given normal background conditions, it was A's act that made the difference between it happening or not. These facts may have little moral relevance in the case in which A is entirely without fault, where it was not his purpose to harm anyone, much less C, and in which he did not know, nor had any reason to expect, that he was creating an unreasonable risk of harm to anyone. At the other extreme, A's relatively remote causal connection to C's harm may have great moral relevance if it is also true that he intentionally caused harm to C (or if not to C personally, then to some unknown persons of C's type) or caused such harm in conscious disregard of a known unreasonable risk, or caused it with gross and culpable negligence. Suppose, for example, that A is a racist who produces a TV drama showing white lynch mobs in a favorable light and depicting their black victims as subhuman savages, all in the hope of causing a revival of the charming old practice of terrorizing blacks. Predictably, several hundred viewers with the appropriate predispositions kidnap and torture blacks, much to A's delight. A has used these various B's as dominoes—mere instruments to produce the desired harms—but they were all perfectly willing dominoes, acting voluntarily on the idea A has suggestively implanted in their receptive minds. In this case, where A's fault is so conspicuous, what further harm is there in saying that he caused the voluntary actions of others and is coresponsible with them for the harms?

Olivia's suit against NBC apparently failed because the plaintiff could not show that the television film *advocated* or *encouraged* the violent and depraved act that it depicted for purely dramatic purposes.[25] Without that advocacy, A's causal contribution to the harm could not be shown to be intentional, and thus one of the culpability conditions of great importance to the criminal law would be missing. Also a good part of the point in the judgment that A harmed C would be missing. A harmed C only if his wrongful (unjustified and inexcused) conduct was a cause of B's harm. Simply being a prior causal condition of the resultant set-back interest is not enough. If we add either evil intention or foreknowledge to "but-for cause," however, the combination would be enough. Similarly, if we added conscious disregard of a substantial and unreasonable risk (recklessness) or acting in ignorance of an unreasonable risk one ought to have known (negligence), the combination would be enough. Even if A's action was a but-for cause of C's harm, it would not be true that A harmed C (in the sense required by the harm principle) if he acted neither intentionally, knowingly, recklessly, nor negligently in respect to the resultant harm. In most of the imitative harm cases, the fault of the film producer, at most, is negligence. Often it is plausible to charge that he *ought* to have known that some unstable person would voluntarily cause harm to a victim, whether he knew in fact or not. But unless the negligence is extraordinary—action in the teeth of an enormous and conspicuous risk—then it does not necessarily manifest the insensitivity or indifference that would be morally culpable, and the criminal law, which uses moral condemnation and punishment, would be out of place. In that case, however, it would still be true that A harmed C, and the tort remedy would be C's appropriate recourse.[26]

Still another reason against allowing criminal prosecution for the producers of imitated dramas applies even to those who harm victims recklessly or negligently by means of the voluntary actions of third-party viewers. This is a practical rather than a moral reason, one for legislators, not for philosophers: namely that it is, at best, extraordinarily difficult to establish that the drama was even a "but-for cause" of the harm, much less that the producer was in the appropriate way at fault. The adolescents who "artificially raped" Miss Olivia were clearly not angels suddenly and thoroughly corrupted by one television drama. They were already disposed to be cruel and violent when they saw the program, and those dispositions cannot be blamed on the producer. If they had never seen the program, perhaps (how could one know?) they would not have harmed Miss Olivia on the day they did. Perhaps they would have harmed her anyway but in a less imaginative and gruesome way. Perhaps they would have harmed a different victim on that day—perhaps a little boy. Perhaps they would have harmed no one on that day, but Miss Olivia or some one else on a later day. Only two things seem highly probable: (1) they would have caused just as much cruel and violent harm in the long run had they not seen the drama, and (2) they would not have caused precisely *this* harm in precisely this way to precisely this victim at precisely this time, had they not seen the program. In a way it is a mistake to impute the production of harm to the producer so much as its time and manner and direction toward one particular victim and not another. A suit for damages, against this background, suggests that NBC is being charged with diverting harm that would have been produced anyway to someone, say to Miss Doe, to Miss Olivia instead; or transforming the harm, which would have taken one form, say beating with a club or throwing acid in the eyes, into "artificial rape" instead; or re-timing harm that would have happened at one date, say Tuesday afternoon, to another, the preceding Saturday morning. (How uncertain these counterfactual conjectures are!) If something like this interpretation is correct, then if Miss Olivia has a grievance against NBC, Miss Doe (if only she knew) has a debt of gratitude.

It is just as difficult to establish that the harm suffered by an actual victim was merely diverted to her from someone else (as opposed to being a harm caused afresh that would not otherwise have landed on anyone) as it is to establish any of the other counterfactual conjectures mentioned above. But assuming that C's harm caused directly by B as a consequence of an idea suggested by A is indeed a "merely diverted harm," what implications should that have for legal liability? It should make no difference, I think, to the question of whether A should be civilly liable to C for her damages. Even though the harm she suffered was harm that someone would have suffered eventually anyway, it became *her* harm as a consequence (in part) of the conduct of A, the defendant, and *she* is the one who needs compensation. The question of criminal liability is more difficult, because the defendant in a criminal trial is not merely responding to the personal grievance of a specific victim; rather, the grievance is said to be that of the whole community, and it is the state that brings the formal charges against him. It is less clear in the criminal context that society has a grievance against A, above and beyond the personal grievance of the victim C, when it is given that the same amount of harm would have been produced eventually by B even without A's contribution, and that A's role was simply to cause its diversion from some unknown D (a social gain) to poor C (a counterbalancing social loss).

There are many other reasons why legislatures, even those that endorse the harm principle, should be leery of passing criminal legislation against the "indirect causation" of harm through film broadcasts. If we allow a special value and legally privileged position to the interest in free expression (not only of opinion but also of dramatic and aesthetic works), as the United States Constitution does, then we can argue, as American courts have, against any legal restraints on expression that do not fall squarely within the standard exceptive categories—obscenity, defamation, incitement, etc. "Dangerous suggestiveness" is not one of those categories; nor should it be if we wish to avoid general terrorization of writers and producers, discour-

agement of experimental styles, dampening of creativity, and similar undermining of the socially vital interest in free expression. But even if we do not
accept so absolute an immunity for aesthetic expression, there are powerful
practical reasons against using the criminal law to control the indirect harms
of film productions. Causal connections are simply too speculative, and risk
appraisals too uncertain, to support so solemn a sanction as criminal liability. Kent Greenawalt sums up these practical difficulties succinctly:

> Even if one puts aside any special value of communication, substantial argu-
> ments can be advanced against any general principle of imposing liability on
> speakers who recklessly or negligently create a risk that someone else will
> commit a crime. In contrast to more ordinary cases, like the one in which a
> stray bullet aimlessly fired into a lighted house strikes an occupant, it is more
> difficult to ascertain the risk that speech creates to determine whether the harm
> occurred as a consequence of the speech. [Greenawalt uses "speech" as a ge-
> neric term for "expression," wide enough to include film dramas and works of
> literature.] One strongly doubts the capabilities of juries to make the assess-
> ments of substantiality of risk, and consequence, particularly if its members
> are unsympathetic with the ideas communicated. . . .
>   . . . Since punishment for negligence should be used sparingly in any
> event, these arguments strongly suggest that punishment should generally be
> eschewed for speakers who inadvertently risk intentional wrongful action by
> listeners. And even apart from the special value of communication, punish-
> ment of speech that recklessly produces criminal action would be tolerable, if
> at all, only upon unmistakable proof of risk and cause. . . . [27]

Greenawalt does not mention the special case of film productions designed *intentionally* to get audience members to commit crimes, like that in
our previous example of the drama about abusing and torturing blacks
produced for the purpose of suggesting modes of mistreatment to susceptible members of the audience. In a way, intention is much easier for a jury
to judge than recklessness or negligence since the jury does not have to
appraise the reasonableness of risks or decide what a defendant "ought to
have known." If there is credible testimony that the producer disclosed his
intentions to others, then that counts clearly as evidence for his culpable
purpose. And if violent incidents of the depicted sort occur immediately,
although they had not occurred for many years, a causal linkage is strongly
suggested. But cases of deliberate harm production by film drama would be
extremely rare, and credible evidence of deliberate intention would be rarer
still. There would hardly ever be a prosecution, and almost never a conviction. Still the bare possibility of prosecution would cast something of a chill
on the creative community. It must be remembered, moreover, that severe
sanctions are available for the punishment of the direct and primary
offenders.

Most of the above considerations tell equally against permitting damage suits against "indirect causes" of harm through dramatic suggestion, but nevertheless, I find the case against tort actions to be less overwhelmingly convincing. After all, television dramas witnessed by millions of people make enormous profits for the television companies, while the victims of rapes, tortures, and shootings must pay their own losses and endure their own sufferings. One impulse of justice, at least, would be satisfied by a scheme that transferred the costs incurred by the innocent victims to shoulders better able to bear them, indeed to parties who actually *profited* from the very actions that led to the losses occuring. If we required fault for tort liability in these cases, then probably we would judge that straightforward negligence suits should not succeed because of the evidential obscurities already mentioned. These difficulties would also undermine most cases where the producer's conscious recklessness toward others or purposeful harming of others is suspected, though in the rare cases where there is clear evidence of deliberate intention or conscious disregard of a known risk, traditional fault-based civil suits are more feasible, partly because of the greater clarity of the evidence, and partly because evil intention and recklessness toward others are more culpable states of mind, morally speaking, than negligence. There is an argument, however, for *not* requiring proof of fault in each case, but for assigning responsibility in advance to all production companies for all harms of which their dramas are a cause. The argument would be that the parties who make a profit from a general activity serving the public ought to shoulder the risk of any severe harms they cause to elements of the public, and factor them into their general budget of business expenses. As between totally faultless victims of violence, on the one hand, and the profit-making producers, on the other, it is fair that the latter pay the costs of the injuries which would not have occurred but for their profit-making activities.[28] (The actual costs, of course, would be spread very widely among advertising agencies, commercial sponsors, and insurance companies.) Such a scheme would not require proof of fault but only proof of causation—which would be difficult enough.

It is probable that this sort of "strict liability" scheme for imitative harms, because of the difficulty of establishing causation, would not be an expensive one. I suspect that the clearest evidence of the requisite causation would be the correlation between film-viewing and action when there is a short time-gap between the two, and when the imitated crime is an especially novel one, rarely depicted in drama, film, or literature, and almost equally rarely committed in real life. Then the coincidence would be striking circumstantial evidence of causal influence. Predictability or foreseeability would not have to be shown, since they bear on fault. But since it is much more difficult to show that the actor would not have caused *some* kind of harm in *some* manner or other, routine or novel, perhaps even to *this* victim, even if he had not viewed the producer's show, the producer might be held liable only for the *incremental harms* beyond what might have been expected anyway. (The store robbers might not have forced their victims to swallow Drano had they not seen the Clint Eastwood film, but they might well have committed the crime anyway omitting only that ghoulish increment. Any victim who recovered from his shooting then might sue for the injuries caused by the Drano.) The incremental injuries suffered by the victim are manifestly harms in the sense of set-back interests, but can they be said to be harms in our special sense—set-back interests caused by acts of *harming?* They were produced by the criminal's acts of harming, but the civil suit we are imagining is against the producer, and if he acted without fault (as we are supposing he might have) then *he* did not harm the victim even though his faultless conduct was a cause of the setback to the victim's interest. Relative to him the harming is only a fiction, and in fact the harm principle as we have formulated it would not legitimize imposing liability on him. The harm principle, however, is a principle for legitimizing *criminal* prohibitions, and no question of criminal law is involved here. A strict liability statute in the criminal law, if it threatened penal sanctions, could not be justified by the harm principle, for it would permit persons to be punished for some reason other than that they had harmed (wronged) anyone. I exclude from this judgment, however, so-called public welfare offenses that require producers of such products as milk, which are vital to public health and safety, to keep their products safe, and automatically impose a fine for discovered impurities even without evidence of fault. Such a penalty lacks the reprobative symbolism of genuine punishment, and the statute that specifies it, therefore, should not be classified as part of the criminal law.[29]

In any case, policy decisions of the kinds we have considered here are in large part matters for interest-balancing and assessments of cost effectiveness. They are practical matters and open questions, properly debated in legislatures. The same is true of proposals to grant regulatory agencies the power to order films "recalled" after evidence of their harm production has mounted, though again that evidence would so rarely be compelling that occasions for properly exercising the power would be rare, and the utility of the regulatory scheme, given its general desuetude, would be counterbalanced by the danger to free expression posed by the bare possession of the power.

We can now summarize our answers to the four questions about imitative harms raised at the beginning of this section. (1) Provided that *A* was in a relevant way at fault when he produced his dangerously suggestive drama (either his deliberate purpose was to cause harm, or he caused it knowingly, recklessly, or negligently), and that the production really was an occurrence but for which the harm to *C* would not have occurred (and not merely a coincidence), there is no denying that *A* harmed *B*, in the sense of "to harm" used by the harm principle. (2) Consequently, the need to prevent indirect harming through expectable imitation is *a* reason for criminalizing the production of dangerously suggestive films and performances. (3) Nevertheless, because of various severe practical difficulties, such a reason would probably never be a sufficient reason for criminalization. Reasons on the other side of the legislative scales would probably always outbalance it. (4) Similar counterbalancing reasons would probably outweigh harm prevention and tell against regulative restrictions of dangerous films and against permitting recovery of civil damages against an indirect harmer also, but the case against compensation through tort action is by no means as decisive as that against criminalization, and an argument from justice even has some force in favor of imposing a kind of strict liability against the whole film industry for imitative harms. Such a scheme would still require that a causal connection between the film broadcast and the harm be established, and that would be no easy achievement, since in many cases the primary wrongdoer would have produced the harms in any case, and the film model determined only the manner or timing of the harm. Even without the need to prove fault, suits for recovery would probably succeed only rarely given the difficulty of the causal question. One party *can* be a cause of the voluntary actions of another party, and thus be coresponsible with him for the harmful consequences to a third party, but the evidence is not often clear that this has happened.

6. Summary of additional restrictions on the harm principle

We can now conclude the list of restrictive interpretations of the concept of harming and mediating maxims for the application of the harm principle, begun in Chapter 5.

12. The thwarting of *competitive interests* does not count as a harm unless it also is a wrong, which it is when:
   a. it is inflicted unfairly (through cheating, force, or fraud), *or*
   b. consent to the competitive risk has not voluntarily been given, *or*
   c. the form of competition is itself illegitimate.
   A form of competition is illegitimate if it is "avoidable" in Mill's sense, *and*, also, it is *either:*

a. so structured that voluntary consent to serious risks is very difficult to secure or impossible to confirm, *or*

b. it is necessarily harmful to interests of third parties or the public at large.

13. In the case of accumulative harms where single occurrences up to a threshold are harmless but general performance *would be* harmful, legislators should acquire the best empirical information they can get about the readiness of persons to engage in the conduct in question. Then the conduct should be permitted if in fact the likely number of persons who will engage in it falls below the threshold of harm, *unless* all have an interest in engaging in the conduct, but sufficient numbers refrain out of moral scruple or civic spirit to keep below the threshold of public harm. In the latter case, the conduct is "harmless" only because of unfair sacrifices, and should be prohibited. That the avoidance of accumulative harm should not be made to depend on the sacrificial forbearances of the virtuous to the greater advantage of the selfish is a mediating maxim for the application of the harm principle.

14. When pollutants and similar threats to the public interest accumulate as the result of the joint and/or successive uneven contributions of numerous parties, each of which is "harmless" in itself except that it moves the condition of the environment closer to the threshold of harm, and most of which are positively beneficial in other ways, then blanket prohibitions of these contributions will often be as harmful as continued blanket permissiveness. The simple harm principle yields no solution to the problem, but it does legitimize the establishment of a regulatory system that can provide meaning to imputations of harmful conduct (e.g. excessive emissions), which can in turn support authoritative orders backed up by criminal sanctions. To be "wrongful," a contribution toward public accumulative harm must be a violation of an authoritative scheme of allocative priorities already in force. In the absence of such a background there is no nonarbitrary method for imputing accumulative harms to individual parties. The regulatory system in turn must balance values of efficiency, equity, and feasibility. Its priorities must be determined by the entire range of relevant reasons for policy decisions.

15. When *A* presents a fictitious drama to the public whose plot suggests to *B* a harm he might inflict on some victim, and only because of that, *B* voluntarily inflicts that harm on *C*, then the harm can be imputed to *A* as well as to *B*, provided his fiction was a "but-for cause" of the harm, and he was at fault in producing it because either his deliberate purpose was to cause the harm, or he contributed to the harm knowingly,

recklessly, or negligently. But even though the harmfulness of acts of A's kind is a reason for statutes creating criminal liability, it is probably never a sufficient reason, given the many countervailing practical reasons on the other side. In principle, however, the harmfulness of A's conduct could be a ground for rules permitting him to be civilly liable for C's damages.

Not all of the restrictions recommended in the summaries of this and the previous chapter have, by any means, been supported by decisive argument. In some instances, legislators employing the harm principle may well use different mediating maxims that better reflect their own moral viewpoints. But they will have to use *some* supplementary criteria, because otherwise the harm principle is a mere empty receptacle, awaiting the provision of normative content before it can be of any use. Not just *any* normative content, of course, can plausibly be provided; there must be some congeniality with the animating spirit of the harm principle, insofar as it can be presumptively reconstructed. Our full elaboration of the harm principle will now appear to the reader to have much more in it than was even suggested by its original bare formulation. But however the harm principle has been supplemented by additional principle, however thoroughly it has been refined and shaped by conceptual analysis, and however complicated the set of mediating maxims prescribed to guide its application, that principle will still not suffice to legitimize prohibition of conduct on the grounds that it is offensive to others, harmful to the actor himself, or inherently immoral. Elastic it may be, but it cannot stretch *that* far.

Notes

General Introduction

1. John Stuart Mill, *On Liberty*, Chap. 1, para. 1.
2. C. L. Ten, *Mill On Liberty* (Oxford: Clarendon Press, 1980), p. 2. The quotation is from Mill's *On Liberty*, chap. I, para. 5. Alexis de Tocqueville thought that even ruthless punishments by the absolute monarchs of Europe were not as effective in repressing unpopular opinions as social pressure was in America. Not that an author "is in danger of an *auto-da-fe*, but he is exposed to continued obloquy and [social] persecution." *Democracy in America* (New York: Vintage Books, 1945), vol. 1, pp. 273–74.
3. For the distinction between policies and principles, see Ronald Dworkin, *Taking Rights Seriously* (Cambridge, Mass.: Harvard University Press, 1977), pp. 22–28, 71–80, and 90–100.
4. In many cases it is equally "useless" to have a liberty conferred by the silence of the law without the protection of a legal claim-right to the noninterference of others with its exercise. It is good that I am left at liberty by the state to buy what I wish with the $100 bill now in my wallet, but if others are equally at liberty to take my money if they can, and flee with impunity, then the value of my liberty is much diminished. In the language suggested below (Chap. 19, §3), one might say that I am at liberty to spend my $100 as I wish (the law permits me to do so), but I am not in fact *free* to do so (other persons can effectively prevent me from doing so). There are, of course, still other ways of being *unable* to do so even though one is free and at liberty, for example because of one's being diseased and comatose.
5. The classic statement of the moral and general utilitarian arguments for the presumption in favor of liberty is Chapter 3 of Mill's *On Liberty*.

6. See Sanford Kadish, "The Crisis of Overcriminalization," *Annals* 157 (1967): 374ff.
7. Maurice Cranston, *Freedom: A New Analysis* (London: Longmans, Green & Co., 1953), p. 65.
8. Mill, *On Liberty*, chap. 1, para. 9.
9. *Ibid.*, chap. 5, para. 7.
10. As quoted by John A. Jenkins in "Free Thinkers," *T.W.A. Ambassador*, March 1980, p. 54.
11. This point was made decisively by J. S. Mill. See his *Principles of Political Economy*, in *Collected Works*, ed. F. E. Mineka and D. N. Lindley (Toronto: Toronto University Press, 1972), pp. 31–44. See also L. T. Hobhouse, *The Elements of Social Justice* (London: George Allen & Unwin, 1922), pp. 161–63, and Fred R. Berger, "Mill's Substantive Principles of Justice: A Comparison with Nozick," *American Philosophical Quarterly* 19 (1982): 372–80.
12. See my two reviews of John Rawls: "Justice, Fairness, and Rationality," *Yale Law Journal* 81 (1972): 1004–31, and "Duty and Obligation in the Non-Ideal World," *Journal of Philosophy* 70 (1973): 263–75. Some remarks can be found there favorable to the view Rawls calls "intuitionism," that there is an irreducible plurality of equally basic moral principles.
13. George Santayana, *Winds of Doctrine* (New York: Charles Scribner's Sons, 1913), p. 147.
14. For more detailed and persuasive accounts of the "coherence method" in ethics see my "Justice, Fairness and Rationality," *op. cit.* (see note 12), pp. 1018–21; A. C. Ewing, *Ethics* (New York: Macmillan, 1953), pp. 1–15; Jonathan Glover, *Causing Death and Saving Lives* (Harmondsworth, Middlesex: Penguin Books, 1977), pp. 22–38; and especially John Rawls's account of "reflective equilibrium" in *A Theory of Justice* (Cambridge, Mass.: Harvard University Press, 1971), pp. 17–22.
15. In the passage criticized by Santayana, Russell is arguing, in a manner as old as Plato, against hedonism:

> For instance, to show that the good is not pleasure, he [Russell] can avowedly do nothing but appeal "to ethical judgments with which almost everyone would agree." He repeats, in effect, Plato's argument about the life of the oyster, having pleasure with no knowledge. Imagine such mindless pleasure, as intense and prolonged as you please, and would you choose it? Is it your good? Here the British reader, like the blushing Greek youth, is expected to answer instinctively, No! It is an *argumentum ad hominem* (and there can be no other kind of argument in ethics); but the man who gives the required answer does so not because the answer is self-evident, which it is not, but because he is the required sort of man. He is shocked at the idea of resembling an oyster. Yet changeless pleasure, without memory or reflection, without the wearisome intermixture of arbitrary images, is just what the mystic, the voluptuary, and perhaps the oyster find to be good. . . .
> Such a radical hedonism is indeed inhuman; it undermines all conventional ambitions, and is not a possible foundation for political or artistic life. But that is all we can say against it. Our humanity cannot annul the incommensurable sorts of good that may be pursued in the world, though it cannot itself pursue them. The impossibility which people labor under of being satisfied with pure pleasure as a goal is due to their want of imagination, or rather by their being dominated by an imagination which is exclusively human. (*Winds of Doctrine*, pp. 147–48)

16. For a helpful classification of "legal techniques" (of which direct prohibition backed by threat is only one), see Robert S. Summers, "The Technique Element in Law," *California Law Review* 59 (1971): 733–51, as expanded by Michael D. Bayles in *Principles of Legislation* (Detroit: Wayne State University Press, 1978), pp. 66–70.

17. Bayles, *op. cit.*, p. 70.

18. The practice of awarding "punitive damages" as well as compensatory damages in tort cases is a hybrid device for achieving some of the criminal law's purposes without the constraints of criminal procedure. Although it is subject to erratic variation and other abuses, it can in some cases provide a kind of corrective to the rigidities of criminal law, as the following newspaper story illustrates:

> Florence, Arizona. A Tucson woman who saw the man convicted of raping her go free on probation was awarded $1.1 million dollars in damages yesterday by Pinal County judge, E. D. McBryde.
>
> Denise Moroney [was] awarded $100,000 in compensatory damages and $1 million in punitive damages from Joachim "Jack" Sanchez, who did not appear at yesterday's trial. He is currently being sought on a felony warrant in connection with another rape. . . .
>
> In November 1978, a Florence jury found Sanchez guilty of raping Moroney the previous May 27. . . . A parade of witnesses then testified on Sanchez's behalf at a mitigation hearing, and the presiding judge . . . sentenced Sanchez to five years probation.
>
> Moroney, 27, filed the civil complaint of sexual assault against Sanchez last June. "There has got to be some penalty," she said when she filed the suit. "What's to stop men from doing it if they know they can walk free?"
>
> . . . Two witnesses who have been counseling Moroney since the attack told the court that Moroney has been suffering from depression, loss of sleep and appetite and periods of uncontrollable crying. They also testified that Moroney's concern for her daughter's safety since the incident may require further counseling for her and her daughter.
>
> After McBryde made the award, Moroney said she hadn't expected to collect punitive damages. . . . Collecting the award will be a problem, but Sanchez has some assets and will be liable for making payments for his entire life, Mercaldo [Moroney's lawyer] said. "A punitive award like this cannot be discharged in bankruptcy proceedings . . . (they) give people a fresh start who deserve one—but this is a punitive award." (*Arizona Daily Star*, January 9, 1980)

19. Michael D. Bayles, "Comments," in *Issues in Law and Morality*, ed. Norman Care and Thomas Trelogan (Cleveland: Case Western Reserve University Press, 1973), pp. 122–25.

20. See my essay "The Expressive Function of Punishment" in *Doing and Deserving* (Princeton, N.J.: Princeton University Press, 1970), pp. 95–118.

21. Ernest Nagel, "The Enforcement of Morals," *Humanist* (May/June, 1968), pp. 18–27. Reprinted in Paul Kurtz, ed., *Moral Problems in Contemporary Society* (Englewood Cliffs, N.J.: Prentice-Hall, 1969), from p. 143. See also Martin P. Golding, *Philosophy of Law* (Englewood Cliffs, N.J.: Prentice-Hall, 1975), pp. 64–68. Golding concludes that "there are no theoretical limitations to the law" (p. 67).

22. Nagel, *op. cit.*, p. 27.

23. *Ibid.*, p. 22.

1. Harms as Setbacks to Interest

1. Strictly speaking, this definition is circular, since a person would probably have to know what it is to have an interest in something before he could know what it is to "gain or lose" as well as vice versa. But even a circular definition can have some practical utility in providing an equivalent expression for the word to be defined that is more easily manipulated to good purpose, or which is more suggestive, or productive of insight. The word "stake," for example, brings out with intuitive vividness the connection between interests and risks.

2. Charles Fried, *Contract as Promise* (Cambridge, Mass.: Harvard University Press, 1981), p. 37. The example is my own, not Fried's. For a defense of the position opposed to Fried's, see P. S. Atiya, *Promises, Morals, and Law* (Oxford: Clarendon Press, 1981), pp. 212–15.

3. Nicholas Rescher, *Welfare: The Social Issue in Philosophical Perspective* (Pittsburgh: University of Pittsburgh Press, 1972), p. 6.

4. *Ibid.*, p. 5.

5. Brian Barry, *Political Argument* (London: Routledge & Kegan Paul; New York: Humanities Press, 1965), p. 183.

6. C. L. Stevenson, *Ethics and Language* (New Haven: Yale University Press, 1944), p. 203. Since a person may have more than one focal aim, Stevenson's definition should be amended as follows: ". . . if anything else is not a means to this, *or to another focal aim*, it will be without predominating value."

7. On this point my earlier work was mistaken. See my *Social Philosophy* (Englewood Cliffs, N.J.: Prentice-Hall, 1973), pp. 27–28.

8. John Kleinig has pointed out to me that the Epicurean view, as sketchily depicted here, would render rational the Epicurean's suicide as a sure means of eliminating pain and emotional turbulence, assuming of course that he had no other interests. That would seem to follow, except that the Epicureans regarded the absence of pain and turbulence as itself a kind of negative pleasure worth experiencing in its own right. Hence, the sense in which they were hedonists. See Cicero's criticism, *De Finibus Bonorum et Malorum*, trans. H. Rackham (Cambridge, Mass.: Harvard University Press, 1961), Book II.

9. John Kleinig, "Crime and the Concept of Harm," *American Philosophical Quarterly* 15 (1978): 32.

10. *Loc. cit.*

11. A caveat is required about the expression "worse off." Not everything that makes a person worse off harms him, but only that which makes him worse off in respect to his *interests*. He can be made mildly annoyed, offended, bored, even hurt to some degree without his interests being affected, in which case he is, in a sense, "worse off" than he would otherwise be although he has not been harmed.

12. When a person's financial interests are near the "top of the graph," and are then caused to decline a bit, he might be asked if he was harmed by his loss, to which he might reply, "No, not harmed; I could easily afford it." That would be to use a nonrelativistic conception of "harm." What one can "afford" is a loss that is not sufficient to put one's interest in a harmed condition, but which only affects (negatively) its direction of movement.

13. It might be true of course that all defeatings of interest, like all events generally, have their prior determining causes, but it would not follow that all interest-

defeats are "foreordained," in the sense employed in the text. Of the whole class of present interests that will be defeated in the future, only that subclass of interests that will be defeated regardless of what their possessors do are "doomed" from the start. More precisely, those interests are doomed when there is nothing their possessors can do, *or* have a reasonable opportunity to do, *or* indeed any reason to do, that would prevent their defeat. The person driving to the airport to board the plane that will in fact crash, for example, can avoid the crash by turning around and driving home again, and he would do precisely that if he had any reason to suspect that the plane would malfunction. But he has no such reason; nor is there any way he can come to acquire such a reason in his circumstances. Thus, even though there are things he could do to avoid his fate, there is no possibility of his doing those things. Hence, he is doomed. A person who has already contracted a fatal disease may be doomed in an even stronger sense: there may be nothing he could do to avoid his death even if he were fully informed and motivated. There are many other examples, however, of persons whose interests *will* be defeated, but would not be if the person took certain steps that he has the ability and opportunity to take, and *has every reason to take*, to avoid defeat. There may be a causal explanation of why these people suffer the resultant harm, but the interest of theirs that is defeated was at no point *doomed* to defeat.

14. Barry, *op. cit.* (see note 5), p. 183.
15. *Loc. cit.*
16. Anthony Kenny, "Happiness," *Proceedings of the Aristotelian Society* 66 (1965–66): 93–102, as reprinted in J. Feinberg, ed., *Moral Concepts*, (Oxford: Oxford University Press, 1969), p. 48.
17. For a development of this idea, see my "Absurd Self-fulfillment" in Peter van Inwagen, ed., *Time and Cause, Essays Presented to Richard Taylor* (Dortrecht, The Netherlands: Reidel, 1980), pp. 255–81. The higher animals in fact may share with humans an ulterior *interest* in not being in intense and enduring painful states, so that such states, therefore, truly are "harmed conditions" whether harmful or not.
18. Hyman Gross, *A Theory of Criminal Justice* (New York: Oxford University Press, 1979), p. 120.

2. Puzzling Cases

1. "It appears then that virtue is as it were the health and comeliness and well-being of the soul, as wickedness is disease, deformity, and weakness." Plato, *The Republic*, trans. Francis Cornford (London: Oxford University Press, 1941), Bk. 4. 414 (p. 143).
2. For a fuller development of this interpretation of Plato, see H. A. Prichard, *Duty and Interest* (Oxford: Clarendon Press, 1928), espec. pp. 4–25.
3. Brian Barry, *Political Argument* (London: Routledge & Kegan Paul, 1965), p. 183.
4. *Ibid.*, pp. 178–86. This account, therefore, does not imply that what is in one's interests leads to a total satisfaction once and for all. Cf. Thomas Hobbes: ". . . the Felicity of this life consisteth not in the repose of a mind satisfied. For there is no such *Finis Ultimus* or *Summum Bonum* as is spoken of in the Books of

the old Morall Philosophers. Nor can a man any more live, whose Desires are at an end, than he, whose Senses and Imaginations are at a stand. Felicity is a continuall progresse of the desire, from one object to another; the attaining of the former being still but the way to the latter. The cause whereof is, That the object of man's desire is not to enjoy once only, and for one instant of time, but *to ensure for ever the way of his future desire*" (italics added). *Leviathan* (1651), Bk. 1, chap. 2, para. 2.

5. Barry, *op. cit.* (see note 3), p. 185.

6. S. I. Benn, " 'Interests' in Politics," *Proceedings of the Aristotelian Society* 60 (1960): 130–31.

7. Ralph Barton Perry, *General Theory of Value* (New York: Longmans, Green, & Co., 1926), p. 672. His exact words: ". . . a favorable interest in the satisfaction of the interest of a second person."

8. See my "Collective Responsibility" in *Doing and Deserving* (Princeton, N.J.: Princeton University Press, 1970), pp. 233–41.

9. Barry, *op. cit.* (see note 3), p. 77.

10. Cf. *Webster's New International Dictionary*, 2d ed. (1954): "not influenced by regard to personal advantage . . . , " and the *Oxford English Dictionary:* "not influenced by self-interest. . . ."

11. Two kinds of unselfish actions then can be distinguished in terms of the categories in the chart: those in category B and those actions in category A2 that are not done wrongly at the expense of, or in blamable disregard of, the interests (or passing wants) of third parties.

12. This difficulty was first suggested to me by Michael Bayles.

13. Although reciprocal vicarious harms are not subject to any kind of metrical treatment, certain numerical relations suggest an analogy: $1 + \frac{1}{2} + \frac{1}{4} + \frac{1}{8} + \frac{1}{16}$, etc., only approaches 2 as a limit, but it doesn't "approach" 3 or any larger number (much less an infinite number) at all.

14. A possible model for understanding this indeterminacy is that proposed in another context by W. D. Falk. Speaking of the concept of the distinctively moral and the controversy over whether it applies to wholly self-regarding conduct, Falk noted that there is a tendency in ordinary thought to say the one thing and a conflicting tendency to say the other. "This disagreement exhibits the kind of shuttle-service between rival considerations known as the dialectic of a problem. It may be that this shuttle service is maintained by a cleft in the very concept of morality. This concept may have grown from conflicting or only partially overlapping observations, not fully reconciled in ordinary thinking." W. D. Falk, "Morality, Self, and Others," as reprinted in Joel Feinberg, ed., *Reason and Responsibility*, 5th ed. (Belmont, Cal.: Wadsworth Publishing Company, 1981), p. 52.

15. Cf. Barbara Levenbook, "Harming Someone after His Death," *Ethics* 94 (1984).

16. See Ernest Partridge, "Posthumous Interests and Posthumous Respect," *Ethics* 91 (1981): 243–64, for a forceful use of this technique in a thorough rebuttal of my earlier arguments for the harmfulness of death. See also Mary Mothersill's relentless criticisms of Thomas Nagel in her article "Death" in James Rachels, ed., *Moral Problems*, 1st ed. (New York: Harper & Row, 1971), pp. 372–83.

17. See Epicurus, *Letter to Menoeceus*, in Cyril Bailey, ed., *Epicurus: The Extant*

Remains (Oxford: Oxford University Press, 1926). For ingenious attempts to resolve the epicurean paradox, see Thomas Nagel, "Death," in his *Mortal Questions* (Cambridge: Cambridge University Press, 1979), pp. 1–10, and Harry D. Silverstein, "The Evil of Death," *Journal of Philosophy* 77 (1980): 401–24. Nagel's views especially have influenced my own.

18. Levenbook (see note 15) is very convincing on this point.

19. See my "Harm and Self-Interest," in P. M. S. Hacker and J. Raz (eds.), *Law, Morality and Society* (Oxford: Clarendon Press, 1977), p. 308.

20. Partridge, *op. cit.* (see note 16), p. 246.

21. *Ibid.*, p. 260.

22. W. D. Ross, *Foundations of Ethics* (Oxford: Clarendon Press, 1939), p. 300.

23. This judgment is probably too confident if understood to extend to cases where what is wanted is expected to cause actual *disappointment*. Derek Parfit has reminded me of the distinction between cases where fulfillment *can't possibly* produce satisfaction because the person will never be in a position to know that his want has been fulfilled, and cases where fulfillment can produce satisfaction but in fact won't. In the former case, all would agree that the important thing is that what we want to happen will happen (our desire will be fulfilled). But in the latter case, if people know or confidently expect that fulfillment will not only "not cause joy" but will actually produce disappointment, it is not so clear, as Parfit points out, that the important thing is "to get what one wants." There is some question, however, whether the existence of the want could even survive such conditions.

24. The most vivid example I know in literature of "positively harmful" death is that foreseen by Pip at the hands of the villainous Orlick in Charles Dickens's *Great Expectations*, Chap. 53 (Penguin edition, p. 436). Orlick is about to murder Pip and dispose of his body in a kiln in a remote marsh. "I'll put your body in the kiln," he says. "I won't have a rag of you, I won't have a bone of you, left on earth. . . . Let people suppose what they may of you, they shall never know nothing." Pip's reaction is revealing: "My mind, with inconceivable rapidity, followed out all the consequences of such a death. Estella's father would believe I had deserted him, would be taken, would die accusing me; even Herbert would doubt me, when he compared the letter I had left for him, with the fact that I had called at Miss Haversham's gate for only a moment; Joe and Biddy would never know how sorry I had been that night; none would ever know how I had suffered, how true I had meant to be, what an agony I had passed through. The death close before me was terrible, but far more terrible than death was the dread of being misremembered after death. And so quick were my thoughts, that I saw myself despised by unborn generations—Estella's children and their children—while the wretch's [Orlick's] words were yet on his lips."

25. C. D. Broad, "Egoism as a Theory of Human Motives," in *Ethics and the History of Philosophy* (London: Routledge & Kegan Paul, 1952), p. 220.

26. *Ibid.*, p. 221.

27. Aristotle, *Nicomachean Ethics*, trans. J. A. K. Thomson (Baltimore: Penguin Books, 1953), 1.10.

28. *Ibid.*, first paragraph. Aristotle's primary concern in this chapter, however, was not to show that a person's interests can be affected after his death, but rather

that well-being, whether before or after death, cannot be utterly destroyed by the caprice of events, but at worst, only somewhat tarnished. The point about interests surviving death he simply assumed as beyond need of argument.

29. George Pitcher, "The Misfortunes of the Dead," forthcoming in *American Philosophical Quarterly*.

30. *Ibid.*

31. *Ibid.*

32. *Ibid.*

33. *Ibid.*

34. *Ibid.*

35. In this last example, Pitcher would say that the loving father is already harmed by the impending death, quite apart from whether he knows the facts yet or not. See his own example of Bishop Berkeley's son.

36. The remainder of this paragraph summarizes the argument suggested by pp. 254–61 of "Posthumous Interests and Posthumous Respect" (see note 16).

37. See my article "The Forms and Limits of Utilitarianism," *Philosophical Review* 76 (1967): 368–81. I call arguments like the one sketched above "Actual-Rule Utilitarian," as opposed both to "Ideal-Rule Utilitarian" arguments and to "Generalization" arguments.

38. L. W. Sumner, *Abortion and Moral Theory* (Princeton, N.J.: Princeton University Press, 1981), pp. 143–54.

39. See my article "Abortion" in Tom Regan, ed., *Matters of Life and Death* (New York: Random House, 1979), pp. 182–217.

40. The legal rights corresponding to a fetus's "future interests" are often called "contingent rights," or rights contingent on its being born. The fetus's present right to property, for example, is a legal protection offered now to its future interest, contingent upon its birth, and instantly voidable if it dies before birth. As Coke put it: "The law in many cases hath consideration of him in respect of the apparent expectation of his birth" (as quoted by William Salmond, *Jurisprudence*, 12th ed. [London: Sweet & Maxwell, 1966], p. 303)—but this is quite another thing than recognizing a right actually to be born. *Assuming* that the child will be born, the law seems to say, various interests that he will come to have after birth must be protected from damage that they can incur even before birth. For a more detailed discussion, see my essay "Is There a Right To Be Born?" in Joel Feinberg, *Rights, Justice, and the Bounds of Liberty* (Princeton, N.J.: Princeton University Press, 1980), pp. 207–20.

41. *Bundesgericht*, 20.XII.195a, *Juristenzeitung*, 1953, 307. See the discussion in G. Tedeschi, "On Tort Liability for 'Wrongful Life,'" *Israel Law Review* 1 (October 1966): 513–38.

42. *Zepeda v. Zepeda*, 41 Ill. App. 2d 240, 190 N.E. 2d 849.

43. *Williams v. State of New York*, 46 Misc. 2d 824, 260 N.Y.S. 2d 953 (Ct. Claims, 1965); *reversed*, 25 A.D. 2d 906, 264 N.Y.S. 2d 786 (App. Div. 1966); *reversal affirmed*, 18 N.Y. 2d 481, 233 N.E. 2d 343 (1966).

44. Judge Sidney Squire quoted the court in *Zepeda v. Zepeda* (see note 42), as follows: "What does disturb us is the nature of the new action and the related suits which would be encouraged. Encouragement would extend to all others born into the world under conditions they might regard as adverse. One might seek damages for being born of a certain color, another because of race, one for

being born with a hereditary disease, another for inheriting unfortunate family characteristics; one for being born into a large and destitute family, another because a parent has an unsavory reputation. . . ."

45. We have seen that it *can* be inflicted before conception or after conception and before birth.

46. Judge Kenneth Keating in *Williams v. State of New York*, 223 N.E. 2d 344.

47. In *Gleitman v. Cosgrove* (49 N.J. 22, 227 A. 2d 689), a typical case, Mrs. Gleitman (the plaintiff's mother) contracted rubella during the first month of pregnancy but was told (she claimed) by Dr. Cosgrove that there was no risk to her child in continued pregnancy. Technically, this is a wrongful-birth case, rather than wrongful conception, but from the point of view of the infant plaintiff, the central issue is the same.

48. Derek Parfit, "On Doing the Best for Our Children," in M. D. Bayles, ed., *Ethics and Population* (Cambridge, Mass.: Schenkman, 1976). Parfit used his example to make another point in another context, namely to show that a plausible version of utilitarianism must condemn not only harms to specific persons but also evils of a more impersonal kind. See also Jonathan Glover, *Causing Death and Saving Lives* (Harmondsworth, Middlesex: Penguin Books, 1977), pp. 67–69, and Michael D. Bayles, "Harm to the Unconceived," *Philosophy and Public Affairs* 5 (1976): 292–304. I have used Parfit's ingenious example for still another purpose, namely to illustrate what I call "non-grievance evils." (See Chap. 28, §§7, 8).

3. Harming as Wronging

1. We do speak of "injured feelings" as well as "wounded feelings," perhaps to emphasize the point of analogy with broken bones and injured organs—that they are all subject to "healing" in time. Similarly our "wounds" leave "scars" (sensitive places) in both cases.

2. American Law Institute, *Restatement of the Law of Torts* (St. Paul, Minnesota: American Law Institute Publishers, 1934).

3. *Ibid.*, chap. 1, §7, "Injury," Comment a, p. 12.

4. I am told that old English law characterized surgery as "justified grievous bodily harm," but I have been unable to verify this.

5. The reader interested in these matters might begin by consulting Herbert Morris's useful anthology *Freedom and Responsibility: Readings in Philosophy and Law* (Stanford, Cal.: Stanford University Press, 1961).

6. J. L. Austin, "A Plea for Excuses," *Proceedings of the Aristotelian Society* 57 (1956–57): 1.

7. *Loc. cit.*

8. There is some reason to think that J. S. Mill himself would have favored this restriction had he clearly comprehended it. See *On Liberty*, chap. 5, para. 3.

9. I refer to those called "legal positivists," most notably Jeremy Bentham who wrote (in *Anarchical Fallacies*): "Right . . . is the child of law: from real laws come real rights; but from imaginary laws, from laws of nature, fancied and invented by poets, rhetoricians, and dealers in moral and intellectual poisons, come imaginary rights, a bastard brood of monsters. . . . Natural rights is simple nonsense: natural and imprescriptible rights, rhetorical nonsense—non-

sense upon stilts." *The Works of Jeremy Bentham*, ed. J. Bowring, 11 vols. (Edinburgh, 1838–43), vol. 2, pp. 501–2, 523.

10. For a discussion of its role and history in English tort law, see *Winfield and Golowicz on Tort*, ed. W. V. H. Rogers, 10th ed. (London: Sweet & Maxwell, 1975), pp. 614–16.

11. Aristotle, *Nicomachean Ethics*, bk. 5, chaps. 8, 9, 11.

12. Some liberties are taken here with Aristotle's sketchy argument. His actual conclusion, in the English translation of W. D. Ross (London: Oxford University Press, 1925), is that no one can *wish* to be unjustly treated (p. 129). "If a man assigns more to another than to himself," he does not voluntarily treat himself unjustly (wrong himself), "for he suffers nothing contrary to his own wish, so that he is not treated unjustly so far as this goes, but at most only suffers harm" (p. 130).

13. John Salmond, *Salmond on Jurisprudence*, ed. Glanville Williams, 7th ed. (London: Sweet & Maxwell, 1957), p. 261.

14. *Webster's New World Dictionary of the American Language* (1970).

15. Similarly, the word "harm" will be used primarily in the narrow sense referring to setbacks to interest wrongfully inflicted, though from time to time the context will make it clear that the word is being used in its broader sense to refer to set-back interest whether wrongfully caused or not. In the same way "victim" will be used in the sense linked to wrongfully set-back interest, though from time to time the context will make it clear that the reference is to one who suffers harm (set-back interest) however produced.

16. Morris, *op. cit.* (see note 5), 282.

17. See the essay "Sua Culpa" in my *Doing and Deserving* (Princeton, N.J.: Princeton University Press, 1970), pp. 177–221. The same distinction is made by H. L. A. Hart and A. M. Honoré in the language of "causes" versus "mere conditions." See their *Causation in the Law* (Oxford: Clarendon Press, 1959), pp. 32–41.

18. Hart and Honoré, *op. cit.*, p. 117.

19. Morris, *op. cit.*, (see note 5), p. 284. I have changed Morris's letter variables.

20. Based on J. A. McLaughlin, "Proximate Cause," *Harvard Law Review* 39 (1925–26): 149. See also Hart and Honoré, *op. cit.*, pp. 219 ff.

21. Hart and Honoré, *op. cit.*, p. 117.

22. D. D. Raphael wisely suggests that "results held too remote for liability should be called 'results' or 'effects' and not 'consequences,' " just as conditions too remote to be causes should be called causal factors or the like and not "*the* cause." I have tried to follow his recommendation. See the symposium "The Consequences of Actions" between Raphael and A. N. Prior in the *Proceedings of the Aristotlelian Society*, Supp. vol. 29 (1956): 91–115.

23. Hart and Honoré, *op. cit.*, p. 127.

24. These three examples are from Herbert Morris, *op. cit.* (see note 5), p. 285.

25. These facts closely resemble those in the actual case of *Hines v. Garrett*, 131 Va. 125, 108 S.E. 690 (1921). The railroad was held civilly liable for the criminal assault.

26. Morris, *op. cit.* (see note 5), p. 284.

27. *Loc. cit.*

28. William Dray, *Laws and Explanation in History* (London: Oxford University Press, 1957), p. 100.

29. H. L. A. Hart and A. M. Honoré, "Causation in the Law," *Law Quarterly Review* 72, pt. 1 (1956), as reprinted in Morris, *op. cit.* (see note 5), p. 331.

4. Failures to Prevent Harm

1. Luke 10:25–37.
2. Aleksander W. Rudzinski, "The Duty to Rescue: A Comparative Analysis," in James M. Ratcliffe, ed., *The Good Samaritan and the Law* (Garden City, N.Y.: Doubleday Anchor Books, 1966), p. 92. The countries listed are Portugal (1867), the Netherlands (1881), Italy (1889 and 1930), Norway (1902), Russia (1903–17), Turkey (1926), Denmark (1930), Poland (1932), Germany (1935 and 1953), Roumania (1938), France (1941 and 1945), Hungary (1948 and 1961), Czechoslovakia (1950), Belgium (1961), and Switzerland (various cantons at various dates). Finland joined the ranks in 1969.
3. Vt. Stat. Ann., tit. 12 §519 (Supp. 1971).
4. Mark A. Franklin, "Vermont Requires Rescue: A Comment," *Stanford Law Review* 51 (1972): 59 n. 56, as cited by Anthony Woozley, "A Duty to Rescue: Some Thoughts on Criminal Liability," *Virginia Law Review*, 69 (1983), p. 1273.
5. Francis H. Bohlen, "The Moral Duty to Aid Others as a Principle of Tort Liability," *University of Pennsylvania Law Review* 56 (1908): 217.
6. Jeffrie G. Murphy, "Blackmail: A Preliminary Inquiry," *The Monist* 63, no. 2 (1980): 168 n. 6. Italics added.
7. Lance K. Stell, "Dueling and the Right to Life," *Ethics* 90 (1979): 12. The Mill quotation is from *Utilitarianism* (New York: Bobbs-Merrill, 1957), p. 61.
8. Judith Thomson, "A Defense of Abortion," *Philosophy and Public Affairs* 1, no. 1, pt. 6 (1971): 62–64.
9. Mill, *op. cit.*, p. 61.
10. I discuss the distinction between desert and entitlement in some detail in the essay "Justice and Personal Desert" in my *Doing and Deserving* (Princeton, N.J.: Princeton University Press, 1970), pp. 55–87.
11. James Barr Ames, "Law and Morals," *Harvard Law Review* 22 (1908), as reprinted in Ratcliffe, *op. cit.* (see note 2), p. 19 (italics added). Ames here advocates change of the traditional rule.
12. Lord Thomas Macaulay, "Notes on the Indian Penal Code," in *Works*, 8 vols. (New York: Longmans, Green and Co., 1897), vol. 7, p. 497.
13. H. B. Acton, "Symposium on 'Rights,' " *Proceedings of the Aristotelian Society*, Supp. vol. 24 (1950): 107–8. See also the essay "Duties, Rights, and Claims" in my *Justice and the Bounds of Liberty* (Princeton, N.J.: Princeton University Press, 1980), pp. 130–42.
14. Richard Epstein, "A Theory of Strict Liability," *Journal of Legal Studies* 2 (1973): 200.
15. See my essay "Supererogation and Rules" in *Doing and Deserving* (Princeton, N.J.: Princeton University Press, 1970), p. 13.
16. Henry Sidgwick, *Methods of Ethics*, 7th ed. (London: Macmillan, 1963), p. 219. Cf. Roderick Chisholm, "Supererogation and Offence: A Conceptual Scheme for Ethics," *Ratio* 5 (1963): 1–14.
17. Epstein, *op. cit.* (see note 14), p. 201.
18. *Ibid.*, p. 198.

19. Macaulay, *op. cit.* (see note 12).
20. *Ibid.*, p. 494.
21. *Ibid.*, p. 495.
22. *Loc. cit.*
23. *Ibid.*, p. 494.
24. Edward Livingston, *Code of Crime and Punishments*, in *Complete Works* (New York: National Prison Association of U.S.A., 1873), vol. 2, pp. 126–27.
25. Macaulay, *op. cit.* (see note 12), p. 495.
26. *Ibid.*, pp. 496–97.
27. Thomas C. Grey, *The Legal Enforcement of Morality* (New York: Random House, 1983), pp. 159–60.
28. *Ibid.*, p. 160.
29. In litigious twentieth-century America one of the risks incurred by good samaritans (particularly physicians) is civil liability for negligence if they should somehow accidentally make things worse despite their good intentions. For that reason a criminal bad samaritan statute should create not only a duty to rescue but also a rescuer's immunity from civil suit except perhaps for *gross* negligence. Many states already exempt physicians in this way when they provide voluntary emergency care. The immunity is good policy when there is no legal duty to offer assistance; it is required by justice when there is such a duty.
30. Macaulay's treatment of these cases is precisely parallel to his treatment of the river-fording case. "We are unable to see where . . . we can draw the line. If the rich man who refuses to save a beggar's life at the cost of a little copper is a murderer, is the poor man just one degree above beggary also to be a murderer if he omits to invite the beggar to partake his hard-earned rice? Again, if the rich man is a murderer for refusing to save the beggar's life at the cost of a little copper, is he also to be a murderer if he refuses to save the beggar's life at the cost of a thousand rupees? . . . The distinction between a legal and an illegal omission is perhaps plain and intelligible; but the distinction between a large and a small sum of money is very far from being so, not to say that a sum which is small to one man is large to another." *Op. cit.* (see note 12), p. 496. With the addition of the appropriate moral premise, Macaulay's argument can be converted into an argument for the modern welfare state financed by the graduated income tax.
31. The points in this paragraph are suggested by Grey, *op. cit.* (see note 27), and developed in a convincing way by Ernest J. Weinrib, "The Case for a Duty to Rescue," *Yale Law Journal* 90 (1980): 291–92.
32. Weinrib, *op. cit.*, p. 292. Italics added.
33. Cf. Eric D'Arcy, *Human Acts* (Oxford: Clarendon Press, 1963), pp. 43ff.
34. We can now distinguish "not-acting," "failing to act," "neglecting to act," "refraining from acting," and "omitting to act," as follows. Inaction is the genus of which the others are ever more determinate species and subspecies. *Not-acting merely* is inaction that is neither failing, neglecting, refraining, nor omitting to act, because the nonactor lacked either opportunity to act, ability to act, or both. Not-acting is *failing to act* when the nonactor did have the opportunity and ability to act, but did not act anyway either because he had no way of knowing that he had the opportunity and ability, or because he neglected to act or refrained from acting. Failing to act is *neglecting to act* when the nonactor had

both opportunity and ability to act, but either did not know it (though he should have known it), or, knowing it, nevertheless did not realize at the time that he had the ability and opportunity: it never entered his head. Failing to act is *refraining from acting* when the nonactor had the opportunity and ability to act, and that realization entered his head but he nevertheless declined to act. Not-acting is *omitting to act* when (1) it is a refraining from acting and (2) the disjunctive "reasonable expectation" condition is satisfied. These distinctions are rendered diagrammatically as follows:

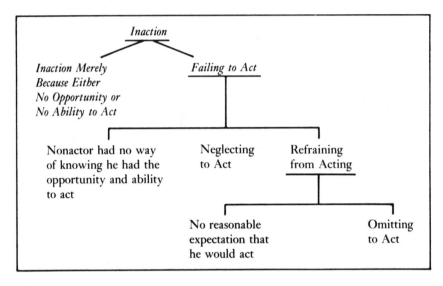

35. See Richard B. Brandt's sensitive account in "The Concepts of Obligation and Duty," *Mind* 73 (1964): 374–93. See also my "Supererogation and Rules" (note 15) and John Rawls, *A Theory of Justice* (Cambridge, Mass.: Harvard University Press, 1971), p. 113.
36. I owe this suggestion to Bruce Landesman's unpublished comments on Woozley (see note 4).
37. Grey, *op. cit.* (see note 27), p. 163.
38. Elizabeth Wolgast seizes on this element of bad luck, and pleads the case for the "unlucky bad samaritan" by contrasting him with the "scheming bad samaritan" who uses his foresight to evade samaritan obligations—"he has earplugs in his ears when someone is calling for help, and he has turned off the road before reaching the needy stranger." Wolgast prefers rewarding the good (minimally decent) samaritan rather than punishing the (unlucky) bad one, because that way "we shall not be putting the unlucky in jail for their lack of guile." The quotations are from her still-unpublished comments on Woozley (see note 4).
39. Woozley, *op. cit.* (see note 4) p. 1300. Landesman adds to Woozley's list of unforseeable affirmative legal duties, the duty to sit on juries. *Op. cit.* (see note 36).
40. Landesman, *op. cit.*
41. Woozley points out that "allowing to happen" when contrasted with "causing to

happen" can refer to two quite different cases, one an omission and the other an action: "I allow something to happen if I do not put in the way an obstacle which would prevent its happening or if I remove an obstacle which is now preventing its happening." Woozley, *op. cit.*, p. 1295. Thus a physician allows a mortally ill patient to die both when he does not connect him to a respirator (omission) and when he disconnects him from a respirator (action). In labeling the latter case as "letting die" rather than "killing" we imply that it is not wrongful. To be a "letting die" merely, the act of disconnecting must permit the resumption of a previously blocked causal process as opposed to being the initiating of a new one (as e.g. by a lethal injection), *and* it must be done legitimately. If it is done, as Woozley puts it, "against the declared wishes of parents or guardian," or "by somebody who has no authority in the case at all, e.g. an enemy agent or a hospital orderly" (p. 1297), it is a killing and not merely an allowing-to-die, even though it does not initiate an altogether new causal process.

42. Grey, *op. cit.* (see note 27). See also the famous examples proposed by James Rachels in "Active and Passive Euthanasia," *New England Journal of Medicine* 292 (1975): 78–80, and Michael Tooley in "Abortion and Infanticide," *Philosophy and Public Affairs* 2 (1972): 58–60.

43. The phrase is Tooley's (note 42) for the principle that "there is no moral difference between intentionally performing" an act that initiates a causal process leading to another's harm and "intentionally refraining" from stopping that process before the harmful outcome occurs, assuming that minimal effort was required to stop the outcome and that there is "identical motivation in both cases" (p. 58).

44. Heidi Malm, "Good Samaritan Laws and the Concept of Personal Sovereignty," typescript, University of Arizona (1983), p. 11.

45. *Loc. cit.*

46. Richard Trammel, "Saving Life and Taking Life," in Bonnie Steinbock, ed., *Killing and Letting Die* (Englewood Cliffs, N.J.: Prentice-Hall, 1980), p. 167.

47. *Loc. cit.*

48. That "positiveness" and "negativeness" have no relevance whatever in the case where the required effort *is* minimal is shown by an example suggested by Bruce Russell in his "On the Relative Strictness of Negative and Positive Duties" in the Bonnie Steinbock collection, *op. cit.* (see note 46), p. 226. The driver of a runaway railway train has only two choices: to let the train continue on its present course toward a person (*A*) who is tied to the track or to steer on to a branch track and run over a different person (*B*) who is tied to *that* track. If negative duties are necessarily more strict than positive ones, everything else being equal, then he must *not* intervene to steer down the alternate track for that would be to *do* something "active" (turn a wheel or pull a lever) and thus *cause* *B*'s death. If he does not do that, and thus honors his negative duty, he will merely "allow" *A*'s death to occur, and that would be to violate only a less strict positive duty. But as Russell concludes, "Most of us would judge that it is morally indifferent which alternative the driver adopts," that is that the conflicting duties are of equal strictness, even though the only difference between them is that one is positive and the other negative.

49. Trammel, *op. cit.* (see note 46), p. 168.

50. That is, assigning *all* of this social task equally to *everybody* would be irrational.

Another interpretation of the injunction to love one's neighbor is suggested by this point, namely that there is a uniquely efficient (hence "rational") coordination scheme in which each person is assigned primary responsibility for people in serious peril that he encounters in his own proximity ("neighborhood") as he moves about, when no others with special assignments to rescue can be found in that area.

51. On this point I am in agreement with J. L. Mackie (see his "Responsibility and Language," *Australasian Journal of Philosophy* 33 (1955): 152–53, and in disagreement with John Harris, "Bad Samaritans Cause Harm," *Philosophical Quarterly* 32 (April 1982): 60–69.

52. H. L. A. Hart and A. M. Honoré, *Causation in the Law* (Oxford: Clarendon Press, 1959), p. 118.

53. *Ibid.*, p. 108.

54. R. G. Collingwood, "On the So-Called Idea of Causation," *Proceedings of the Aristotelian Society* 38 (1938): 89.

55. Joel Feinberg, "Sua Culpa," in *Doing and Deserving* (Princeton, N.J.: Princeton University Press, 1970), pp. 202–5.

56. Max Black, "Making Something Happen," in Sidney Hook, ed., *Determinism and Freedom in the Age of Modern Science* (New York: New York University Press, 1958), p. 20.

57. Eric Mack, "Bad Samaritanism and the Causation of Harm," *Philosophy and Public Affairs* 9 (1980): 241.

58. *Ibid.*, p. 244.

59. Hart and Honoré, *op. cit.* (see note 52), p. 115.

60. *Loc. cit.*

61. *Ibid.*, p. 114.

62. Mack, *op. cit.* (see note 56), pp. 243–44.

5. Assessing and Comparing Harms

1. "Harmful" is used here in the generic sense distinguished in Chapter 4, §2. The disparity between the elevated location of *A*'s interest curve as it would have been without preventive coercion (the baseline for comparison) and its depressed location on the interest graph as a consequence of the preventive coercion is greater than the disparity between *B*'s normal interest condition as it would be in the absence of *A*'s projected conduct (the baseline for comparison) and the worsened condition it would be in as a consequence of *A*'s projected conduct.

2. E.g. Zechariah Chafee, *Free Speech in the United States* (Cambridge, Mass.: Harvard University Press, 1964).

3. The wording of the "rationale" of the clear and present danger test in this paragraph is taken from my "Limits to the Free Expression of Opinion" in J. Feinberg and H. Gross, eds., *Philosophy of Law*, 2d ed. (Belmont, Cal.: Wadsworth, 1980), pp. 205–6.

4. *Rogers v. Elliot*, 146 Mass. 349, 15 N.E. 768 (1888).

5. Merchants who must keep large amounts of cash in their stores in order to transact business, on the other hand, would more easily qualify for licenses under the more restrictive licensing policy.

6. During the period of the Vietnam War many states lowered their legal drinking

age to nineteen or eighteen. The experience of New Jersey was typical. The average number of persons killed by eighteen-to-twenty-year-old drivers rose 176 percent after the state lowered its drinking age to eighteen. Now twenty of the twenty-five states that lowered their drinking age in the early 1970s, including New Jersey, have raised it again. The most thorough and influential statistical study of the effect of such legislative actions on accident rates is that of Alexander C. Wagenaar of the Transportation Research Institute of the University of Michigan. Wagenaar found that collisions involving nineteen- and twenty-year-old drivers in Michigan fell 20 percent after the drinking age was raised from nineteen to twenty-one in 1978. See Samuel G. Freedman, "Will Raising the Drinking Age Lower the Death Rate," *New York Times*, Dec. 23, 1982.

7. We are dealing in this section with harms in the sense of setbacks to interest only. The other component of harm in the full sense, actions that are wrongs by some prior moral standard, is not under discussion. Before the element of wrongfulness can be determined, interest-balancing must be done. Then resultant legislation incorporating the interest rankings will create the (legal) rights and wrongs to complete the analysis. Moral rights and wrongs in these cases are derivative from, not prior to, the created legal ones.

8. If we remember the analysis in Chapters 1 and 2 of what it is to have an interest (a distinguishable component of a person's good), and the distinction between interests and mere wants, we must be skeptical that there are such things as sadistic and morbid *interests*. Clearly there are such things as sadistic and morbid erratic desires contrary to the desirer's self-interest. But how many persons have desire networks such that inflicting pain on others as an end in itself (say) is good for them, a way of promoting their own well-being? The question is, of course, an open empirical one, but surely there cannot be many such odd birds. Perhaps the legendary Satan is one.

9. Isaiah Berlin, "Two Concepts of Liberty," in *Four Essays on Liberty* (London: Oxford University Press, 1969), p. 130n.

10. *Loc. cit.*

11. *Ibid.*, p. 130. I think that this passage in a long footnote is an aberration from Berlin's arguments in the main text, with which I am largely in agreement.

12. This account of the nature of liberty is enlarged and improved in Chap. 19, §3, below.

13. Strictly speaking, the conflicting interests are: one party's interest in a specific open option and another party's interest in another specific open option. These are "interests in liberty" only in the sense that they are interests in the "liberty category," as opposed, for example, to the "life," "property," or "privacy" categories. Fecundity is a property, strictly speaking, of the options themselves, not of the interests.

14. In many of these "most exceptional cases," the party who is tempted to capture, detain, kidnap, or hijack is driven to such desperate means by threats to his own fecund liberties that are ultimately of his own making, or the consequences of his own wrongdoing, e.g. his need to escape arrest and eventual incarceration for some earlier crime. In some other very exceptional cases, the detainer may have the justification of "necessity" or forced choice of the lesser evil, as when one "borrows" another's automobile in an emergency, leaving the owner at least temporarily stranded and immobile. The "lesser evil" in this case could be an infringement of a less fecund liberty.

15. Except insofar as a woman is legally capable of committing rape herself as an accomplice to the main perpetrator who must, legally speaking, be male. This is a trivial qualification of the point in the text, and deserves at most a note.

16. Consider, for example, mandatory curfew laws, ordinances forbidding minors from purchasing alcoholic beverages or from lingering in places where they are sold, statutes prohibiting the sale of obscene books or the showing, even to audiences of willing and eager adults, of pornographic films. If such laws are justified, it is because they protect interests other than the interest in liberty, for they open nowhere near as many or as fecund options as they close.

6. Fairly Imputing Harms

1. John Stuart Mill, *On Liberty*, chap. 5, para. 3.

2. Lance K. Stell has written a carefully argued essay, "Dueling and the Right to Life" (*Ethics* 90 [1979]: 7–26), maintaining that duels no more than voluntary euthanasia and suicide should be criminal acts. In the light of Stell's article, my brief dismissal of dueling may seem somewhat glib. But see Chapter 23 for a more thorough treatment of coercive force as a voluntariness-reducing factor, and Chapter 30, §7, for a discussion of consent as a defense in criminal law. Stell is right when he claims that not every logically possible instance of a duel in the legal sense ("the act of fighting with deadly weapons between two persons in pursuance of a previous agreement") is necessarily less than fully voluntary on both sides. And insofar as a duel is wholly voluntary, its legal status should not be markedly different from voluntary suicide and voluntary euthanasia. But Stell underestimates, I think, the voluntariness-reducing influence of "codes of honor" and prevalent standards of social esteem. I suspect that our own complex society, even though lacking a formal code, is not without such coercive influences.

   We do not have to look to medieval Europe for familiar examples of dueling under social pressure. The Scotch-Irish immigrants who settled the American South brought with them their own code of honor and the practice of family feuds and duels, all part of their "persistent inbred, timeless customs and traditions of ancient origins" (C. Vann Woodward). See Bertram Wyatt-Brown's definitive *Southern Honor: Ethics and Behavior in the Old South* (New York: Oxford University Press, 1982). The coercive effect of the "code" on consent is well expressed in C. Vann Woodward's review (*New York Review of Books*, Nov. 18, 1982): "The male ego had to establish 'manliness,' virility, honor. Declining to bet, to drink, or to fight meant loss of self-esteem and community evaluation. Dueling served these purposes among the upper ranks, though it was not confined to them, and feuding was common in the hills and back country. *Duels, like other rituals of virility and violence, were not assertions of individualism but responses to the demands of community opinion*, the Southern variety of the American tyranny Tocqueville deplored. Behind the genial and convivial, behind the hunts, barbecues and joyful rituals lurked dangerous and unmanageable rages." (Italics added).

3. Jeremy Bentham, *An Introduction to the Principles of Morals and Legislation* (1789), ed. J. H. Burns and H. L. A. Hart (University of London, Athlone Press, 1970), Chap. 16, §1, 9 (p. 189).

4. Brian Barry, *Political Argument* (London: Routledge & Kegan Paul, 1965), p. 196.
5. *Ibid.*, p. 196.
6. This fifth characteristic distinguishes this class of harms from the simpler accumulative harms like those caused by *littering*, which *can* be handled by simple across-the-board prohibitions. It is also mainly in virtue of this fifth feature that the pollution cases differ from the famous paradigm example of accumulative harms, forbidden walking on the grass in a public park. In that example, if only one person takes a shortcut to his destination across a plot of well-tended lawn, no harm will be done to the lawn and there will be a net gain in utility, but if everyone were to be equally free to do the same, the consequences would be hard indeed on the grass. Its roots and blades would be brought over the threshold of harm. Since there are no workable and nonarbitrary methods of permitting only some but not all a license to walk in the sensitive areas, and the cost to individuals of their loss of liberty in this respect is only minor inconvenience, we have good grounds for legislating a general prohibition. Clearly it would be better to have a general prohibition than none at all. But in the pollution cases the social costs of blanket prohibition are as great as those of blanket permission, so we *must* find a workable and nonarbitrary middle way.
7. See Kenneth Culp Davis, *Discretionary Justice: A Preliminary Inquiry* (Urbana, Ill.: University of Illinois Press, 1971), esp. chap. 4, "Structuring Discretion."
8. The seven pollutants controlled under the 1970 amendments are: sulfur dioxide, particulate matter, nitrogen dioxide, carbon monoxide, photochemical oxidents (as ozone), nonmethane hydrocarbons, and lead.
9. Problems of pollution control are not different in kind, but much more difficult politically, in those regions ("nonattainment areas") where ambient pollution concentrations exceed their assigned ceilings. See Lewis T. Kontnik, "Comment. Increment Allocation Under Prevention of Significant Deterioration: How to Decide Who Is Allowed to Pollute," *Northwestern Law Review* 74 (Feb. 1980): 936–69. I am heavily indebted to Kontnik's article in what follows.
10. *Ibid.*, p. 941.
11. *Loc. cit.*
12. *Ibid.*, p. 949.
13. *Ibid.*, p. 947.
14. See the UPI dispatch, December 30, 1980, in the *Chicago Tribune* and elsewhere.
15. Bernard Williams, ed., *Obscenity and Film Censorship: An Abridgement of the Williams Report* (Cambridge: Cambridge University Press, 1981), p. 65. The report mentions numerous other alleged examples of this sort on pp. 63–65.
16. Gene Lyons, review of *Victim* by Gary Kinder (Delacort, 1983), in *Newsweek*, Sept. 13, 1982, p. 81. The book under review is the story of the mass murder from the point of view of the victims: "We first see the victims as *things*, animate technical problems brought . . . by ambulance to an Ogden, Utah, emergency room. A middle-aged woman and a teen-age boy, suffering gunshot wounds to the head. The woman was gone moments after arriving, the boy diagnosed as terminal. The doctors argued over the ethics of trying to save him. Besides a bullet in his skull, he 'was spewing blood from his lungs nearly three feet into the air.' Nobody knew why." The cause, of course, was the Drano.

17. Marilyn Beck, *Arizona Daily Star*, May 22, 1982.
18. Robert Hatch, *The Nation*, May 9, 1981, p. 581.
19. *Loc. cit.*
20. App. 141, Cal. Rptr. 511.
21. *Ibid.*, p. 512.
22. See H. L. A. Hart and A. M. Honoré, *Causation in the Law* (Oxford: Clarendon Press, 1959), pp. 129–50.
23. Fla. App., 361 So. 2d 776 (1978).
24. See my essay "Causing Voluntary Actions," in *Doing and Deserving* (Princeton, N.J.: Princeton University Press, 1970), pp. 152–86.
25. Even if the drama had in some sense "advocated" such conduct, it would not be outside the scope of first amendment protection unless it was directed to inciting or producing imminent lawless action and was likely to succeed in inciting or producing such action—the test espoused by the Supreme Court in *Brandenburg v. Ohio*, 395 U.S. 444, 447–48, 89 S. Ct. 1827 (1969).
26. The tort remedy was not available, however, to poor Miss Olivia. She was harmed by a film that enjoyed first amendment protection as a work of artistic expression that was neither obscene, incitive, defamatory, or in any other standard category of expression not protected by the first amendment. The Supreme Court does not permit lower courts to balance in particular cases the harm negligently produced to the plaintiff against the degree of aesthetic merit or other social value in the drama. Once the drama is placed in a protected category, its protection is absolute (see *New York Times Co. v. Sullivan*, 376 U.S. 254–84, S. Ct. 710 [1964]).
27. Kent Greenawalt, "Speech and Crime," *American Bar Foundation Research Journal*, 1980, no. 4:667–68.
28. Similar schemes have recently been proposed, though not usually under the candid label "strict liability," to hold the manufacturers, distributors, and sellers of handguns (except to police departments) liable to the victims of crimes and accidents in which the guns cause harm. Usually the plaintiff lawyer in suits against gun distributors and manufacturers argues from an extremely stretched interpretation of "products liability" rules imposing liability on manufacturers for harms caused by "defects" (key word) in their product. They argue that industry defendants should be held (in effect) strictly liable on the theory that the "inherent hazard" of handguns outweighs any social utility of their private use, thus creating a "defect." They find support in the ruling in *Barker v. Lull Engineering Co.* (Cal. 573 P. 2d 443): "A product is defective in design if . . . the benefits of the challenged design do not outweigh the risk of danger inherent in such design." See James Podgers, "Handguns New Target for Tort Lawyers," *A.B.A. Journal* 67 (Nov. 1981): 1443–44. This reinterpretation of "defect" may be stretching things too far, but its legal flaws should not preclude *legislative* decisions to impose industry-wide strict liability regardless of fault. On balance, that might have fatal difficulties too, but it would be supported *prima facie* by considerations of justice and efficient harm reduction outside of the criminal law.
29. For developments of this point, see my essays "Collective Responsibility," pp. 223–25, and "The Expressive Function of Punishment," pp. 95–118, both in *Doing and Deserving* (see note 24).

INDEX

DATE DUE